Pride and Profit

Capitalist Thought: Studies in Philosophy, Politics, and Economics

Series Editor: Edward W. Younkins, Wheeling Jesuit University

Mission Statement

This book series is devoted to studying the foundations of capitalism from a number of academic disciplines including, but not limited to, philosophy, political science, economics, law, literature, and history. Recognizing the expansion of the boundaries of economics, this series particularly welcomes proposals for monographs and edited collections that focus on topics from transdisciplinary, interdisciplinary, and multidisciplinary perspectives. Lexington Books will consider a wide range of conceptual, empirical, and methodological submissions. Works in this series will tend to synthesize and integrate knowledge and to build bridges within and between disciplines. They will be of vital concern to academicians, businesspeople, and others in the debate about the proper role of capitalism, business, and businesspeople in economic society.

Advisory Board

Books in Series

Economic Morality: Ancient to Modern Readings by Henry C. Clark and Eric Allison

The Ontology and Function of Money: The Philosophical Fundamentals of Monetary Institutions by Leonidas Zelmanovitz

Andrew Carnegie: An Economic Biography by Samuel Bostaph

Water Capitalism: Privatize Oceans, Rivers, Lakes, and Aquifers Too by Walter E. Block and Peter Lothian Nelson

Capitalism and Commerce in Imaginative Literature: Perspectives on Business from Novels and Plays edited by Edward W. Younkins

Pride and Profit: The Intersection of Jane Austen and Adam Smith by Cecil E. Bohanon and Michelle Albert Vachris

Pride and Profit

*The Intersection of
Jane Austen and Adam Smith*

Cecil E. Bohanon and
Michelle Albert Vachris

LEXINGTON BOOKS
Lanham • Boulder • New York • London

Published by Lexington Books
An imprint of The Rowman & Littlefield Publishing Group, Inc.
4501 Forbes Boulevard, Suite 200, Lanham, Maryland 20706
www.rowman.com

Unit A, Whitacre Mews, 26-34 Stannary Street, London SE11 4AB

British Library Cataloguing in Publication Information Available

Library of Congress Cataloging-in-Publication Data
Names: Bohanon, Cecil E., author. | Vachris, Michelle Albert, author.
Title: Pride and profit : the intersection of Jane Austen and Adam Smith / by Cecil E. Bohanon and Michelle Albert Vachris.
Description: Lanham, Maryland : Lexington Books, 2016. | Series: Capitalist thought: studies in philosophy, politics, and economics | Includes bibliographical references and index.
Identifiers: LCCN 2015040418| ISBN 9780739191835 (cloth : alk. paper) | ISBN 9780739191842 (electronic)| ISBN 9781498530262 (pbk : alk. paper)
Subjects: LCSH: Austen, Jane, 1775-1817--Criticism and interpretation. | Austen, Jane, 1775-1817--Knowledge--Economics. | Economics and literature--Great Britain--History--19th century. | Capitalism and literature--Great Britain--History--19th century. | Smith, Adam, 1723-1790--Influence. | Economics in literature.
Classification: LCC PR4038.E25 B64 2016 | DDC 823/.7--dc23 LC record available at http://lccn.loc.gov/2015040418

Printed in the United States of America

Contents

Acknowledgments

This book is the by-product of a professional collaboration that traces its origins to a conference in Cleveland, Ohio, in the summer of 2007. We along with a dozen or so assorted academics discussed two works of early twentieth-century American literature: Theodore Dreiser's *Sister Carrie* and Frank Norris's *McTeague*. From that conference the two of us began collaborating on a number of academic works on the intersection of literature and economics. We are grateful to the hosts of that Socratic conference—Indianapolis-based educational foundation Liberty Fund and all the participants from the Cleveland event.

Liberty Fund has also supported our attending a number of other conferences including ones on Adam Smith, Jane Austen, and a variety of other topics that have undoubtedly contributed to the current work. It is quite common for academics to bemoan overspecialization in higher education. Calls for interdisciplinary interaction are common. Liberty Fund is one of the few organizations that actually does something about academic myopia by providing a number of venues that foster interdisciplinary interactions.

We also wish to express our gratitude to the Association of Private Enterprise Education (APEE), the Public Choice Society (PCS), and the Virginia Association of Economists (VAE) for providing formats where we presented earlier versions of this work. We envisioned this book with our editor Joseph Parry in the lobby of the Monteleone Hotel in New Orleans at the PCS's fiftieth-anniversary meeting in 2013. Also special thanks to the Students for Liberty group who participated in the virtual class on the topic of Adam Smith and Jane Austen.

We both earned our PhDs in economics departments that were (are) characterized as being part of the Virginia School of Political Economy. We were both lucky to be trained in a tradition that encouraged broad thinking and academic risk taking. We would like to thank our respective institutions, Ball State University and Christopher Newport University, for providing academic support and sabbaticals that allow us to pursue this work. The Branch Banking and Trust (BB&T) Charitable Foundation also provided research support, including the funding of a student researcher, Elizabeth Samios. Thanks to all our colleagues, students, and student organizations (especially the BSU Econ Club) who have listened, asked questions, and encouraged us in this effort.

A special thanks to an anonymous referee and to our special friend and colleague Lynne Kiesling who read our first manuscripts and provided detailed insights and critiques, both stylistic and substantive, which improved our final draft. The usual disclaimer applies. Finally we'd both like to thank our families: Barbara, Denis, and Dmitri Bohanon, and Scott, Kyle, and Brendan Vachris and Irene Albert, for their insights, encouragement, and emotional support. They always stand by us.

Abbreviations

The following abbreviations are used for the novels of Jane Austen. All citations are from *The Complete Novels of Jane Austen*, New York: Penguin Books, 1983.

E   *Emma*
MP   *Mansfield Park*
NA   *Northanger Abbey*
P   *Persuasion*
PP   *Pride and Prejudice*
SS   *Sense and Sensibility*

The following abbreviations are used for the works of Adam Smith. All citations are from the Liberty Fund editions as listed in the bibliography.

LJ   *Lectures on Jurisprudence*
TMS   *The Theory of Moral Sentiments*
WN   *An Inquiry into the Nature and Causes of the Wealth of Nations*

Chapter One

Introduction

Why Jane Austen and Adam Smith?

Jane Austen and Adam Smith? What could the two writers possibly have to do with one another and why is this of interest to twenty-first-century readers? Adam Smith was born in 1723 and died in 1790. His lesser known philosophical work *Theory of Moral Sentiments* was first published in 1759 and his better-known economic treatise *Wealth of Nations* was published in 1776. Jane Austen was born in 1775 and died in 1817. Her six novels, all of them about the trials and travails of young unmarried English ladies of the gentry class, were published between 1811 and 1818. Austen was fifteen years old when Smith died at age sixty-seven. She lived another twenty-six years until her untimely death at age forty-one. Chronologically Smith could have been a rather old father or grandfather to Austen; roughly speaking Austen was about a generation or so after Smith.

Smith's work is about political and economic issues: free markets, the invisible hand, commercial activitiy, and all that. Austen's work is about the comic-tragic interactions of relatively well-off young people courting and eventually marrying in the very restricted and prudish society of early nineteenth century England. Smith is aware of the major social issues of his time and makes extensive comments on British policies. Austen makes no mention of politics and scant reference to the wars that were raging at the time of her novels. There is no mention of Napoleon and little reference to other contemporary political, social, or economic issues of her day.

Fast forward 200+ years to our time; social mores and conditions have radically changed. Divorce, unthinkable and scandalous then, is common and socially acceptable today. Young women from middle class backgrounds had few options in Smith's and Austen's day except to marry shrewdly, or face spinsterhood. Today, independent of one's view on gender disparity, it is unquestionable that young women from various income classes and social backgrounds attend and graduate from universities, enter the business world and professional occupations, and serve as governors, senators, cabinet secretaries, and high court justices. In Smith's and Austen's time wealth flowed primarily from ownership of agricultural property, although the rising merchant and nascent manufacturing classes were also accumulating fine houses and estates and participating in high society. Today new wealth flows not so much from these enterprises as from information technology and creative endeavors.

The Church was an established institution in the world of Austen and Smith, and while it still plays a ceremonial role in British government today, it has a very different and much more muted voice in the United Kingdom now than it had in their time. The modern state's role as provider and guarantor of health, welfare, and education services was hardly imagined in their day. Class and social distinctions in the United Kingdom in Austen's and Smith's times were much more pronounced and enforced than they are today and quite different from those in the United States even in their time.

The values and manners reflected in Smith and Austen seem to the modern mind to be stiff, formal, and antiquated. At best they are quaint and amusing, at worst misogynistic and oppressive. Our egalitarian worldview seems far superior to the class-based view that Smith and Austen struggle with but ultimately seem to accept.

Even if we are convinced that Austen and Smith are of little relevance for our time it might be an interesting exercise to investigate ways in which the novelist and economist overlap. A first place to search for overlaps between Austen and Smith is to ask what was occurring in the United Kingdom during the sixty-year period between publication of Smith's *Theory of Moral Sentiments* and Austen's *Persuasion*? For one there was a rise in what we today call scientific thinking.

An early twentieth-century historian of the era of Smith and Austen noted that, "It was not until the middle of the 18th century that the broad conception of an immutable order in nature became part of the mental heritage of all educated persons . . . Even in the year 1720 a woman in Godalming [England] declared that she was giving birth to rabbits, and several doctors, including the King's anatomist, believed her story" (Buer, 1926, 112). We can presume that both Smith and Austen would not have believed that story and that they both ascribed to the view of an immutable order in nature.

This rise of reason and decline of superstition is often called the Enlightenment. It is generally described as an awakening of thought during the seventeenth and eighteenth centuries in Western Europe and America. Enlightenment movements were especially prevalent in England, Scotland,

and France. There is little question that both Smith and Austen lived in a world being influenced by Enlightenment thinking.

There are certain themes of the Enlightenment that we might expect to see reflected in the work of a social philosopher and novelist of the era. We list three that are potentially interesting and can readily be seen in both Smith and Austen. In a world influenced by the Enlightenment:

1. People think for themselves on issues of morality and propriety instead of deferring to authority figures. This independent thinking corresponds to a decline in the influence, authority, and respect for church and aristocracy (Broadie, 2001). Smith demonstrates independent thinking when he aims his policy advice in *Wealth of Nations* to an explicit critique of the mercantile policies of his day. It is also very clear that Austen's characters are willing to defy the authority of rank. For example, Austen's protagonist in *Pride and Prejudice*, Elizabeth Bennet, is certainly unwilling to accept the commands of the higher ranking Lady Catherine de Bourgh as to her potential marriage to Lady Catherine's nephew Mr. Darcy.

2. People are tolerant and open to ideas of others, even ideas of which they do not approve (Broadie, 2001). Free and open discussion of different ideas is an important component of the discovery process that can lead to developments in the sciences and the arts, a point also emphasized by Mokyr (2009, 33). Throughout *Wealth of Nations* Smith illustrates the discovery process of markets and innovations. There are many examples of tolerance and openness to new ideas in Austen's work, even between those of different rank. In *Mansfield Park* the rigid and authoritarian Sir Thomas Bertram is quite upset with his niece Fanny Price for refusing to marry the eligible Henry Crawford. Although he does not approve of Fanny's decision he certainly tolerates it.[1] He respects her wishes and informs her "Your feelings are as well known to me, as my wishes and regrets must be to you. . . . You will have nothing to fear, or to be agitated about. You cannot suppose me capable of trying to persuade you to marry against your inclinations" (*MP*, 636).

3. There is a movement away from asking "how can I be good?" toward asking "how can I be happy?" (Porter, 1981). Furthermore, an optimistic drive for improvement is a commonly recognized feature of the Enlightenment Age, according to Broadie (2001, 38). Both the individual drive for improvement and search for happiness feature strongly in Smith's *Theory of Moral Sentiments*. Likewise, Austen's female protagonists play an active role in seeking their own happiness by the only course available to them, their choice of marriage partner. There are few pre-arranged marriages in her works.[2] At another level, both

Smith and Austen can be seen as thinking about how the individual's pursuit of happiness also relates to her moral improvement.

These Enlightenment themes are very interesting and are deserving of serious scholarly treatment. While we will refer to these and other Enlightenment themes, they are not our main story. Our claims are much more specific than the congruity of broad-brush Enlightenment themes that show up in Smith and Austen.

We note along with a number of Austen scholars that much of Adam Smith's thinking is reflected in Jane Austen's novels. Most of the connections we and other scholars draw between the two are from Smith's less well-known *Theory of Moral Sentiments*. It is important to know that while Smith is understood by most today as an economist interested in real world policy questions, these issues are not his exclusive or even primary focus in *Theory of Moral Sentiments*. Rather, in TMS, he develops a theory of interpersonal interaction among individuals founded on the notion that humans are by definition morally regarding creatures. From this foundation he derives a number of insights about human behavior that are quite applicable to non-commercial activities.

Our claim in this book is simple: Jane Austen is channeling Adam Smith in her stories and characters. But more than this: we also think that Austen embellishes, refines, and explains Adam Smith. Our understanding of Smith is improved and expanded by reading Jane Austen because she brings his insights to life and adds insights of her own. A reader of Smith can get a lot out of Austen just as the reader of Austen can get a lot out of Smith, because the rhetoric of both coincide so well.

We are not particularly interested in nor offer any original insight as to the specific channel of the Smithian influence on Austen. Did she read and refer to Smith when she wrote her novels? Had she read Smith in the past and inadvertently adopted his views?[3] Or were Smith's views simply something in the intellectual air of her time and a reflection of popular thinking of the period? We do not know and we leave it to others to investigate this most interesting question.

Our job is to take you, our reader, through a number of the overlaps between Smith and Austen in a way that we hope you find interesting. No specialized knowledge of Smith or Austen is required, although an interest in and familiarity with the basic plot and characters of Austen's novels will, we suspect, make the journey a lot more fun! We also encourage our readers to watch any of the many film adaptations of Austen's novels that are available and/or to pick up and read the novels. You will enjoy them and be in good economic company.[4]

For those readers needing an introductory primer or refresher on Smith's moral philosophy, we provide an overview of his work in chapters 2 and 3.

Chapter 2 introduces the reader to the overall Smithian project in TMS and chapter 3 summarizes his thinking on the virtues and vices in TMS that also play a prominent role in Austen's novels. For those readers needing an introductory primer or refresher on Austen's novels, we provide an overview of all six of them in the appendix.

Readers who are somewhat familiar with Smith and are interested in specific Austen novels can move right to chapters 4–9. In each of these chapters, Austen's novels are matched up with a specific Smithian concept. Chapter 4 examines the virtue of Self-Command in Austen, primarily in *Sense and Sensibility*, but also in *Mansfield Park* and *Emma*. Chapter 5 uses characters in *Mansfield Park* to illustrate the Smithian triad of virtues Prudence, Benevolence, and Justice. (We will refer to these as the PB&J virtues.) After the virtues come the vices, beginning with an analysis of Vanity in chapter 6 using examples from *Persuasion* as well as from *Sense and Sensibility*, and *Mansfield Park*. The vice of Pride is viewed, perhaps as expected, solely through the novel *Pride and Prejudice* in chapter 7. We then turn to other important components of Smith's moral philosophy found in Austen. Chapter 8 discusses Smith's views on greed and promises through the lens of *Northanger Abbey* with additions from *Mansfield Park*, *Persuasion*, and *Sense and Sensibility*. Finally, in chapter 9, we draw parallels between Smith's conceptualization of the "man of system" and "impartial spectator" in Austen's characters from all six novels, especially in *Emma*. We round out the intersection of Adam Smith and Jane Austen in chapters 10–12 where we discuss the economic life of Austen's world, the emergence of commercial society, and the changing attitudes about social rank. In chapter 13, we offer some concluding remarks.

So why should twenty-first-century folks pay attention to eighteenth- and nineteenth-century thinking? Yes, many aspects of the world of Adam Smith and Jane Austen seem out-of-date and even repugnant to many modern readers. And, no, we could not reestablish, reconstruct, or return to all the mores and values of their time even if we wanted to. Nonetheless, many of the issues these authors raise are timeless, and we moderns might learn something about how to live life by carefully considering their perspectives.

Then, as now, we seek to be loved by our fellow creatures. Then, as now, we desire the approval and admiration of those around us. At a deeper level we want not just to be loved, but to be lovable, not just to be admired but to be worthy of admiration. And yet, then and now, we are subject to being deceived, especially by our own delusions about ourselves. Right and wrong, good and bad, virtue and vice are remarkably the same over time. In our estimation both Smith and Austen were keenly interested in how to live a life of moral rectitude in rapidly changing and confusing circumstances where there were many temptations to take a less elevated path. Sound familiar? We think it does. Two centuries later, both Adam Smith and Jane Austen continue to be read and analyzed. We suspect it is because they are examining, in interesting ways, issues that are timeless and universal parts of the human condition. Let us see what they have to say.

NOTES

1. Cox (1990, 78) points out that by Austen's time it was a common view that to marry "without affection" was problematic—but that "in 1700 it would have been no sin at all."

2. Thompson (1990, 152–153) argues convincingly that "mutual consent of child and parent" is Austen's requirement for a good marriage.

3. For example, Collins (1998, 179–180) explains that Jane Austen's uncle had given her a copy of David Hume's *History of England*. Smith's works were widely read by men, so in all probability, Austen's father and brothers would have been familiar with *Theory of Moral Sentiments* and *Wealth of Nations*. Knox-Shaw (2004, 17–18) describes a collection of moral lessons for children based on Enlightenment works (*A Father's Instructions: Tales, Fables and Reflections, by Thomas Percival*, 1775) that was given to Austen by her brother. He points out that this work is used in the education of the character Catherine Morland in *Northanger Abbey*, providing further evidence that Jane Austen was familiar with it. Furthermore Eleanor Tilney refers fondly to works of Mr. Hume in *Northanger Abbey* (*NA*, 1062).

4. Whether one agrees with his perspective or not it is undoubtedly the case that John Maynard Keynes was one of the most influential economists of the twentieth century. He was also apparently an Austen reader. A contemporary of his, Austin Robinson, reported that "He crossed the Atlantic always by ship when he could. . . . The crossings in some measure provided a short holiday, for he would mix lighter reading (Jane Austen on this occasion) with his work and relax a little." Robinson (1947).

I

Adam Smith's *Theory of Moral Sentiments*: A User's Guide for Jane Austen Readers

Chapter Two

A General Introduction to Smith's Moral Theory

PART 1: SMITH'S THEORY

Adam Smith was a major figure of the Scottish Enlightenment, a movement that also included Smith's teacher Francis Hutcheson, David Hume, and others. The Scottish version of the Enlightenment is known for its pragmatism and skepticism. The Scots did not view human perfection as likely to be obtained, but thought we could and should strive for improvement. Yes, we use reason to understand and improve our world, but the Scots also recognized that our reason is sometimes clouded by our passions. They concluded that we must be realistic in our expectations about how far reason can take us.

Smith's first book, *The Theory of Moral Sentiments* was published in 1759. It was an attempt to identify the nature or the *science* of moral judgment, provide a roadmap for improvement of moral character, and explain the moral order of the social world. Smith, like other Enlightenment thinkers, was trying to apply a Newtonian framework to the study of human nature (Skinner, 1974). Sir Isaac Newton's laws of physics revolutionized the way people thought about the physical world by illustrating the order that exists in nature. Moral philosophers of the Enlightenment, such as Smith, looked for systems of order in the moral and social world.

Smith's *Theory of Moral Sentiments* maintains that sympathy leads to social order in moral development. Smith's second book, *An Inquiry into the Nature and Causes of the Wealth of Nations* (1776) holds that self-interest leads to social order in our commercial life. With the publication of *Wealth of Nations*, Smith separated himself from the rest of the moral philosophers of his time. No longer was he one of many philosophers of the Enlightenment.

Rather, this publication distinguished him as the founding father of economics: a separate discipline. In *Wealth of Nations* Smith asks why is it that some countries prosper while others remain poor? His answer is that prosperous countries trade. Indeed he maintains that people have a natural "propensity to truck, barter, and exchange" (*WN*, 25). This propensity leads us to specialize in what we can produce most efficiently and trade for the rest, in other words, it leads to the division of labor. Division of labor makes people more productive because we can focus on getting better at specific endeavors instead of trying to be jacks of all trades. More productivity improvements increases the size of the economic pie, that is, productivity leads to economic growth. To Smith, commercial activity is the key to the wealth of nations.

Smith had planned to publish a third book on Jurisprudence, or the study of law. While he died before he could draft this book, his *Lectures on Jurisprudence* from his years teaching at the University of Glasgow were published long after his death. In part of these lectures, Smith elaborates on the necessity of commerce for economic progress. He laments the fact that pre-commercial societies place a high value on obtaining wealth through conquests or inheritances and look down on trade as a way of making a living. The attitudes of most of the landed gentry of Jane Austen's novels reflect this pre-commercial way of thinking as is further explored in chapter 11.

While Adam Smith is best known for his work *Wealth of Nations*, his *Theory of Moral Sentiments* preceded WN by seventeen years. Smith revised TMS six times indicating he had an inordinate interest in the work. In fact, he was working on revisions of the work until his death, and the sixth edition was released two weeks before his death. Most but not all of the congruence found between Smith and Austen is between his TMS and her novels. So a somewhat more detailed analysis than the thumbnail sketch of TMS offered above is necessary for the readers to appreciate the congruence.

Smith is both transparent and frustrating to the modern reader. He is a writer of great eloquence and wit. In both TMS and WN he offers striking examples that illustrate his points. In fact many contemporary writers use Smith's examples when commenting on current events and problems. For example, in TMS Smith reflects on the probable response of a European "man of humanity" to a great earthquake in China, noting that in the final analysis the loss of such a man's "little finger" would be of more concern to him than "the ruin of hundreds of millions of his brethren" (*TMS*, 136–137). This example is commonly referred to in philosophical and academic treatises, as well as in the popular press (see for example, Miller, 2005). While contextual use of Smith is hardly inappropriate it is rare that these contemporary uses of Smith's work give a comprehensive view of Smith's thinking in TMS.

In fact coming up with a summary of TMS that fits on a bumper sticker, a one-page executive summary, or an elevator talk is difficult. The writing style of an eighteenth-century philosopher is alien and off-putting to even the most educated and motivated modern reader. We do not approach intellectual topics in the same way Smith did in the second half of the eighteenth century. TMS is hardly a linear work with clear and precise propositions followed by extensive mathematical proofs so common in modern economics. And thank heavens! Smith's style allows discussion of a plethora of issues and offers a number of ways of illustrating points about those issues.

A careful and conscientious reading of TMS gives us a work that is internally coherent as well as colorful and interesting. But this does not belie the task of summarizing TMS for the work at hand. Our best shot at a summary is: we humans crave approval and we also want to be able to look ourselves in the mirror and like what we see. Smith presents a system of virtues that, if practiced, lead to human flourishing. However, this summary is not quite enough. Therefore, we offer Jane Austen readers a guide, a tour, of TMS that is brief, usable, and accurate. We hope this basic skeletal outline of Smith's thinking coupled with a few well-honed insights about TMS will yield many returns in understanding Austen.

A BASIC SKETCH OF TMS

Adam Smith did not approach the issue of moral sentiments by offering a formal model. Yet his thinking is rigorous and thoughtful. We begin with a simple sketch of TMS that is summarized in the first section of this work. We believe this is a tractable and valid description of Smith's basic view of human nature and human interaction.

Smith begins his book with an account of human interdependence. His opening line is: "How selfish soever man may be supposed, there are evidently some principles in his nature, which interest him in the fortune of others, and render their happiness necessary to him, though he derives nothing from it except the pleasure of seeing it" (*TMS*, 9). At a superficial level this may seem puzzling coming from the author who also insisted in WN "It is not from the benevolence of the butcher, the brewer, or the baker, that we expect our dinner, but from their regard to their own interest" (*WN*, 26–27). Note that in TMS, Smith is excluding purely instrumental interests in others' well-being that seems to be at the heart of his description of market transactions in WN. In TMS, he is not talking about desiring to see another happy because there will be a commercial gain from their happiness. Instead, we desire to see others happy just because we like to see it.

However, in the opening sentence of TMS Smith does not dismiss self-regard. It is also inherent in human nature. He ends the paragraph by noting that the ability to show guileless interest in others' happiness is even found in the most self-regarding individual we can imagine. "The greatest ruffian, the most hardened violator of the laws of society, is not altogether without it" (*TMS*, 9).

Another insight is Smith's observation that this other regarding tendency in human nature is among "the original passions of human nature . . . " (*TMS*, 9). Human passions, or what we may call today human emotions, are at the heart of human nature. Part, but clearly not all, of our emotional makeup includes a tendency to unaffectedly regard the welfare of others.

Smith suggests that this interest in others is part of the biological nature of humans. He comments that when we see a stick ready to strike the leg of another, we instinctually flinch and through imagination can feel the pain of the sufferer. Smith calls this affinity "sympathy" or "fellow-feeling" and notes that humans feel mutual sympathy in regards to both joys and sorrows (*TMS*, 10).

Smith knows we are not creatures of pure instinct; we also use our intellect in making judgments about our fellow men. This includes when they are expressing joy or grief. Our immediate response to the visceral signals of joy or grief of another is to inquire as to its cause. We find this knowledge is necessary to inform an appropriate response. Or as Smith states, "our sympathy with the grief or joy of another, before we are informed of the cause of either, is always extremely imperfect" (*TMS*, 11). We might add, it is also quite problematic to know all the relevant components that led to the joy or grief even upon serious inquiry.

The tension between what we think is the case, what we fancy and imagine to be the case, and what is actually true is also at the heart of the human condition. Our knowledge is limited, especially our knowledge of the condition and feelings of our fellow man. So what is our recourse? There is none except to draw on our own personal experiences. I can understand your pain only because I have felt pain. At best, we can only approximate the feelings of another by referring to similar experiences we have gone through. "Every faculty in one man is the measure by which he judges of the like faculty in another. I judge of your sight by my sight, of your ear by my ear, of your reason by my reason, of your resentment by my resentment, of your love by my love. I neither have, nor can have, any other way of judging about them" (*TMS*, 19).

When we have a joy or sorrow, what we are looking for from our fellow man is something more than the superficial sympathy that they may instinctually provide. Rather we seek, we crave, a deeper sense of agreement or approbation or approval from our fellow man. Seeking and obtaining this approval in times of sorrows, especially ones that call for resentment, is the height of human camaraderie and a deep source of human satisfaction.

And so how do we obtain this approval? We know that the other person's sympathy is based on his own experience, which we don't completely understand and suspect may be far different from ours. We know that no other person is quite capable of feeling our joy or sorrow to the extent we do. We know we can never effectively communicate all the pre-conditions of our joy or sorrow. Therefore we must soften our own passions about our joy or sorrow in our communication with our counter-part, or in Smith's words, "He must flatten, if I may be allowed to say so, the sharpness of its natural tone, in order to reduce it to harmony and concord with the emotions of those who are about him" (*TMS*, 22). We can never really feel what others feel, so our passions will not be flattened to exactly equal another's, but they will become similar enough. Rather "[t]hough they will never be unisons, they may be concords, and this is all that is wanted or required" (*TMS*, 22).

This process of seeking mutual sympathy of sentiments along with tempering one's passions is the foundation of Smith's approach to moral theory. It recognizes and balances the emotional and rational components of human nature. It provides an iterative process of social interaction that ultimately forms social mores, rules, laws, and all social institutions. It lionizes neither unrestrained passion nor calculating reason. It emphasizes the social nature of man, yet leaves ample room for individual autonomy.

So what are our prospects for obtaining sympathy? Smith quite rightly states, "We expect less sympathy from a common acquaintance than from a friend" (*TMS*, 23). He goes on to note that the necessary and appropriate degree of tempering our passions increases the less well we know the other person. We show more control over our emotions in front of people that we do not know very well.

And to what extent should we expect to receive sympathy? This is an especially poignant question given our own natural favoring of ourselves and our own lack of knowledge of others. Is the sympathy we expect appropriate? Is the sympathy we receive appropriate? Have we tempered our appeal enough or perhaps too much? To what extent should we expect to give sympathy? Is the sympathy we give enough, given our own natural favoring of ourselves? Is it too much?

This is where Smith introduces his concept of the "impartial spectator" (*TMS*, 24). This is the entity to which we refer when we make our judgments on matters of morality. Smith mentions the impartial spectator throughout TMS, sixty-six times by our count, and yet never gives a technical definition of the term. The impartial spectator is something more than the individual human conscience; it is conscience tempered by a consideration of what an impartial morally upright person would regard as right and true. We know we are partial in favor of ourselves and our friends, and against our enemies. The impartial spectator is the proper corrector of these biases. He seems more than a mere heuristic device, but less than something we can model in any precise way. For our purposes we shall have to be content with the fuzzy notion that we know what Smith is getting at without requiring the precision we might like. Jane Austen's narrators are often impartial spectators of her characters' behaviors and every once in a while she invites the reader to imagine the feelings of one of her characters. Some characters serve as impartial spectators to others, as we will explore in chapter 9.

The impartial spectator is part of the iterative process of moral development in both the individual and the larger society. We learn to act virtuously by getting feedback about our behavior from others. We, in turn, provide similar feedback to others about their behavior. This constant feedback mechanism leads us to develop the impartial spectator that judges and guides our behavior. In the early years of our moral development, we act morally because we do not want others to judge us badly. As we use the feedback from others to develop our own impartial spectator, we then do not need judgments of others so much. Instead we judge ourselves. Our impartial spectator helps us to act virtuously, not so much because we are afraid to get caught by others and have to bear their disapproval. Rather we act virtuously because otherwise our own guilt will weigh us down. In this way social order emerges from our ability to sympathize and our desire for approval from ourselves and others.

From these very simple precepts about human behavior, Smith derives insights about the virtuous life. Although not explicit at this point it is clear that Smith sees the virtuous life as the best life, the one most amenable to generating human happiness both for the individual and the larger society. Again it may seem strange to those with a superficial acquaintance with WN, with its emphasis on trade and commerce, on gain and advantage, to think of Smith as viewing virtue as the fount of human happiness. But Smith seems convinced of this, and had his analysis in WN convinced him otherwise he surely would have expressed such sentiments in later revision of TMS.

Smith first informs us: "To feel much for others and little for ourselves, that to restrain our selfish, and to indulge our benevolent affections, constitutes the perfection of human nature" (*TMS*, 25). And what could be more plausible? Who is the person we admire most? Is it not the person who is attentive to the desires of others and not so concerned about themselves? We all revere the parent, child, teacher, colleague, friend who can cheer us up but does not require a lot of maintenance in return.

Smith goes on to describe the virtue that is essential in this perfection of human nature. He rightfully notes that virtue is not the same as good manners. "Virtue is excellence, something uncommonly great and beautiful, which rises far above what is vulgar and ordinary" (*TMS*, 25).

So if virtue is the key to happiness in Smith, how and why does virtue lead to happiness? Moreover, what obstacles do humans face in attaining the happy and virtuous life. Or put it another way, why are so many people so unhappy? To answer these questions let us now examine in more detail Smith's notion of what the virtuous life looks like. This discussion will be followed by an examination of Smith's views of how human nature impedes and/or misdirects this pursuit of virtue.

SMITH'S HAPPY PICTURE OF HUMAN VIRTUE

In a passing reference about wealth, Smith shows his hand and indicates that in his opinion "the chief part of human happiness arises from the consciousness of being beloved" (*TMS*, 41). Although being beloved may not exactly coincide with acquiring the approval and avoiding the disapproval of others it is clear that consistent attainment of the approval of others is very close to being beloved. And what causes one to be beloved?

It is easy to see how Smith's definition of human perfection and virtue is equivalent to being lovable. The person who cares much for others and little for herself; the person who can offer exquisite tenderness and simultaneously exert astonishing self-control is the object of our affection and approbation. But Smith goes a bit farther. To be truly virtuous and happy, one must not only obtain the admiration of one's fellow man (and make no mistake approval does and should please) one must also *deserve* the admiration. In fact being deserving of approval is, for the true man of virtue, *more* important than actually receiving approval. Or in his words "Man naturally desires, not only to be loved, but to be lovely. . . . He desires, not only praise, but praiseworthiness . . . " (*TMS*, 113–114). Smith goes on to point out that, "To be pleased with such groundless applause is a proof of the most superficial levity and weakness" (*TMS*, 115).

Smith argues that nature has given humans both the desire to be praised and to be praiseworthy (*TMS*, 117). The same proposition holds for blame and blameworthiness; both are things we instinctively wish to avoid. Smith even postulates avoiding being blameworthy is a more powerful force than simply avoiding blame. Smith argues that the fear of "inward disgrace" is the greatest fear of the "most commonly honest man" (*TMS*, 138).

By this reading, Smith seems an optimist. He sets his sights for individual humans to attain a very high degree of virtue. The mechanism he alludes to in this attainment is the aforementioned impartial spectator. The man of virtue is constantly referring his behavior and his internal feelings to the judgment of the spectator. In fact, "He does not merely affect the sentiments of the impartial spectator. He really adopts them. He almost identifies himself with, he almost becomes himself that impartial spectator" (*TMS*, 147). Smith makes much of the impartial spectator, and at one level it appears to be internal to the individual. Smith often refers to it as residing within one's breast. Yet as the quote above suggests it also has an existence external to the individual. Why is the impartial spectator so emphasized by Smith?

If part of the Enlightenment project is to free man from the slavish restraints of state and church, what will ensure moral order? One answer is individual conscience. If each individual is subject to an internal restraint, an internal voice, that directs, constrains, and improves his behavior, there is hope that a viable social order can emerge. The impartial spectator becomes "a hero of the Enlightenment" (Broadie, 2001, 101) as it is he (it?) that guides mankind, person by person, away from moral turpitude to moral rectitude. Such an internal-external entity that teaches, uplifts, corrects, and directs is not really so strange, even in contemporary culture.

One example can be found in youth organizations. The Boy and Girl Scouts of America are one of the largest youth organizations in the United States, having over five million youth members. Both organizations emphasize a code of behavior consistent with good manners, scrupulous honesty, and spirited benevolence. A song used to close many evening events in both organizations entreats the scout to seriously examine whether he/she has followed the ideals of scouting that day. Scouting tries to inculcate its participants in the habit of an internal moral dialogue at day's end.

Compare these sentiments and habits to Smith's comments about the impartial spectator:

> If in the course of the day we have swerved in any respect from the rules which he prescribes to us; if we have either exceeded or relaxed in our frugality; if we have either exceeded or relaxed in our industry; if, through passion or inadvertency, we have hurt in any respect the interest or happiness of our neighbour; if we have neglected a plain and proper opportunity of promoting that interest and happiness; it is this inmate who, in the evening, calls us to an account for all those omissions and violations, and his reproaches often make us blush inwardly both for our folly and inattention to our own happiness, and for our still greater indifference and inattention, perhaps, to that of other people. (*TMS*, 262)

For another example of an impartial spectator, we turn to Christian theology. Each part of the Christian trinity plays a definitive role in the lives of believers. If the second part of the trinity, Jesus Christ, is in heaven how can he advise and direct his followers on earth? In the Gospel of John, Jesus gives an answer: "But the Comforter, which is the Holy Ghost, whom the Father will send in my name, he shall teach you all things, and bring all things to your remembrance, whatsoever I have said unto you" (John 14:26 KJV). The Holy Ghost is God and external to the believer. The Holy Ghost is an immediate and available part of God. The Holy Ghost will inform and teach the faithful on earth as to correct conduct.

Smith asks how moral calculations are to be made when there are conflicting demands, for example, between gratitude and friendship? Smith postulates a faith in the impartial spectator as advisor and teacher. Compare his answer to the Gospel of John from above. According to Smith, we look to "the supposed impartial spectator, the great judge and arbiter of our conduct. If we place ourselves completely in his situation, if we really view ourselves with his eyes, and as he views us, and listen with diligent and reverential attention to what he suggests to us, his voice will never deceive us" (*TMS*, 226–227). The impartial spectator takes on near-divine characteristics in Smith, for better or worse.

Smith offers a second mechanism that complements the impartial spectator and is a much more down-to-earth ballast against evil and for a good life and good society, namely, access to general principles and rules of conduct. Although we are all inclined to follow our own selfish inclinations Smith notes:

> Nature, however, has not left this weakness, which is of so much importance, altogether without a remedy; nor has she abandoned us entirely to the delusions of self-love. Our continual observations upon the conduct of others, insensibly lead us to form to ourselves certain general rules concerning what is fit and proper either to be done or to be avoided. (*TMS*, 159)

> Those general rules of conduct, when they have been fixed in our mind by habitual reflection, are of great use in correcting the misrepresentations of self-love concerning what is fit and proper to be done in our particular situation. (*TMS*, 159–160)

The supplement and likely predecessor of Smith's impartial spectator, then, are general rules. These rules ensure the good conduct necessary for individual moral development and necessary for maintaining the social order. Put another way, the impartial spectator is rather powerless in the heart of a man or woman in the absence of their comprehensive respect for general rules. "Without this sacred regard to general rules, there is no man whose conduct can be much depended upon. It is this which constitutes the most essential difference between a man of principle and honour and a worthless fellow" (*TMS*, 163).

In his famous China earthquake example mentioned earlier, Smith makes two major points. First, although we all bemoan disasters that are far away, these do not influence our behavior as much as the small problems of our immediate world. Indeed, we would be more upset at the loss of our little finger than we would be upon learning of millions of deaths across the globe. But, turning to Smith's second point, would we be willing to trade the lives of millions in China in order to save our little finger? According to Smith, "Human nature startles with horror at the thought" (*TMS*, 137). But why? We maintain that Smith's second, often-missed, point in the China earthquake story is that our horror does not emerge just from our own nature but rather from inculcated moral rules or *principles*. Yes, we have "that feeble spark of benevolence" that makes us care for others, but that spark is not enough to completely offset our self-love. The "stronger power" that makes us unable to purchase back our little finger with millions of Chinese earthquake victims "is reason, principle, conscience, the inhabitant of the breast, the man within, the great judge and arbiter of our conduct" (*TMS*, 137). Our moral behavior, then, is guided by the impartial spectator, with the helping hand of general rules and principles.

SMITH'S REALISTIC PICTURE OF HUMAN NATURE

And now for the rest of us. Although Smith sets a high mark for virtue and seems optimistic in our ability to attain it, he is quite aware of the problems humans have in attaining such virtue; and he is well aware of the flaws in human nature. Desire for approbation from others causes us to reduce the pitch of our passions. Our amenability to rules and impartial spectator constrains but does not completely tame our natural self-love.

Smith recognizes that we may not be able to attain true virtue, even though we may often act with propriety, and he draws an important distinction between the two concepts.

> There is, in this respect, a considerable difference between virtue and mere propriety; between those qualities and actions which deserve to be admired and celebrated, and those which simply deserve to be approved of. Upon many occasions, to act with the most perfect propriety, requires no more than that common and ordinary degree of sensibility or self-command which the most worthless of mankind are possest of, and sometimes even that degree is not necessary. (*TMS*, 25)

Smith gives us a striking example

> Thus, to give a very low instance, to eat when we are hungry, is certainly, upon ordinary occasions, perfectly right and proper, and cannot miss being approved of as such by every body. Nothing, however, could be more absurd than to say it was virtuous. (*TMS*, 25)

Our behavior, then, can fall along a spectrum from vice to virtue, and propriety is seen as a sort of borderline where we move from vice into virtue. Proper behavior is that which would attain the *approval* from the impartial spectator, but virtuous behavior would attain his *admiration*.

The human tendency to moral behavior never works perfectly because humans are subject to systematic flaws. The predisposition for human bias and subsequent error in action and corruption in character is a constant theme in TMS. Our judgment, especially as to our own rectitude is biased. No one wants to think ill of themselves as Smith states:

It is so disagreeable to think ill of ourselves, that we often purposely turn away our view from those circumstances which might render that judgment unfavourable. He is a bold surgeon, they say, whose hand does not tremble when he performs an operation upon his own person; and he is often equally bold who does not hesitate to pull off the mysterious veil of self-delusion. . . . This self-deceit, this fatal weakness of mankind, is the source of half the disorders of human life. (*TMS*, 158)

Human beings want to believe themselves to be worthy of the admiration of others, but we have a difficult time making an accurate assessment of our own worthiness. This is especially true when it comes to our behavior on matters deemed right and wrong. Our stubbornly flawed self-judgments lead us astray.

This insight is not original or unique to Smith. Socrates, a fount of wisdom in the Western tradition, called on us to "know thyself." Russian writer Fyodor Dostoevsky lists self-deceit is the source of most maladies in the human soul. As his Father Zossima states, "Above all don't lie to yourself. The man who lies to himself . . . loses all respect for himself and others" (Dostoevsky, 1987, 20). Twentieth-century Russian writer Alexander Solzhenitsyn sees evil as emerging from a drive for good. "To do evil a human being must first of all believe that what he's doing is good, or else that it's a well-considered act in conformity with natural law. Fortunately, it is in the nature of the human being to seek a justification for his actions" (Solzhenitsyn, 1974, 173). He goes on to note that such self-deceptions are often fueled by all-encompassing ideologies so prominent in his time which "helps to make his acts seem good instead of bad in his own and others' eyes, so that he won't hear reproaches and curses but will receive praise and honors" (Solzhenitsyn, 1974, 173).

T. S. Eliot, modern English-American poet and playwright, notes, "Half the harm that is done in this world is due to people who want to feel important. They don't mean to do harm; but the harm does not interest them. Or they do not see it, or they justify it because they are absorbed in the endless struggle to think well of themselves" (Eliot, 1950, 47).

This theme of self-deception and systemic bias continues to play a large role in the modern field of behavioral economics. Behavioralists combine the insights of economics with that of psychology in an attempt to better understand human decision making. On the one hand, yes, individuals often make mistakes when assessing costs and benefits especially when uncertainty is involved. On the other hand, our decision making can improve and social order can emerge when we interact with others. Roberts (2014) views this field as owing an intellectual debt to Smith. Indeed many in the field specifically cite *Theory of Moral Sentiments*.

When Smith indicates that half of human problems result from an unwillingness to critically evaluate ourselves, he also offers an insight into the source of most of the rest of our problems. It is human to misestimate the felicity/misery of one situation compared to another. Professor B at XYZ State U estimates his happiness will markedly increase if he lands a position at Ivy U. He also estimates he will be miserable if he is forced out of XYZ State U to Podunk State. He is in fact wrong; his ability to lead a virtuous life is pretty much the same at all three locations, yet this illusion directs his behavior. As Smith puts it:

> The great source of both the misery and disorders of human life, seems to arise from over-rating the difference between one permanent situation and another. Avarice over-rates the difference between poverty and riches: ambition, that between a private and a public station: vain-glory, that between obscurity and extensive reputation. The person under the influence of any of those extravagant passions, is not only miserable in his actual situation, but is often disposed to disturb the peace of society, in order to arrive at that which he so foolishly admires. (*TMS*, 149)

So Smith is cognizant of the importance yet difficulty of self-assessment. Most people don't make the mark of the "wise and virtuous man" (*TMS*, 247). Smith illustrates this difficulty in perception in his discussion of the self-estimation by great men and by less-than-great underachievers. Both types misestimate and their misestimating leads to regrettable consequences for all. "The principle of self-estimation may be too high, and it may likewise be too low. It is so very agreeable to think highly, and so very disagreeable to think meanly of ourselves, that, to the person himself, it cannot well be doubted, but that some degree of excess must be much less disagreeable than any degree of defect" (*TMS*, 246). Humans prefer to think well of themselves; and therefore, tend to err on the side of overestimation.

But Smith goes further. Thinking well of oneself is, more often than not, a prerequisite to being a success. "Great success in the world, great authority over the sentiments and opinions of mankind, have very seldom been acquired without some degree of this excessive self-admiration" (*TMS*, 250). And this often leads to disaster for all involved. Smith refers to the madness and cruelty of Alexander the Great, who betrayed and executed his true friends in fits of paranoid insanity. The lavishness of the leader's self-estimation causes him to suspect those faithful confidants whose "sober and just esteem falls so far short of the extravagance of his own self-admiration, that he regards it as mere malignity and envy. He suspects his best friends. Their company becomes offensive to him. He drives them from his presence, and often rewards their services, not only with ingratitude, but with cruelty and injustice" (*TMS*, 254). This picture foreshadows the criminal excesses of the twentieth century's Hitler, Stalin, Mao, and Pol Pot. But one need not be a psychotic sociopath to suffer and make others suffer from one's excessive self-estimation.

What of those whose self-estimation is too low? Smith's picture is not very hopeful there either.

> Men of merit considerably above the common level, sometimes underrate as well as over-rate themselves. Such characters, though not very dignified, are often, in private society, far from being disagreeable. His companions . . . may have some kindness for him, they have seldom much respect; and the warmth of their kindness is very seldom sufficient to compensate the coldness of their respect. (*TMS*, 259–260)

Such a man is always under achieving and turning down opportunities: "He seems doubtful himself, they say, whether he is perfectly fit for such a situation or such an office; and immediately give the preference to some impudent blockhead who entertains no doubt about his own qualifications" (*TMS*, 260). And although Smith may not have said it, letting the blockheads rule hardly makes the world a better place. Moreover, we can hardly envy the frustration such a man inevitably faces. Smith notes that such a man usually ends up with "an insignificant, complaining, and discontented old age" (*TMS*, 260).

The truly modest and virtuous man of Smith's imagination is not a meek and mild character, nor is he averse to ambition. In fact what in Smith's time was called *mean spirited* is the underachiever who fails to take on the vicissitudes of life. As Smith says

> A person appears mean-spirited, who does not pursue these with some degree of earnestness for their own sake. We should despise a prince who was not anxious about conquering or defending a province. We should have little respect for a private gentleman who did not exert himself to gain an estate, or even a considerable office, when he could acquire them without either meanness or injustice. A member of parliament who shews no keenness about his own election, is abandoned by his friends, as altogether unworthy of their attachment. Even a tradesman is thought a poor-spirited fellow among his neighbours, who does not bestir himself to get what they call an extraordinary job, or some uncommon advantage. This spirit and keenness constitutes the difference between the man of enterprise and the man of dull regularity. Those great objects of self-interest, of which the loss or acquisition quite changes the rank of the person, are the objects of the passion properly called ambition; a passion, which when it keeps within the bounds of prudence and justice, is always admired in the world. (*TMS*, 173)

Smith's path to the virtuous and happy life as given in TMS looks straightforward but its actual attainment is rather difficult. Getting one's self-assessment *just right* seems impossible, but misestimating leaves one prone to folly, disaster, and misery. Yet who is to blame? Most of our problems reside in our own nature, not the stars. We misunderstand others, but more important we misjudge ourselves; and so humans are a mixture of joy and sorrow, gratitude and resentment, vice and virtue. These are clearly themes that arise in Jane Austen's world, in her stories, her plots, and her characters.

We will now follow with some additional insights Smith makes about the human condition that are often echoed in Austen, the specific vices and virtues outlined in Smith.

Chapter Three

Virtues and Vices in Smith

As we have seen in the previous chapter, Smith's TMS is a theory about the formation and implementation of human moral sentiments. The life of virtue, the best way to a satisfying life of happiness and tranquility, is understandable to the ordinary man and yet elusive. The moral instinct is part of human nature, yet its impediments are also part of human nature.

We do not ascribe to Jane Austen a wholesale adoption of Smith's theory. However, what we do note is that many themes and specifics in TMS seem to resonate strongly in Austen's novels. In the spirit of providing the reader a guide to this Smith-Austen overlap, we now offer an analysis of the specific virtues and vices outlined by Smith in TMS in some detail. We will find uncanny overlaps in Jane Austen's novels to be explored in later chapters.

In terms of virtues, Smith offers a kind of holy trinity of PB&J: Prudence, Benevolence, and Justice grounded in the separate and necessary virtue of Self-Command. Smith calls prudence a self-directed virtue, while benevolence and justice are other-directed virtues. All these must be crowned with the virtue of self-command. "The man who acts according to the rules of perfect prudence, of strict justice, and of proper benevolence, may be said to be perfectly virtuous. But the most perfect knowledge of those rules will not alone enable him to act in this manner: . . . The most perfect knowledge, if it is not supported by the most perfect self-command, will not always enable him to do his duty" (*TMS*, 237).

Smith divides virtue into two distinct classes. "The amiable virtues consist in that degree of sensibility which surprises by its exquisite and unexpected delicacy and tenderness" (*TMS*, 25). These are contrasted to but not opposed to "[t]he awful and respectable, in that degree of self-command which astonishes by its amazing superiority over the most ungovernable passions of human nature" (*TMS*, 25). (Note that "awful" here means awe-inspiring, as opposed to bad.)

The amiable virtues (such as benevolence) are other directed; they are the best of what we can give when we offer sympathy to others. They are amiable precisely because they comfort and encourage others. The awful virtues (such as prudence) are self-directed and consist of constraining our own passions out of regard for the well-being of others. Smith also refers to another term relating to self-directed virtue that is crucial in his moral theory: self-command. (We count it showing up in TMS fifty-one times.)

The crucial vices Smith discusses flow from the tendency to excessive self-estimation and can be classified as those of pride and vanity. "[W]e cannot enter into and sympathize with the excessive self–estimation of those characters in which we can discern no such distinguished superiority. We are disgusted and revolted by it. . . . We call it pride or vanity; two words, of which the latter always, and the former for the most part, involve in their meaning a considerable degree of blame" (*TMS*, 255).

Let us now turn our attention to what Smith has to say about these six topics: Prudence, Benevolence, Justice, Self-Command, Vanity, and Pride.

PRUDENCE

Prudence is a Smithian virtue that concerns our *own* happiness, as opposed to the virtues of benevolence and justice that involve our concern for others. Prudence is "both supported and rewarded by the entire approbation of the impartial spectator" (*TMS*, 215). According to Smith, "We suffer more . . . when we fall from a better to a worse situation, than we ever enjoy when we rise from a worse to a better" (*TMS*, 213); therefore we practice prudence to obtain security from a fall. Prudence can be best seen as a set of life-style habits that can be adopted and developed.

A prudent woman takes care of her health, her fortune, and her reputation in an attempt to find security. She is frugal, sincere, and does not meddle with business or affairs that are not her own. The prudent woman is honest, she is not a braggart, she knows her own business, and is constantly improving her knowledge of her trade, profession, or occupation. The prudent woman is quite capable of friendships although she is not inclined to sociability beyond that which is necessary and proper. She is not a reveler but observes proper decency. A prudent woman hates faction. In short, a prudent woman is a very boring lady.

And it takes more than prudence alone for us to be fully virtuous. A woman may live a life where she harms no one, is always proper and polite and acts with propriety and decency, yet fails to draw the deep admiration of others. As Smith says, "Prudence . . . is regarded as a most respectable and even, in some degree, as an amiable and agreeable quality, yet it never is considered as one, either of the most endearing, or of the most ennobling of the virtues. It commands a certain cold esteem, but seems not entitled to any very ardent love or admiration (*TMS*, 216).

Smith insists that prudence must be augmented with the other virtues. "Prudence is, in all these cases, combined with many greater and more splendid virtues, with valour, with extensive and strong benevolence, with a sacred regard to the rules of justice, and all these supported by a proper degree of self-command. This superior prudence . . . is the best head joined to the best heart. It is the most perfect wisdom combined with the most perfect virtue" (*TMS*, 216).

BENEVOLENCE

When most people think of "benevolence" and Adam Smith, they think of the famous quote from *Wealth of Nations*; "It is not from the benevolence of the butcher, the brewer, or the baker, that we expect our dinner, but from their regard to their own interest" (*WN*, 26–27). Here Smith is describing how self-interested behavior is turned into service to others in market transactions. In this way he offers us a pragmatic defense of capitalism. Far too many people, however, have interpreted Smith here as implying that *greed is good*. On the contrary, benevolence plays a large role in Smith's vision of morality. And as we have seen in the previous chapter on TMS, Smith maintains "that to feel much for others and little for ourselves, that to restrain our selfish, and to indulge our benevolent affections, constitutes the perfection of human nature" (*TMS*, 25).

Smith contends that the degree of our benevolence depends on how close we are to the people needing our assistance. He begins with the notion that "[e]very man . . . is first and principally recommended to his own care" (*TMS*, 219). We know ourselves the best, so we know what is best for us. After ourselves, we know best our own families. Since benevolence is dependent on our sympathy for others, it is only natural that we feel the most sympathy for those we know best. After the immediate family comes the extended family and then friends. To be an object of benevolence, one must be an object of sympathy; and sympathy is contingent on regular and persistent interaction. Smith says as much when he notes "What is called affection, is in reality nothing but habitual sympathy. Our concern in the happiness or misery of those who are the objects of what we call our affections" (*TMS*, 220).

We also owe a special benevolence toward those who have been previously generous to us. In summary, we are most benevolent and least self-interested with those closest to us. As the level of familiarity falls, the amount of benevolence decreases and the amount of self-interest increases. When dealing with complete strangers in a commercial setting, then, we are motivated almost solely by self-interest. Otteson (2002) and others call this Smith's *familiarity principle* in that benevolence and familiarity are positively related to one another.

The economist and legal scholar Ronald Coase made a similar point. Smith knew the division of labor necessary for living standards in his time depended on the cooperation of literally a "multitude" (*WN*, 22). As Smith points out in his example of the woolen coat, and as Leonard Read points out in his famous 1958 essay on the pencil, most of the people who do the work of providing us even the simplest of products are strangers who will not, cannot be motivated by benevolence to provide us with our wants. Coase concludes,

> Adam Smith's argument for the use of the market for the organization of economic activity is much stronger than it is usually thought to be. The market is not simply an ingenious mechanism, fueled by self-interest, for securing the co-operation of individuals in the production of goods and services. In most circumstances it is the only way in which this could be done. (Coase, 1976, 544)

Going back to the China earthquake example, Smith comments that the thought of millions dying in China to save a single European man's little finger "startles (us) with horror at the thought . . . " (*TMS*, 137). Yet we act as if we don't care much about the dying Chinese (or slaughtered Syrians, Iraqis, Sudanese, Ukrainians, Uighurs . . .). We sleep well at night despite our knowledge. So Smith asks, "But what makes this difference? When our passive feelings are almost always so sordid and so selfish, how comes it that our active principles should often be so generous and so noble?" (*TMS*, 137). Recall his answer is that "it is not that feeble spark of benevolence. . . . [i]t is reason, principle, conscience, the inhabitant of the breast . . . " (*TMS*, 137). In other words, it is the impartial spectator, coupled with the proclivity to understand and accept moral precepts, that makes us recognize that "we are but one of the multitude" (*TMS*, 137).

Smith cannot make this point enough when reflecting on how we respond nobly to distant catastrophes "[i]t is not the love of our neighbour, it is not the love of mankind, which upon many occasions prompts us to the practice of those divine virtues. It is a stronger love, a more powerful affection . . . the love of what is honourable and noble, of the grandeur, and dignity, and superiority of our own characters" (*TMS*, 137).

This all confirms Smith's view that benevolence is not the virtue we exhibit when we deal with others outside our immediate circle. Benevolence is very limited in its ability to make humans behave properly toward strangers and those who are unseen in the larger social order, because truly benevolent actions require direct sympathy which is by all accounts quite local.

Do not be tempted to infer, however, that Smith views benevolence as merely an outgrowth of self-love; it is to be distinguished from prudence. Indeed, having a selfish motive for benevolent actions "seems often to sully the beauty of those actions" (*TMS*, 304). Smith further maintains that "[t]he wise and virtuous man is at all times willing that his own private interest should be sacrificed to the public interest" (*TMS*, 235).

That man in *Theory of Moral Sentiments* is assumed to be motivated by sympathy, while man in *Wealth of Nations* is assumed to be motivated by self-interest has long been referred to as "the Adam Smith problem." Otteson (2002) offers the familiarity principle as a solution to this perceived problem. Our moral development is based upon sympathy, and we feel the most sympathy for those we hold most dear. It is only natural, then, for our interactions with family and friends to be based upon benevolence. Our interactions with strangers, say the butcher, the brewer, or the baker, are based upon self-interest because we do not know them well enough to sympathize with them. Our impartial spectator and our ability to be subject to principles and rules, however, ensure that our dealings with strangers are also within moral bounds, for we are always constrained by the rules of justice.

JUSTICE

While benevolence and justice are both virtues that concern our relationships with others (social virtues), Smith makes an important distinction between the two (*TMS*, 78–82). It is virtuous to be both benevolent and just, but one only has a *duty* to be just; one has no obligation to be benevolent. Benevolent acts are always the result of free will and we are indeed encouraged by our impartial spectator and by God to perform them. Justice, however, may be implemented by force. To act without benevolence does no harm to another, but to act unjustly is to inflict harm on others. "Justice . . . is the main pillar that upholds the whole edifice. If it is removed, the great, the immense fabric of human society . . . must in a moment crumble into atoms" (*TMS*, 86). Benevolence, however, "is the ornament which embellishes, not the foundation which supports the building" (*TMS*, 86).

So what does Smith mean when he says an individual is to practice justice? Smith calls the keeping of serious promises as "that most sacred rule of justice" (*TMS*, 330). Promises, therefore, should not be taken lightly. "A brave man ought to die, rather than make a promise which he can neither keep without folly, nor violate without ignominy" (*TMS*, 332). Smith gives as an example of justice the repayment of debts. "If I owe a man ten pounds, justice requires that I should precisely pay him ten pounds, either at the time agreed upon, or when he demands it" (*TMS*, 175). He likens the rules of justice to the rules of grammar in that they are "precise, accurate, and indispensable" (*TMS*, 175). Furthermore, just as we can learn to write correctly by following the rules of grammar, so too can we learn to act justly by following the rules of justice. Justice is strict, impartial, and incorporates the interests of the larger community. Smith refers to the case of the Roman leader Brutus who "led forth his own sons to a capital punishment, because they had conspired against the rising liberty of Rome" (*TMS*, 192). As a father, this had to be difficult, but as a Roman citizen Brutus was able to condemn and properly punish the traitors.

To Smith, the practice of the three virtues of prudence, benevolence, and justice (PB&J) together produce human happiness. Furthermore, our recognition of these virtues in others, through our sympathy, also increases our happiness.

> In our approbation of the character of the prudent man, we feel, with peculiar complacency, the security which he must enjoy while he walks under the safeguard of that sedate and deliberate virtue. In our approbation of the character of the just man, we feel, with equal complacency, the security which all those connected with him, whether in neighbourhood, society, or business, must derive from his scrupulous anxiety never either to hurt or offend. In our approbation of the character of the beneficent man, we enter into the gratitude of all those who are within the sphere of his good offices, and conceive with them the highest sense of his merit. (*TMS*, 264)

Of course, as noted above, the trinity of PB&J requires the development of self-command.

SELF-COMMAND

Self-command is not a term we use in contemporary discussion. Our equivalent phrase is "self-control." Smith sees self-command as having two parts. On the one hand it allows us to constrain the excesses of immediate passion of the moment, for example controlling our excessive anger. But self-command also refers to constraining one's desire for immediate "ease, pleasure . . . and other gratifications" (*TMS*, 238) so as to complete tedious but necessary duties, to fulfill obligations, and finish useful projects. In other words the second part of self-command allows us to gain the benefits of delayed gratification. "The command of the former . . . denominated fortitude, manhood, and strength of mind; that of the latter, temperance, decency, modesty, and moderation" (*TMS*, 238).

Smith notes that a young child has no self-command. But then when it[1] is introduced to the company of other children it quickly learns that it must restrain its own desires and passions to get along with its playmates. "It thus enters into the great school of self-command, it studies to be more and more master of itself, and begins to exercise over its own feelings a discipline which the practice of the longest life is very seldom sufficient to bring to complete perfection" (*TMS*, 145).

Although self-command is part of the set of respectable (awful) virtues it is not at all in conflict with the amiable virtues.[2] In fact it is self-command that allows us to properly practice the amiable virtues.

> Our sensibility to the feelings of others, so far from being inconsistent with the manhood of self-command, is the very principle upon which that manhood is founded. The very same principle or instinct which, in the misfortune of our neighbour, prompts us to compassionate his sorrow; in our own misfortune, prompts us to restrain the abject and miserable lamentations of our own sorrow. (*TMS*, 152)

Self-command is the prerequisite for avoiding vice and a first among equals in the practice of virtue. "Self-command is not only itself a great virtue, but from it all the other virtues seem to derive their principal lustre" (*TMS*, 241).

VANITY

Smith offers a number of examples, definitions, and insights into vanity that are quite interesting. For a comprehensive understanding of Smith's view of vanity we must now stray from the task of outlining Smith's views as they relate to the relationships and interactions among families, friends, and acquaintances which are central to Austen's work. Instead, we will explore Smith's thinking on vanity as it applies to the larger social order.

Vanity, it ends up, is quite related to our desire to accumulate wealth, status, or improved social standing. Smith argues that "[i]t is because mankind are disposed to sympathize more entirely with our joy than with our sorrow, that we make parade of our riches, and conceal our poverty. . . . it is chiefly from this regard to the sentiments of mankind, that we pursue riches and avoid poverty" (*TMS*, 50). Note Smith makes reference to his foundation of human nature, the desire for mutual sympathy. He posits an asymmetry in obtaining mutual sympathy between joys and sorrows; folks go along with good news more than the bad. And, of course, there is no better good news to share than the newly acquired trinkets, the baubles, the conveniences, the contraptions, those items of consumption that we can show off to our neighbor. All this, however, requires income and wealth; which in turn requires income-producing activity of some form. We not only want to keep up with the Joneses, we want to one-up the Joneses. And get the Joneses to admire us and offer their approbation by admiring our fortune as evidenced by the goods and services we consume.

Smith is very explicit about this. The point of getting goods and services that come with wealth, rank, and power is *not* the utility those goods offer us. It is not the pleasure, it is not the convenience, rather it is the desire to be admired by others, which he identifies as vanity. As a matter of fact, all upward mobility, through trade and commerce or any other means, is driven by vanity, that is, the desire to be praised and admired by others.

> From whence . . . (comes) that great purpose of human life which we call bettering our condition? To be observed, to be attended to, to be taken notice of with sympathy, complacency, and approbation. . . . It is the vanity, not the ease, or the pleasure, which interests us. But vanity is always founded upon the belief of our being the object of attention and approbation. (*TMS*, 50)

So riches, preferment, and fame all appear to fulfill our desire to be beloved. Vanity is a cheap substitute for the *real* reason to be beloved and admired, which is to be praiseworthy.

But what of our desire for praise and praiseworthiness? Vanity plays a role here too! In Smith's view it is fine to be praised if one is *worthy* of praise, it is also fine to enjoy that praise. But there is another way to obtain praise that is not so upright, by lying, by claiming to have done things that you have not done, or by putting on airs so as others conclude you are praiseworthy. This, too, is vanity. "To desire, or even to accept of praise, where no praise is due, can be the effect only of the most contemptible vanity" (*TMS*, 117). "To be pleased with such groundless applause . . . is what is properly called vanity, and is the foundation of the most ridiculous and contemptible vices, the vices of affectation and common lying" (*TMS*, 115).

So another way to be vain is to tell tall tales to make one's self interesting or put on airs of greatness. But it is to the same end: getting attention, approbation, and approval on the cheap.

Smith appears shocked that the behavior of the "foolish liar" and "coxcomb" in fact work, but he recognizes it does. The empirical evidence and the vain man's enormous capacity for self-delusion lead to the conclusion that even common sense cannot save him from it.

> [I]f experience did not teach us how common they are, one should imagine the least spark of common sense would save us from [it]. The foolish liar, who endeavours to excite the admiration of the company by the relation of adventures which never had any existence; the important coxcomb, who gives himself airs of rank and distinction which he well knows he has no just pretensions to; are both of them, no doubt, pleased with the applause which they fancy they meet with. But their vanity arises from so gross an illusion of the imagi-

nation, that it is difficult to conceive how any rational creature should be imposed upon by it. (*TMS*, 115)

To desire distinction, to desire to be admired, without being praiseworthy is to be vain. Wealth and greatness, as well as deception and falsehood, facilitate such admiration. This admiration, again, is a misguided desire for recognition and praise, or vanity. "[T]he magnificence of wealth and greatness; and in this consists the sole advantage of these last. They more effectually gratify that love of distinction so natural to man" (*TMS*, 182).

Smith highlights the irony. Wealth derived to attain approbation and attention never quite works out as expected. Smith offers the story of the poor man's son who is cursed by ambition. Admiring the rich and famous, he finds his father's cottage and way of life inadequate. He embarks on improving his situation. He is clearly motivated by his vanity and by "the idea of a certain artificial and elegant repose" (*TMS*, 181) that he thinks his riches will give him, the end-point of vanity. He forges forward improving himself, being the best in his field and advancing as he submits "to more fatigue of body and more uneasiness of mind" (*TMS*, 181) in the first month of his quest than he would otherwise in his entire life. At the end of it all, he is wealthy and successful but "find[s] that wealth and greatness are mere trinkets of frivolous utility . . . " (*TMS*, 181). He ends up with only baubles and trinkets and comes to see that "[p]ower and riches appear then to be, what they are, enormous and operose machines contrived to produce a few trifling conveniencies . . . " (*TMS*, 182).

So much for the Smith of WN who admires profit seeking activity. Isn't this the *real* "Adam Smith problem"? It would seem these lamentations about the futility of wealth and advancement would make Smith join with the cadre of philosophers and moralists who despise wealth, denounce accumulation, and preach against materialism.

But Smith pulls a surprise card in TMS that insulates him from any such critique. As to vanity's ability to delude us to seek wealth, power, and rank, Smith proclaims, "And it is well that nature imposes upon us in this manner. It is this deception which rouses and keeps in continual motion the industry of mankind" (*TMS*, 183). Why is it *well*? Because, if humans did not fall prey to vanity's deception there would be no progress, no civilization for humankind. This deception prompts us "to build houses, to found cities and commonwealths, and to invent and improve all the sciences and arts . . . " (*TMS*, 183). This "industry of mankind" stemming from vanity increases living standards, improves health, and allows for larger populations. Smith recognizes the costs of civilization, but he is no romantic pining for the halcyon days of the savages. He believes civilization is worth the costs. He goes on, "The earth by these labours of mankind has been obliged to redouble her natural fertility, and to maintain a greater multitude of inhabitants" (*TMS*,

184). And so what of those who obtain most of the apparent gains from this expansion of human activity? What of the landlords, the princes, the entre-preneurs, the titans who direct and appropriate most of the gains? Smith tells us, yes, the greedy landlord "in [his] imagination consumes himself the whole harvest . . . " (*TMS*, 184). But in reality, both the rich and poor benefit. The rich,

> consume little more than the poor, and in spite of their natural selfishness and rapacity, though they mean only their own conveniency, though the sole end which they propose from the labours of all the thousands whom they employ, be the gratification of their own vain and insatiable desires, they divide with the poor the produce of all their improvements. They are led by an *invisible hand* [emphasis added] to make nearly the same distribution of the necessaries of life, which would have been made, had the earth been divided into equal portions among all its inhabitants, and thus without intending it, without knowing it, advance the interest of the society, and afford means to the multi-plication of the species. When Providence divided the earth among a few lordly masters, it neither forgot nor abandoned those who seemed to have been left out in the partition. These last too enjoy their share of all that it produces. In what constitutes the real happiness of human life, they are in no respect inferior to those who would seem so much above them. In ease of body and peace of mind, all the different ranks of life are nearly upon a level, and the beggar, who suns himself by the side of the highway, possesses that security which kings are fighting for. (*TMS*, 184–185)

This "invisible hand" reference, which so clearly outlines the unintended consequences of successful vanity, is found in TMS, not WN, which usually gets credit for the concept.[3] In TMS, Smith suggests that yes, personal vanity leads to improved outcomes for the vain, greedy, and often rapacious instiga-tor of economic improvements. But, the lion's share of these benefits go to the masses. This insight may be particularly true in a market-based system, but Smith seems to imply the result is pretty much independent of the eco-nomic system in place.

PRIDE

Pride differs from vanity, although clearly an individual may have both. Both suffer from excessive self-estimation. The vain man craves approbation and praise that he does not deserve and deep down knows he does not deserve it. The proud man really does believe in his own superiority and while he thinks he deserve praise he does not seek it, especially from his inferiors (which includes almost everyone). "The proud man is sincere, and, in the bottom of his heart, is convinced of his own superiority; though it may sometimes be difficult to guess upon what that conviction is founded. . . . He disdains to court your esteem . . . [he] seems to wish, not so much to excite your esteem for himself, as to mortify that for yourself" (*TMS*, 255).

The proud man is really a rather unpleasant fellow. He is not impressed by others' compliments (thinking, isn't it obvious that I am great?) and he is not inclined to offer his approbation to others. The vain man, on the other hand, loves the compliments of others and is quite willing to offer approbation to almost everyone in order to see it reciprocated to himself. He is very amiable fellow, although perhaps not that interesting.

> The vain man is not sincere, and, in the bottom of his heart, is very seldom convinced of that superiority which he wishes you to ascribe to him. . . . Far from despising your esteem, he courts it with the most anxious assiduity. Far from wishing to mortify your self-estimation, he is happy to cherish it, in hopes that in return you will cherish his own. He flatters in order to be flattered. (*TMS*, 255–256)

The vain man is disposed to what economists call *conspicuous consumption*, and he wishes to imitate those of the best class. The vain man is often driven to financial ruin as he tries to keep up appearances to impress those from whom he seeks to be flattered.

> The vain man sees the respect which is paid to rank and fortune, and wishes to usurp this respect, as well as that for talents and virtues. His dress, his equipage, his way of living, accordingly, all announce both a higher rank and a greater fortune than really belong to him. . . . The proud man can very seldom be accused of this folly. (*TMS*, 256)

Smith makes clear who is the best company at a cocktail party or who to invite to a social gathering. Vanity trumps pride. The vain man gives "a pleasant and a sprightly flattery, . . . The proud man, on the contrary, never flatters, and is frequently scarce civil to anybody. . . . vanity is almost always a sprightly and a gay, and very often a good-natured passion. Pride is always a grave, a sullen, and a severe one" (*TMS*, 257).

Typical of Smith's subtle thinking, he views the vices of pride and vanity as often correlated with virtues. We may respect the proud man despite his flaw and may genuinely like the vain man despite his blemish; " . . . pride is frequently attended with many respectable virtues; with truth, with integrity, with a high sense of honour, with cordial and steady friendship, with the most inflexible firmness and resolution. Vanity, with many amiable ones; with humanity, with politeness, with a desire to oblige in all little matters, and sometimes with a real generosity" (*TMS*, 258).

Vanity is never in itself a virtue but is something that can be overcome. Smith sees vanity as a common tendency among the young. The high-spirited nature of the young often leads them to foolish vanity but time, proper education, and life-experience often remedy the vanity of youth.

> The words vain and vanity are never taken in a good sense. . . . Vanity is very frequently no more than an attempt prematurely to usurp that glory before it is due. Though your son, under five-and-twenty years of age, should be but a coxcomb; do not, upon that account, despair of his becoming, before he is forty, a very wise and worthy man . . . the great secret of education is to direct vanity to proper objects. (*TMS*, 258–259)

Pride, on the other hand, is "sometimes taken in a good sense" and is sometimes "confounded with magnanimity" (*TMS*, 258). The virtue of magnanimity is not so much financial generosity as a generosity of spirit, to not take offense, to not give offensive, to be prone to overlook the slights of others, to forgive others, to disdain pettiness, to avoid being mean and nasty to others even when justified.

Smith notes that one can be vain and proud simultaneously, and notes it may be difficult to untangle which is which. "But the proud man is often vain; and the vain man is often proud . . . and we sometimes find the superficial and impertinent ostentation of vanity joined to the most malignant and derisive insolence of pride" (*TMS*, 259).

And finally neither the proud nor the vain are very happy, as they lack the PB&J virtues. "The proud and the vain man, on the contrary, are constantly dissatisfied. The one is tormented with indignation at the unjust superiority, as he thinks it, of other people. The other is in continual dread of the shame which, he foresees, would attend upon the detection of his groundless pretensions" (*TMS*, 261).

These two chapters give an overview of Smith's *Theory of Moral Sentiments*. We surmise that Smith was a shrewd and insightful student of human nature, attentive to its subtleties and nuances. One need not agree with Smith on the whole or part to appreciate his coherence and stature as a moral philosopher. In the next six chapters we turn attention to a different set of works that reveal another shrewd and insightful student of human nature: novelist Jane Austen.

When exploring the intersection of Jane Austen and Adam Smith, it can be noted that their moral thinking reflects the late eighteenth century notion of sensibility; indeed these years are often referred to as the Age of Sensibility. Here, sensibility means being sensitive to others' feelings and it is through this empathy that we develop as moral beings. Smith teaches us that sympathy is the glue that not only "holds together the fabric of society" but also allows for a good society to emerge (Brissenden, 1974, 31). Our sensibility can be seen as a system in which we respond to experiences with others (Warren, 1990, 26). Smith and Austen both illustrate how a feedback system of approbation and disapprobation from others and from our internal impartial spectator results in our moral development.

Sensibility, *feeling* sympathetically to others, is closely related to sentimentality, *responding* sympathetically to others. According to some scholars, Smith's TMS stands as the culmination of sentimentalism in philosophy (see for example Brissenden, 1974, and Schneewind, 1998). The concepts of sensibility and sentimentality spilled over into eighteenth century literature, "particularly in the newly emerging genre of the novel" (Byrne, 2013, 66). In literature, sentimentalism often went overboard leading to novels filled with hand-wringing, overwrought characters ruled by their passions. One such novel is *The Mysteries of Udolpho* by Ann Radcliffe, a book that leads Catherine Morland's imagination to run wild in *Northanger Abbey*. Austen's satirical treatment of Radcliffe's novel provides a critique of the over-sentimentality of her day.

Austen's critique of sentimentalism is best exemplified in the contrast between Elinor and Marianne in *Sense and Sensibility* as we will explore further in chapter 4. Marianne is ruled by her passions, and her sentimentality results in fits of despair and illness. Elinor is sensitive to others but also practices self-command, representing the Smithian ideal of "the best head joined to the best heart" (*TMS*, 216). Both Smith and Austen recognize the importance of sensibility for our moral development, but both caution us against its extremes.

The next six chapters will offer our readers an analysis of the manifestation of Smith's moral thought in Austen's novels with a focus on how she brings alive for us Smith's roadmap to a virtuous life.

NOTES

1. Smith consistently refers to children in the third person impersonal; a child is neither a he nor she but an "it."

2. As justice in the abovementioned example of Brutus might well be! Brutus was just in condemning his sons to death but hardly amiable. In chapter 5 we will see Smith also uses justice in a somewhat different sense than what we have outlined here, and that this second sense is part of justice as a virtue.

3. While Smith's *Wealth of Nations* often gets credit for the invisible hand concept, the idea that private actions could have unintended social benefits was a common concept in eighteenth-century thinking. Smith does use the "invisible hand" metaphor once in WN but it is in the context of foreign trade (*WN*, 456).

II

Austen Reflects and Illuminates Smith

Chapter Four

Self-Command in *Sense and Sensibility*

Elinor Dashwood had developed a deep affection for Edward Ferrars. She had every reason to believe he felt the same. She is puzzled and perturbed by Edward's failure to articulate his affections for her on the two occasions he departed her company after an extended visit. She eventually finds out why he made no such overture.

Lucy Steele is a very vulgar young lady. She is uneducated, overbearing, and has few charms. One day she and Elinor are on a walk. Lucy reveals to Elinor that for a number of years she, Lucy, had been secretly engaged to Edward Ferrars—the light and love of Elinor's life. Upon hearing this news Austen tells us: "Elinor was silent. Elinor's security sunk but her *self-command* did not sink with it" (*SS*, 82, emphasis added).

Their walk and conversation continues. Lucy both reveals information about her history with Edward and inquires of Elinor's interactions with Edward. Although Elinor was "mortified, shocked and confounded" by this newly acquired information she was able to carry on her conversation with Lucy "with a composure of voice, under which was concealed an emotion and distress beyond anything she had ever felt before" (*SS*, 84).

Jane Austen portrays Elinor's actions as admirable, even virtuous; and the foundation for these actions was Elinor's extraordinary sense of self-command. As noted in the previous chapter and by other scholars (Raphael and Macfie, 1982, 6; McCloskey, 2006, 306–307) self-command is a central virtue in Smith's moral theory. But what is self-command? Why is it so important in Austen and Smith?

As noted previously self-command is not commonly used in contemporary English but at a superficial level can be considered akin to self-control, especially in regard to emotions or "passions." We will discover, however, that in Austen and Smith self-command is more than simple self-restraint or self-control, although it certainly includes both attributes.

Those of a certain age may remember a series of commercials for the pain reliever Anacin. In each of the television advertisements the protagonist suffers from a headache and snaps at some innocent by-stander. For example, a middle-aged lady barks at children whose ball falls in her yard saying, "Can't you children play somewhere else!" In another scenario a younger woman cooks over a pot, an older lady approaches her at the stove suggesting, "Don't you think it needs a little salt?" To which the younger woman responds in a very angry tone "Mother please! I'd rather do it myself!" In the commercials the afflicted person takes Anacin and ends up reconciling with those they have snapped at. The middle-aged lady brings the children cookies; the daughter makes a nice cup of tea for her mom.[1] All is well in the world. The improper behavior is forgiven because it is atoned for by acts of beneficence. All because of Anacin.

Well not quite—the tablets have a helper. In these and other Anacin ads of the time, between the outburst and the reconciliation, an inner-voice of the party suffering from a headache says to the sufferer and the TV audience: "Control yourself! Sure you have a headache—but don't take it out on them!" At the end of the commercial Anacin is acclaimed because it allows one to be "in control again."

This is what most of us think when we think of self-control: not losing one's cool so as to be rude to others. And it is interesting that mid-twentieth-century mores made respect for self-control a basis for advertising appeal. We argue that although the self-command of Smith and Austen includes self-control, self-command is much more than simply restraining oneself so as not to be rude.

A richer view of self-command is linked to sensibility, which is quite conveniently in the title of Austen's first novel. Self-command is also linked to having proper principles, a recurring theme in Smith and in *Mansfield Park*; and to having correct knowledge of others and oneself which is a key theme in *Emma*.

MORE ON SELF-COMMAND IN SMITH

What makes self-command more than self-control in Smith? Let us first explore self-command in the context of sensibility. *Sensibility* as used in Smith and Austen's time is not to be confused with the contemporary use of the word *sensible*, which is a synonym for practical or utilitarian: as in, she wore sensible shoes for the day's walking in the city, but is, as noted earlier, more akin to sensitivity.

Stokes (1991, 154) points out that before the mid-eighteenth century sensibility meant "human feelings" in a general way but after 1756 it implied "capacity for refined emotion; delicate sensitiveness to taste . . . readiness to feel compassion for suffering. . . ." Smith's *Theory of Moral Sentiments* was first published in 1759, just at the cusp of this change in meaning and Smith's use of the word is in line with the post-1756 notion; Austen's use of the word is also clearly in this later vein.

To be sensible by this definition is to be sensitive and the more sensitive one is the more sensibility one has. Sensibility can be part of an experience—a viewer of a painting who appreciates a painting with intense depth and passion is more sensible than one who expresses less pleasure. Sensibility can be part of one's own state of mind or feelings—the person who appears to feel more pain from a blow to the leg has more sensibility than one who appears to feel less pain. Sensibility can also be other directed—the person who exhibits more compassion, more mutual sympathy to a grieving widow, has more sensibility than one who shows less sympathy.

In Smith the sensibility one has toward one's own infirmities is in contrast to the sensibility one feels and expresses toward the infirmities of others. Sensibility toward one's own state is rarely praiseworthy—and is more usually blameworthy—while sensibility toward others is almost always praiseworthy. Recall Smith tells us: "to feel much for others and little for ourselves, that to restrain our selfish, and to indulge our benevolent affections, constitutes the perfection of human nature" (*TMS*, 25).

This theme of sensibility toward others paired with restrained sensibility toward self as praiseworthy is recurring in TMS. They are also interrelated to one another. "The man who feels the most for the joys and sorrows of others, is best fitted for acquiring the most complete control of his own joys and sorrows. The man of the most exquisite humanity, is naturally the most capable of acquiring the highest degree of self-command" (*TMS*, 152).

We also recall Smith's notion that "the virtues of *sensibility* and *self-command* are not apprehended to consist in the ordinary, but in the uncommon degrees of those qualities. . . ." To snap at someone because they are irritating is breech of propriety, yet to refrain from yelling at one's mother when she suggests adding salt in the pot is hardly virtuous. To not yell at children when they are irritating shows an ordinary degree of sensibility and self-command that are not particularly praiseworthy. When the middle-aged lady of the Anacin commercial brings the children a plate of fresh baked cookies she is exhibiting virtue because of her "sensibility which surprises by its exquisite and unexpected delicacy and tenderness" (*TMS*, 25). Likewise, for Elinor to show composure when confronted with the news of her beloved's engagement to another (and by that other!) shows extraordinary self-command and is deemed virtuous because it "astonishes by its amazing superiority over the most ungovernable passions of human nature" (*TMS*, 25).

While Smith's moral theory calls for increases in sensibility toward others, Smith does not imply martyrdom is an ethical ideal. There is room for some self-directed sensibility. One can and should stand up for one's own rights and object when one is wronged. Self-command reduced to an unabridged willingness to be abused is no virtue. Self-command is a necessary tool with which to practice all the virtues, but if misapplied as in an ill-conceived masochism, is no virtue at all. Proper sensibility is not completely other regarding; a certain degree of sensibility to one's self is necessary. As Smith states, " . . . the total want of sensibility to personal injury, to personal danger and distress, would, in such situations, take away the whole merit of self-command" (*TMS*, 245).

Yet Smith thinks it is rare for humans to err in the direction of insufficient sensibility to one's *own* problems and woes, he believes human nature inclines error in the opposite direction. He derides the sad-sack complainer, explaining that "[a] fretful temper, which feels, with too much sensibility, every little cross accident, renders a man miserable in himself and offensive to other people" (*TMS*, 244).

Virtuous self-command and sensibility do not come from the bottle of pain-reliever nor is it simple self-control to Smith. Although there may be certain innate components of self-control and sensibility they are also cultivated habits, acquired traits. According to Smith, self-command can be acquired by exposure to adversity. "[T]he wise and just man who has been thoroughly bred in the great school of self-command, in the bustle and business of the world, exposed, perhaps, to the violence and injustice of faction, and to the hardships and hazards of war, maintains this control of his passive feelings upon all occasions . . . " (*TMS*, 146).

Smith also sees social engagement as the best remedy for avoiding excess self-sensibility especially in the presence of adversity. "Are you in adversity? Do not mourn in the darkness of solitude; do not regulate your sorrow according to the indulgent sympathy of your intimate friends, return, as soon as possible to the day-light of the world and of society. Live with strangers, with those who know nothing or care nothing about your misfortune" (*TMS*, 154). Smith's picture is clear: the moral man, the virtuous woman, is one who has the self-command to set his or her own selfish sensibilities aside and the self-command to respond with sensibilities to others.

Recall also in Smith another indispensable tool in pursuit of virtue: principles and adherence to general rules. "Without this sacred regard to general rules, there is no man whose conduct can be much depended upon. It is this which constitutes the most essential difference between a man of principle and honour and a worthless fellow" (*TMS*, 163).

AUSTEN'S DRAMATIZATION OF SMITH: TWO SISTERS OF *SENSE AND SENSIBILITY*

Sense and Sensibility was Jane Austen's first published novel. As with her other novels the plot centers on young ladies who are relatively impoverished aristocrats in search of husbands. The two sisters of this novel are the nineteen-year-old Elinor Dashwood and her sixteen-year-old sister Marianne.

Marianne Dashwood falls in love with the elegant and lively John Willoughby and is subsequently jilted by Willoughby. Elinor Dashwood falls in love with the shy and unaccomplished Edward Ferrars. She has every reason to believe he has similar feelings for her, yet he never seems able to express them. She later learns, as outlined above, that despite their mutual affection a match is impossible because Edward is bound by an old promise to another.

Austen reveals early on the difference in the characters of the two main protagonists Elinor and Marianne:

> [Elinor] . . . had an excellent heart; her disposition was affectionate, and her feelings were strong: but *she knew how to govern them*: it was knowledge her mother had yet to learn, and which one of her sisters had resolved never to be taught. Marianne's abilities were, in many respects quite equal to Elinor's. She was sensible and clever, but eager in everything; her sorrows, her joys, could have no moderation. She was generous, amiable, interesting; she was everything but prudent. (*SS*, 33–34, emphasis added)

Elinor is, at key points of the novel, characterized as having the cardinal Smithian virtue of self-command. Moreover, Austen affirms, like Smith, that feelings are something to be governed, not simply controlled or restrained. Governing, not simply controlling passion, is a key distinction between self-control and self-command.

When the Dashwoods leave Norland, Edward's good-bye to Elinor is tepid and more like that of a brother than a lover. This is noted by her more passionate sister Marianne who notes: "Even now her [Elinor's] self-command is invariable. When is she dejected or melancholy? When does she try to avoid society or appear restless or dissatisfied in it?" (*SS*, 30). Marianne thinks Elinor should be more upset on Edward's leaving without expressing his affection for Elinor. Marianne expects but does not observe outward displays of melancholy from Elinor. More to Smith's point, whatever dissatisfaction Elinor has in her relationship with Edward, she is actively engaged in society just as Smith recommends to a person in distress or mourning.

This theme occurs again later in the novel after Edward visits the Dashwoods at their new home at Barton Cottage in Devonshire. He is gloomy and despondent for much of the visit and leaves rather suddenly in a poor state of mind. This "left an uncomfortable impression on Elinor's feelings especially, which required some trouble and time to subdue. But as it was her determination to subdue it, and to prevent herself from appearing to suffer more than what all her family suffered on his going away" (*SS*, 66). Elinor is a very determined young lady; she does not want to appear to be upset. We are not told whether this is from considerations of propriety, kindness, shyness, or simply stubborn pride, but her desire is fulfilled by a plan of action that accomplishes the restraint:

> Elinor sat down to her drawing-table as soon as he was out of the house, busily employed herself the whole day, neither sought nor avoided the mention of his name, appeared to interest herself almost as much as ever in the general concerns of the family, and if, by this conduct, she did not lessen her own grief, it was at least prevented from unnecessary increase, and her mother and sisters were spared much solicitude on her account. (*SS*, 66)

We see that self-command is more than just gritting one's teeth, or white-knuckling through distress. It is a habit, a method of diverting one's attention to other matters and other concerns coupled with a determined focus on those other matters. When you practice self-command, you do not merely repress your emotions. Rather you govern them, much like a sailor governs the wind in a sail to steer a boat.

As noted above Elinor exhibited extraordinary self-command when Lucy Steele reveals her engagement to Edward. Once Elinor parts from Lucy and has time to reflect on the situation Austen tells us Elinor is at first angry, feeling misled and abused, "[h]er resentment of such behaviour, her indignation at having been its dupe, for a short time made her feel only for herself; but other ideas, other considerations, soon arose" (*SS*, 84). She concludes, quite correctly, that Edward's deeper affection "was not an illusion of her own vanity. He certainly loved her" (*SS*, 84). She then considers Edward's situation and concludes he faces a miserable future. She is sorry to see Edward and Lucy matched up; she sincerely feels sorry for Edward as she knows Lucy to be his inferior. "Could he ever be tolerably happy with Lucy Steele; could he, were his affection for herself out of the question, with his integrity, his delicacy, and well-informed mind, be satisfied with a wife like her—illiterate, artful, and selfish?" (*SS*, 85).

In Elinor's character and actions, Austen gives us further insight as to how to effectively govern one's emotions, and how to attain the degree of self-command necessary to be deemed virtuous. Turn away from personal regard and objectively consider the condition of others in the situation. Balance their perspectives with yours. Tamp down your self-regard, ramp up your other regard, and listen to your impartial spectator.

Very late in the novel when Elinor finally does inform Marianne that she had prior knowledge of Edward's secret engagement to Lucy, she continues to exhibit self-command. Mrs. Jennings has reported to the public the news that Edward and Lucy are engaged, and Elinor feels she owes Marianne an explanation. What is astonishing and virtuous is that Elinor turns the occasion into a teachable moment to help Marianne develop her own self-command. "She was very far from wishing to dwell on her own feelings, or to represent herself as suffering much, any otherwise than as the self-command she had practised since her first knowledge of Edward's engagement, might suggest a hint of what was practicable to Marianne" (*SS*, 153).

Austen does not reveal the exact words Elinor uses when she debriefs her sister on the situation, but she does tell the reader, "Her narration was clear and simple; and though it could not be given without emotion, it was not accompanied by violent agitation, nor impetuous grief.—*That* belonged rather to the hearer, for Marianne listened with horror, and cried excessively. Elinor was to be the comforter of others in her own distresses . . . " (*SS*, 153). By having well-developed self-command Elinor is able to comfort Marianne about Marianne's distress over Elinor's grief.[2]

In the same discussion Marianne is shocked to learn that Elinor has known about the engagement for four months, learned of it from Lucy and had to cope with Lucy's insipid gloating about Edward's great love for Lucy. Marianne inquires quite directly as to how Elinor could possibly have held up such a good face for so long. Elinor gives a series of replies straight from a Smithian playbook; she notes "duty" (*SS*, 153) as she had given her word to Lucy, which, of course, resonates well with Smith's principles. Elinor also notes a concern for others' happiness: "I did not love only him" (*SS*, 154). She sincerely did not want to burden her mother or Marianne.

However perhaps the most important consideration: if Edward and Lucy were to be wed, Elinor was convinced she could still find happiness, observing that "one's happiness depending entirely on any particular person, it is not meant—it is not fit—it is not possible that it should be so" (*SS*, 154). Compare this with Smith's observation, "The great source of both the misery and disorders of human life, seems to arise from over-rating the difference between one permanent situation and another" (*TMS*, 149).

Understanding this insight and internalizing it is yet another way Austen raises simple self-control to virtuous self-command. This distinction has its effect on even the most sensible Marianne who states "if the loss of what is most valued is so easily to be made up by something else, your resolution, your self-command, are, perhaps, a little less to be wondered at.—They are brought more within my comprehension" (*SS,* 154).

Finally, Elinor makes it clear that she has not turned into a robot without feeling: she does not lack proper self-sensibility. Self-command allows Elinor to tell her sister that she now "does not suffer materially" (*SS*, 154) from knowledge of Edmund and Lucy's marriage, but this tranquility is not from an absence of feeling by Elinor or an absence of suffering on her part. Elinor had to exert herself to govern her passions over the situation. She reveals that her "composure of mind . . . have been the effect of constant and painful exertion[3];—they did not spring up of themselves;—they did not occur to relieve my spirits at first" (*SS*, 154–155).

Yes she had suffered, but so what? The point is she has persevered. Elinor is a model of Smithian virtue; she is in control of her emotions, can act in a way consistent with propriety, yet is not without sensibilities as directed toward herself or others. Again this is consistent with Smith's notion that self-command is the foundation of other-directed sensibility. We shall soon see Elinor lapse in her self-command, but a lapse that is quite excusable and proper.

But now to Marianne who is quite the opposite of Elinor. Early in the novel she is unrestrained in her open affection for Willoughby. When Elinor notes the exclusive attachment between Marianne and Willoughby "[Elinor] only wished that it were less openly shown; and once or twice did suggest the propriety of some self-command to Marianne. But Marianne abhorred all concealment . . . and Willoughby thought the same" (*SS*, 79).

Indeed, Marianne disdains self-command as being disingenuous. Recall when Elinor acts as if nothing has happened when Edward unexpectedly leaves and "busily employed herself the whole day . . . "; to Marianne "Such behavior as this, so exactly the reverse of her own appeared no more meritorious to Marianne than her own had seemed faulty to her. The business of self-command she settled very easily: with strong affections it was impossible, with calm ones it had no merit" (*SS*, 66).

When Marianne comes to realize she has been jilted by Willoughby she has a breakdown. She stays in bed all day, removes herself from society, has fits of grief and gloom and burdens all around her, especially Elinor. One critic notes that "Marianne's own selfish indulgence of her own suffering makes her insensitive to Elinor's. . . . Marianne forces Elinor to take over all the unpleasant tasks of practical life, while at the same time scorning her sister's steady self-command because it demonstrates the inferiority of her sensibility" (Watt, 1963, 46). This absence of self-command coupled with a refined and self-directed sensibility is the exact opposite of the Smithian ideal.

Marianne does eventually repent of her ways. After the debriefing about Edward and Lucy's liaison, Marianne agrees to restrain herself in any public discussion of the matter and "[s]he performed her promise of being discreet to admiration" (*SS*, 155). After Marianne suffers and recovers from a debilitating illness, Elinor observes Marianne has a "calmness of spirits" and "apparent composure of mind" (*SS*, 200). Marianne then indicates "I have formed my plan and am determined to enter into a course of serious study" (*SS*, 201). Even her remembrance of Willoughby "shall be regulated, it shall be checked by religion, by reason, by constant employment" (*SS*, 203).

It would be easy to see *Sense and Sensibility* as a simple tale of good sense triumphing over wicked sensibility; just as it is easy to think of *The Theory of Moral Sentiments* as lecture on self-command as an exclusive stand-alone virtue. Central to both Smith and Austen is an emphasis on balance, growth, and improvement, and a kind of unity of virtues. Elinor is the heroine of the novel not because she has a total lack of sensibility; but rather because she exhibits a more appropriate balance between sense and sensibility than her sister Marianne. Elinor is not perfect; she too grows and evolves.

Smith and Austen both recognize that in certain situations a lapse of self-command is excusable and even charming. This is well illustrated by *Sense and Sensibility*'s enchanting ending.

When the presumably married Edward appears at the Barton Cottage, Elinor resolves: "I *will* be calm; I *will* be mistress of myself" (*SS*, 209). After an awkward discourse it is revealed that, yes, Lucy is married and is now a Mrs. Ferrars but *not* Mrs. Edmund Ferrars. Rather she is married to Edward's younger brother, the vain Robert Ferrars. This is when Elinor loses her self-command. "Elinor could sit it no longer. She almost ran out of the room, and as soon as the door was closed, burst into tears of joy, which at first she thought would never cease" (*SS*, 210). But as Watt points out:

> Upon hearing that Ferrars was available for marriage Elinor "almost ran out of the room and as soon as the door was closed burst into tears of joy." The joy was not less intense because Elinor remembered that ladies do not run, and that they always shut the door. But Elinor's sense involves much more than prudent reticence and regard for the forms of social decorum; these may be its surface expression, but its essence is fidelity to the inward discrimination of both head and heart." (Watt, 1963, 49)

Austen goes on to describe,

> But Elinor—How are *her* feelings to be described?—From the moment of learning that Lucy was married to another, that Edward was free, to the moment of his justifying the hopes which had so instantly followed, she was every thing by turns but tranquil . . . it required several hours to give sedateness to her spirits, or any degree of tranquillity to her heart. (*SS*, 212)

Yes, even Elinor can have a lapse of self-command. But Smith is likely OK with it. In his discussion of self-command and whether the impartial spectator approves of it, he notes that for some passion the "excess is less disagreeable than the defect" most notably with: "the passions which the spectator is most disposed to sympathize with . . . (where) the immediate feeling or sensation is more or less agreeable to the person principally concerned" (*TMS*, 242–243). There is no doubt that Elinor's display is one of immense joy and reflects her deep affection for Edward. In such a case Smith tells us "the indulgence even of such excessive affections is, upon many occasions, not only agreeable, but delicious" (*TMS*, 243). This is exactly what we suspect Austen intended. We sympathize, we enter into Elinor's joy; in fact we delight in it.

MANSFIELD PARK: SELF-COMMAND AND PRINCIPLES

Although *Mansfield Park* is primarily about the PB&J virtues (see chapter 5), a sub-theme is that the Bertram sisters lack proper self-command. Maria Bertram is engaged to the dull Mr. Rushworth. Mr. Rushworth wants to improve his estate with physical renovations. He invites his fiancée Maria, her sister Julia, and her brother Edmund (elder brother Tom is in Antigua with his father) along with the Crawford siblings (Mary and Henry), cousin Fanny, and Mrs. Norris to make a day trip to his estate near Sotherton to give him advice.

After they arrive and tour the estate, the younger people in the party break off. However, Julia Bertram, who is not betrothed, ends up stuck with Mr. Rushworth's mother and her own Aunt Norris. She would rather be with the younger folks but Austen notes: "The politeness she had been brought up to practice as a duty, made it impossible for her to escape" (*MP*, 500). But Austen then notes how upset Julia is and attributes it to a lack of self-command. "[W]hile the want of that higher species of *self-command*, that just consideration of others, that knowledge of her own heart, that principle of right which had not formed any essential part of her education, made her miserable under it" (*MP*, 500, emphasis added).

Again, Austen refers to a higher form of self-command that goes beyond simple self-control. If Julia had that "higher species of self-command" she would have still been unable to make a quick exit from her two older companions. However, she would have been able to enter into their interests, recognize and readily dismiss her own selfish desires, and enjoy an interaction with her aunt and her then future in-law. A higher species of self-command allows one to transform a less than desirable social situation into a pleasant social encounter. One makes the best of the situation and does not leave the encounter feeling miserable.

Cousin Fanny Price, on the other hand, has that higher species of self-command. Fanny is madly in love with her cousin Edmund who has always been her advocate and friend. When Sir Thomas Bertram deems a ball ought to be held in Fanny's honor, Cousin Edmund surmises Fanny would require a chain to hold the beautiful jeweled cross she had recently acquired as a gift from her brother William. Edmund instinctively knows she would want to wear the cross at the ball and so he gives her a very nice chain.

When Edmund presents the chain to Fanny he also intimates he is truly in love with Mary Crawford. Upon his exit Fanny is heartbroken as she concludes her beloved Edmund would indeed marry Mary Crawford. Austen reports, "Till she had shed many a tear . . . Fanny could not subdue her agitation" (*MP*, 598–599). However, Austen also reports that after her private outburst of emotion "she felt it to be her duty, to try to overcome all that was excessive, all that bordered on selfishness in her affection for Edmund" (*MP*, 599). She regains her internal composure by seizing on the handwritten note that Edmund had made with the gift. She holds it "as a treasure beyond all her hopes" (*MP*, 599) and thereby cherishes the scrap of paper as a permanent token of his friendly though non-romantic affection. "Having regulated her thoughts and comforted her feelings by this happy mixture of reason and weakness, she was able in due time to go down and resume her usual employments near her aunt Bertram, and pay her the usual observances without any apparent want of spirits" (*MP*, 599).

This is a very high order of self-command, of self-government of one's own passions. It is reminiscent of Elinor's self-command. It would receive the full approbation of Adam Smith. Austen teaches us that being able to carry on as usual is evidence of self-command and is also a tool to promote self-command.

As readers of *Mansfield Park* will recall Fanny is vindicated in the novel. Much to the chagrin of her uncle, Sir Thomas, and even her cousin Edmund, she refuses the marriage proposal of the elegant and well-situated Henry Crawford. She thinks Crawford is an unethical scoundrel as she has observed him toying with the affections of young ladies, notably her cousins. "I cannot think well of a man who sports with any woman's feelings" (*MP*, 655).

After being refused by Fanny, but encouraged by both his sister and Sir Thomas to continue to pursue Fanny's hand, Henry Crawford seems to truly desire to reform his rather vain and selfish ways. He makes some inroads to Fanny's approbation. However, his visit to the London home of Mr. and Mrs. Rushworth is his undoing. Mrs. Rushworth, formerly Maria Bertram, had only married the dull and stupid Rushworth for his money. Long before Crawford takes a fancy to Fanny, Fanny had observed that even though she was engaged to Rushworth, Maria had an inappropriate liaison with Henry. As Mrs. Rushworth, Maria is initially cold to Henry when he visits her home, but they end up having an adulterous affair that leads to a scandalous divorce that shames the Bertram family. In addition, the second daughter Julia elopes, and although not as scandalous as a divorce, it is a blot on the family reputation.

Austen reveals that after these two catastrophes Sir Thomas contemplates what went wrong with his daughters. The major influence on them had been their doting Aunt Norris. He concludes that the constant encouragement and flattery from their Aunt Norris coupled with his stern countenance did not have a good effect on the girls. They learned to be spoiled little hypocrites who hid their true feelings and natures from him.

Yet he reflects that this "had not been the most direful mistake in his plan of education" (*MP*, 714). Rather he concludes that in their education: "principle, active principle, had been wanting; that they had never been properly taught to govern their inclinations and tempers by that sense of duty which can alone suffice" (*MP*, 714). Just as in Smith, then, self-command and right principles are related.

Austen makes this reference to lack of principles in the Bertram sisters earlier on in the novel. Although Maria is engaged to Mr. Rushworth, she enjoys the attention of Henry Crawford. Julia also enjoys Mr. Crawford's flirting and attention. Given his insatiable vanity, Crawford enjoys indulging both sisters. This leads to a bitter rift between the two sisters. "[T]he sisters, under such a trial as this, had not affection or *principle* enough to make them merciful or just, to give them honour or compassion. Maria felt her triumph, and pursued her purpose, careless of Julia; and Julia could never see Maria distinguished by Henry Crawford . . . " (*MP*, 541, emphasis added).

Smithian moral theory rings loud and clear. Both principles and self-command are required for good moral judgments, proper behavior, and internal tranquility. It is not the feeble spark of benevolence but a commitment to what both Smith and Austen call *principles* coupled with a type of self-command going beyond mere self-restraint that does the trick.

In fact, *Mansfield Park* is a story about principle as it directs the lives of its characters. The lack of proper principles trumps amiability, good manners, and good intentions. This is true for the Bertram sisters but perhaps more so for both the Crawford siblings. Fanny's triumph is that she intuitively surmises the Crawford siblings' lack of principles and has both the principles and self-command that allows her to act on that assessment despite enormous pressure to abandon her own judgment.

Henry is at first just trifling with Fanny. He only wants to gain her affection as he had with her cousins. But he then finds he has a deeper affection precisely because of her character. Fanny is more than just a sound judge of principles; Fanny embodies good principles. Henry's pursuit of Fanny is based in large part on his own recognition of her good principles. "Henry Crawford had too much sense not to feel the worth of good *principles* in a wife, though he was too little accustomed to serious reflection to know them by their proper name . . . " (*MP*, 616, emphasis added). We note that Henry was not prone to contemplation about serious issues, yet even he recognizes that a woman with good principles would be good for him, although he may not be able to articulate the exact reasoning.

Fanny is not willing to overlook Crawford's lack of principles even as all are encouraging her to accept him. Even her beloved Edmund encourages her to do so, to consider Crawford as an attractive work in progress. When

Edmund encourages Fanny to accept Crawford's proposal he makes due note of Crawford's lack of serious moral thinking. He tells Fanny that she will complete and improve him because of her rock-solid principles. "Crawford's *feelings*, I am ready to acknowledge, have hitherto been too much his guides. Happily, those feelings have generally been good. You will supply the rest; and a most fortunate man he is to attach himself to such a creature—to a woman who, firm as a rock in her own principles . . . " (*MP*, 648).

Fanny's qualms about Crawford are first, last, and always about his principles. Fanny's original rejection of Crawford's proposal is based on her assessment of his lack of character and principles. When Sir Thomas asks her why she objects to accepting Crawford's marriage proposal, he alludes to a possible flaw in Crawford's demeanor. "'Have you any reason, child, to think ill of Mr. Crawford's temper?' 'No, sir.' She longed to add, 'But of his principles I have'" (*MP*, 628). Fanny's reluctance to refer to Crawford's lack of principles is not based on her meekness, but on the fact she would expose Julia and Maria if she let Sir Thomas know of Crawford's flirtatious nature.

In Crawford's encounter with Fanny the day after her initial rejection he again entreats her take his hand in marriage. This only re-enforces her opinion of his lack of principles. "Here was again a something of the same Mr. Crawford whom she had so reprobated before. How evidently was there a gross want of feeling and humanity where his own pleasure was concerned—And alas! how always known no principle to supply as a duty what the heart was deficient in" (*MP*, 635).

Yet Austen is too clever of an author to make Henry Crawford an overt villain. His insights and appreciation of Fanny's principles are commendable. Early on in the novel, Austen reveals an understanding of his own inadequacies and plants the seed for a desire for self-improvement. William Price, Fanny's favorite brother, is in the naval service. He spends some time at Mansfield in the gatherings which included Henry where "William was often called on by his uncle to be the talker." This is just as Henry's romantic inklings toward Fanny are beginning; Henry admires William's recounting of his life, trials, and adventures at sea.

> He longed to have been at sea, and seen and done and suffered as much. His heart was warmed, his fancy fired, and he felt the highest respect for a lad who, before he was twenty, had gone through such bodily hardships and given such proofs of mind. The glory of heroism, of usefulness, of exertion, of endurance, made his own habits of selfish indulgence appear in shameful contrast; and he wished he had been a William Price, distinguishing himself and working his way to fortune and consequence with so much self-respect and happy ardour, instead of what he was! (*MP*, 582)

After Fanny has rejected Henry twice at Mansfield Park she visits her family back in Portsmouth. Henry visits her there with no pretense except to continue courting her. He appears a much more sober and serious man. He reports he actually exerted himself in the management of his Norfolk estate and also shows a keen interest in the welfare of his tenants. Henry leaves Portsmouth and makes his way to London. A while later Fanny receives a strange letter from Henry's sister Mary. In it Mary warns Fanny she will likely hear some gossip about Henry and Maria, and instructs her to ignore it. However, when her own rough-hewed father reads a newspaper report of "a matrimonial *fracas*" (*MP*, 700) between a Mr. R. of Wimpole Street in London with a Mr. C., over a Mrs. R., Fanny sadly concludes the truth of the report and concludes that Henry's "unsettled affections, wavering with his vanity, *Maria's* decided attachment, and no sufficient principle on either side, gave it possibility—Miss Crawford's letter stampt it a fact" (*MP*, 701).

Henry Crawford's downfall lies in his principles being defective. He is left with his passions unbridled and unrestrained. When he encounters Maria he falls back on his habits; he flirts, she accepts, and they both fall together.

Henry's sister Mary Crawford also lacks principles. Recall Fanny's true love, her cousin Edmund, has declared his love for Mary Crawford. But when Edmund encounters Mary Crawford after the scandal has erupted, her thoughts focus on covering up and recovering from the social disaster created by her brother's scandal. She suggests that Henry and Maria should marry and try to reincorporate into society. She is solely concerned with managing the blame of the scandal and not at all with the blameworthiness of the parties involved. Edmund is shocked and concludes that she is lacking in principles.

This difference between Mary and Edmund is not from a lack of kindness or a cruel nature on Mary's part. As Edmund explains to Fanny "She would not voluntarily give unnecessary pain to any one, and though I may deceive myself, I cannot but think that for me, for my feelings, she would—Hers are faults of principle, Fanny; of blunted delicacy and a corrupted, vitiated mind" (*MP*, 710).

Interestingly, both Mary Crawford and Aunt Norris place the blame for the scandal on Fanny, because she had not accepted Henry Crawford's hand in marriage. Both Sir Thomas and Edmund will have none of that. Fanny eventually marries Edmund and emerges as the heroine of Mansfield Park.

EMMA: THE MANDATE OF SELF-COMMAND

The balance of self-command and sensibility that we found in *Sense and Sensibility* is also commended throughout the novel *Emma*. Emma urges her mentee Harriet to practice self-command in the face of the considerable embarrassment and disappointment over a failed match with Mr. Elton who is marrying another. Emma encourages Harriet to exert " . . . a habit of self-

command in you, a consideration of what is your duty, an
priety, an endeavor to avoid the suspicions of others, to sav
credit, and to restore your tranquility" (*E*, 874). Indeed Harri
good student. When Emma invites her to a dinner for Mr. E
bride, Harriet shows great "fortitude" in declining the invi
Emma is further impressed with Harriet's ability to exhibit "great self-
command" (*E*, 946) over the prospect of a match with Frank Churchill.
"Whatever she might feel of brighter hope, she [Harriet] betrayed nothing"
(*E*, 946). Emma is further surprised by the level of self-command exhibited
by Harriet when they find out that Churchill had been secretly engaged to
Jane Fairfax all along. However, what looked like self-command to Emma
was in reality disinterest on Harriet's part. Harriet was not interested in Mr.
Churchill at all, and had instead mistakenly thought Emma had been attempt-
ing to make a match for her with Mr. Knightley.

The importance of self-command plays a large role in one of the most
important scenes in the novel, Emma's cruel insult to Miss Bates at the Box
Hill outing. Ironically, the scene opens with Emma contrasting Frank
Churchill's composure at the outing with his loss of self-command the previous day saying, "You are comfortable because you are under command."
Churchill replies "Your command?—Yes." Emma then clarifies, "I meant
self-command. You had, somehow or other, broken bounds yesterday, and
run away from your own management" (*E*, 934).

Shortly after this reproach, Emma found that "she could not resist" (*E*,
935) lobbing a stinging barb at Miss Bates for her dullness of speech. Once
Mr. Knightley points out the hurtfulness of the public shaming, Emma is
"vexed beyond what could have been expressed" (*E*, 938). Emma's loss of
self-command brings her far from the reader's introduction to the character
as someone who was "handsome, clever, and rich, with a comfortable home
and happy disposition, seemed to unite some of the best blessings of existence; and had lived nearly twenty-one years in the world with very little to
distress of vex her" (*E*, 723).

Jane Fairfax is described by Mr. Knightley as possessing the combination
of the Smithian virtues of self-command and sensibility. "Jane Fairfax has
feeling . . . I do not accuse her of want of feeling. Her sensibilities, I suspect,
are strong, and her temper excellent in its power of forbearance, patience,
self-control . . . " (*E*, 887). No wonder Emma is so jealous of Jane!

SUMMARY OF AUSTEN AND SMITH ON SELF-COMMAND

Jane Austen and Adam Smith certainly seem on the same page with regard to
the virtue of self-command. They affirm its importance and see it as aligned
with other virtues. Smith's abstract discussions of the workings of self-

ommand are played out in Austen's stories and by her characters. Austen affirms and augments Smith's picture; together they give a number of insights to the modern reader about self-command. These include:

- Self-command is more than self-control. A better word is self-government; it is the ability to direct one's emotions to proper ends.
- Self-command can be learned, it must be developed but this requires exertion and effort; the more one practices the more natural and automatic it becomes.
- Self-command must be aligned with proper principles.
- Although requiring exertion, self-command is more than just raw will-power; it includes certain strategies to direct one's attention away from the source of the emotional irritation. This includes forcing oneself to interact with others, with strangers with the larger world; and keeping busy in useful tasks.
- Self-command is also developed by becoming more *other regarding*, by examining and carefully considering the interests and perspectives of others.
- The impartial spectator that resides "in the breast" is an ally of virtuous self-command.
- Self-command yields great rewards; it allows one to act with propriety, dignity, and grace.

Self-command may seem old-fashioned and stilted. We excuse, allow, and even encourage more open displays of self-regard and emotion. Yet there may be much to be gained from a recaptured sense of self-command. In both Smith and Austen, virtue is an attribute that is developed and is essentially a matter of balance. That self-command, sense, and sensibility play such an important role in both writers' work is of interest and potential importance. The prudent but sensible man of Smith or woman of Austen attains a virtue that is lively, attractive, and adaptive, exactly the virtue we suspect makes for a thriving society where humans flourish.

NOTES

1. Anacin commercials can be found on-line at http://www.historicfilms.com/search/?type=all&q=Mother+Please+I%27d+rather+do+it+myself#p1t9782i1898o1963 and http://www.historicfilms.com/search/?type=all&q=Anacin#p1t13565i1563o1625.

2. Elinor's debriefing of Marianne after the public announcement of Edward and Lucy's engagement is depicted in a very different way in the 1995 film production of *Sense and Sensibility*. In that production Elinor is as emotional as Marianne about the situation. The 2008 BBC production of *Sense and Sensibility* is truer to Austen's account of the debriefing, but gives no hint of Elinor using it as a teachable moment for Marianne. We argue there is little basis in Austen's text for a hysterical, weeping Elinor in the 1995 version, and trace its film depiction to contemporary notions of propriety which view open emotional displays and re-

straints thereof, in a very different light. A similar insight can be applied to the omissions of Austen's intent in the 2008 production.

3. See Stokes (1991, 89–91) for a similar analysis of relation between exertion and self-command in Austen's context.

Chapter Five

Prudence, Benevolence, and Justice in *Mansfield Park*

As outlined in the last chapter when Fanny Price refuses the rich and elegant Henry Crawford's marriage proposal, her uncle and patron Sir Thomas chides her, condemns her, and accuses her of obstinacy, much to Fanny's distress. Sir Thomas favors the match and is surprised, perplexed, and distressed that his niece, who is by every account a poor relation, does not enthusiastically embrace the proposal.

After his tempestuous discussion with her on the matter, he is sensitive enough (or sexist enough?) to allow her some time to gather her thoughts. He suggests she take a long walk through the mall of Mansfield Park. Fanny complies and is relieved in doing so. When her aunt, Mrs. Norris, finds out that she walked on the mall instead of to Mrs. Norris's house she is furious and makes a point of scolding Fanny at the family dinner. It seems Mrs. Norris had some task that she would have liked Fanny to do.

This lording over Fanny by Mrs. Norris, here and at other junctures, is inconsistent with prudence. Smith tells us a prudent person is void of "arrogant airs" (*TMS*, 213); the opposite can be said of Mrs. Norris. Smith also tells us the prudent person does not "assume(s) impertinently over anybody" (*TMS*, 214) which Mrs. Norris clearly does with Fanny. In addition to not being prudent, Mrs. Norris's behavior is certainly not benevolent and even unjust. It reminds us of Smith's observation:

> What chiefly enrages us against the man who injures or insults us, is the little account which he seems to make of us, the unreasonable preference which he gives to himself above us, and that absurd self-love, by which he seems to imagine, that other people may be sacrificed at any time, to his conveniency or his humour. The glaring impropriety of this conduct, the gross insolence and

injustice which it seems to involve in it, often shock and exasperate us more
than all the mischief which we have suffered. (*TMS*, 96)

When Sir Thomas informs Mrs. Norris that he was the one who suggested
Fanny walk among the shrubbery, Mrs. Norris does not let up on Fanny,
remarking: "[T]here is something about Fanny, I have often observed it
before—she likes to go her own way to work; she does not like to be dictated
to; she takes her own independent walk whenever she can; she certainly has a
little spirit of secrecy, and independence, and nonsense, about her, which I
would advise her to get the better of" (*MP*, 632).

It is interesting to note Sir Thomas's silent reaction to Mrs. Norris's
adamant hostility toward Fanny: "As a general reflection on Fanny, Sir
Thomas thought nothing could be more unjust, though he had been so lately
expressing the same sentiments himself, and he tried to turn the conversation:
tried repeatedly before he could succeed; for Mrs. Norris had not discernment enough to perceive, either now, or at any other time, to what degree he
thought well of his niece, or how very far he was from wishing to have his
own children's merits set off by the depreciation of hers. She was talking at
Fanny, and resenting this private walk half through the dinner" (*MP*, 632).

Toward the end of *Theory of Moral Sentiments* Adam Smith offers a
compilation of virtues that comes close to fitting on a bumper sticker. Follow
the path of prudence, benevolence, and justice, ground it in self-command,
and you will win the affection of many, know you are beloved by your fellow
man, and live a happy and virtuous life.

Prudence is pretty easy to understand. Take care of yourself, don't spend
beyond your means, don't take unnecessary risks. Smith adds: the prudent
person avoids the "arrogant airs of an assuming pedant" and is "cautious
in . . . actions" and "reserved in his speech." The prudent person never
"rashly or unnecessarily obtrudes his opinion" nor "assumes impertinently
over anybody" and is an "exact observer of decency" (*TMS*, 214). There is a
good dose of *mind your own business* in this fuller description of prudence.

Benevolence is also pretty straightforward. Take amiable and genuine
interest in the well-being of others; or, to put it another way, make sacrifices
to promote other people's happiness. In the Smithian view it is related to
affections as in to "indulge our benevolent affections" which is part of "the
perfection in human nature" (*TMS*, 25). Smith tells us "What is called affection, is in reality nothing but habitual sympathy. Our concern in the happiness or misery of those who are the objects of what we call our affections;
our desire to promote the one, and to prevent the other; are either the actual
feeling of that habitual sympathy, or the necessary consequences of that
feeling" (*TMS*, 220). Smith is skeptical of universal benevolence and sees
benevolence as dependent on sympathy for others, so we naturally feel the
most sympathy for those we know best. No person should be forced to be

benevolent, but no person will ever be happy unless they are benevolent toward others. "Those whose hearts never open to the feelings of humanity, should, we think, be shut out in the same manner, from the affections of all their fellow-creatures, and be allowed to live in the midst of society, as in a great desert where there is nobody to care for them, or to inquire after them" (*TMS*, 82).

A casual reading of Jane Austen yields any number of characters that are prudent in their life-choices, and others that are benevolent toward others. Charlotte Lucas in *Pride and Prejudice* is prudent, as is Anne Elliot in *Persuasion*. Both Colonel Brandon and Mr. Darcy show a great deal of benevolence in *Sense and Sensibility* and *Pride and Prejudice*. However, we find that the overall PB&J theme of prudence, benevolence, and justice is best represented in *Mansfield Park*. This is because one of its central characters, Mrs. Norris, is so totally absent the virtues while in contrast, Sir Thomas Bertram and Edmund Bertram, though less than perfect in all three virtues, develop in all three virtues in the story.

But first a problem to be resolved: prudence and benevolence are personal virtues; but what about justice as a personal virtue? Most of Smith's discussion of justice in TMS is about legal justice that he views as standards that are "precise, accurate, and indispensable" (*TMS*, 175). If by *justice* Smith means that one must always scrupulously follow the law there is little in Jane Austen that speaks of this virtue; for indeed, with few exceptions, everyone in Austen's novels seem to be following the law.[1] Austen did not write detective novels or crime novels.

In the common English of our day one definition of justice has to do with the "administration of law or equity" (OED). In this sense an injustice can and probably should trigger a legal action, either criminal or civil. There is no doubt Smith was thinking of this sense of justice in most of his discussions in TMS on the topic. We can surmise that at an individual refraining from injustice or pursuing justice certainly includes this: don't break the law.

But there are other definitions and uses of the word *justice*. Particularly, "The quality of being just or right, as a human or divine attribute; moral uprightness; just behaviour or dealing as a concept or principle. . . . the exhibition of this quality or principle in action; integrity, rectitude" (OED). This sense of justice goes beyond the law; one can be unjust and yet not criminal or subject to civil suit. If one has two elderly aunts who live together and have different birthdays, to send one a birthday greeting without sending the other a birthday greeting can be labeled an injustice, but it will never trigger legal action.

Smith certainly, on occasion, uses *justice* in this second sense in TMS. In his discussion of praise he indicates that to "desire it [praise] where it is really due, is to desire no more than that a most essential act of justice should be done to us" (*TMS*, 117). Smith also notes the wise man "often feels very severely the injustice of unmerited censure" (*TMS*, 121) which does not necessarily coincide with any legal action brought against such a man. Smith also notes that an older person who has been subject to the "injustice of the world" has learned to shrug it off "and do[es] not even deign to honour its futile authors with any serious resentment" (*TMS*, 144). Also recall Smith's proud man who thinks you ought to view him in the same high esteem he views himself and "demands no more of you than, what he thinks, justice" (*TMS*, 255). He would be deluded, however, if he believes he can compel your good opinion by taking you to a court of law.

Although Smith is not as clear as we may like, we suspect this second sense of justice is included in his maxim of prudence, benevolence and justice. Smith states that benevolence and justice are "other-directed" virtues unlike prudence and self-command, the self-directed virtues. Smith draws a conceptual line between the two "other-directed" virtues; "the virtues of justice and beneficence; of which, the one restrains us from hurting, the other prompts us to promote that happiness" (*TMS*, 262). But the line is not a bright line. What Smith does not make clear is when a personal action that is not illegal is an injustice or merely a failure to be beneficent. [2]

One may do an injustice to Aunt Minnie by stealing from her bank account, which is clearly illegal. One may promote her happiness by beneficently taking her on a trip to Las Vegas. Whether failing to send her a birthday card, when one has been sent to her sister Aunt Maude is simply the absence of beneficence or an active injustice may be an open question. No matter. We can deem personal actions other than legal violation as just or unjust in our reading of Jane Austen. If a character acts in a way that primarily harms another person without a good cause, then they have been unjust.

At the beginning of *Mansfield Park*, at a superficial level, Mrs. Norris *appears* to be prudent, benevolent, and just. She certainly thinks she is. As she tells Sir Thomas, "My dear Sir Thomas, with all my faults I have a warm heart; and, poor as I am, would rather deny myself the necessaries of life than do an ungenerous thing. . . . My own trouble, you know, I never regard" (*MP*, 451). After all she initiates bringing her niece, ten-year-old Fanny Price, to live with the extended family in and around Mansfield Park. Fanny's family is poor and the move will not only enhance Fanny's life prospects but also relieve the Price family of the burden of a child.

However, Austen clues us in early on as to Mrs. Norris's real character; her prudence is limited to frugality and devoid of the other positive characteristics of prudence. Her benevolence consists of directing others to be generous with their resources so that it requires no sacrifice of resources on her part.

At the novel's outset she has convinced Sir Thomas and Lady Bertram to go along with her scheme to bring their mutual niece to live in the neighborhood. The Bertrams assume that Fanny would live with Mrs. Norris and her husband, Reverend Norris. Only later do they discover that Mrs. Norris's plan is for Fanny to live with the Bertrams, a condition to which they acquiesce. Austen notes: "the pleasures of so benevolent a scheme were already enjoyed. The division of gratifying sensations ought not, in strict justice, to have been equal; for Sir Thomas was fully resolved to be the real and consistent patron of the selected child, and Mrs. Norris had not the least intention of being at any expense whatever in her maintenance" (*MP*, 452).

It is interesting that Austen thinks it *unjust* that Mrs. Norris receives so much pleasure given the lack of her personal commitment to her proposed project. Austen goes on to tell us more about Mrs. Norris's character. "As far as walking, talking, and contriving reached, she was thoroughly benevolent, and nobody knew better how to dictate liberality to others; but her love of money was equal to her love of directing, and she knew quite as well how to save her own as to spend that of her friends" (*MP*, 452).

Of course, frugality is part of prudence but not its whole. The "love of directing" is at odds with prudence.[3] Mrs. Norris falls into the trap of Smithian self-delusion, of wanting to think highly of oneself, which Mrs. Norris undoubtedly does. "[I]t was impossible for her to aim at more than the credit of projecting and arranging so expensive a charity; though perhaps she might so little know herself as to walk home to the Parsonage, after this conversation, in the happy belief of being the most liberal-minded sister and aunt in the world" (*MP*, 452).

Mrs. Norris's frugality appears elsewhere in the novel. When her husband dies, it is suggested that Fanny move in with her. Fanny is not at all enthusiastic about such an arrangement, but Mrs. Norris quashes any such thought by, again, pleading her own poverty. "I must live within my income, or I shall be miserable; and I own it would give me great satisfaction to be able to do rather more, to lay by a little at the end of the year" (*MP*, 464). To which her sister Lady Bertram, who is usually clueless on these matters, presciently notes that: "I dare say you will. You always do, don't you?" (*MP*, 464).

For Mrs. Norris, frugality is a habit that directs and delights her world. While Sir Thomas is away in Antigua, his children and their friends are busily arranging to rehearse and stage a play at Mansfield Park. Austen tells us that Mrs. Norris's approval was founded on the play having "very little expense to anybody, and none at all to herself," and it also allowed her to save on her expenses because it made "herself obliged to leave her own house, where she had been living a month at her own cost" (*MP*, 522). Her main role with the play consists of managing little details about the production "and saving, with delighted integrity, half a crown here and there" (*MP*, 541). Mrs. Norris lacks superior prudence because she is devoid in justice and benevolence from the very beginning.

At the novel's onset Sir Thomas agrees that Fanny should leave her home in Portsmouth and live at Mansfield Park, but he anticipates a problem and engages Mrs. Norris to help him:

> "There will be some difficulty in our way, Mrs. Norris," observed Sir Thomas, "as to the distinction proper to be made between the girls as they grow up: how to preserve in the minds of my daughters the consciousness of what they are, without making them think too lowly of their cousin; and how, without depressing her spirits too far, to make her remember that she is not a Miss Bertram. I should wish to see them very good friends, and would, on no account, authorise in my girls the smallest degree of arrogance towards their relation; but still they cannot be equals. Their rank, fortune, rights, and expectations will always be different. It is a point of great delicacy, and you must assist us in our endeavours to choose exactly the right line of conduct." (*MP*, 453)

Mrs. Norris is the main tutor and influence on the two Bertram girls, because their mother, Lady Bertram, is quite incapable and uninterested in exerting much influence on anybody. Sir Thomas is amenable to bringing Fanny to his home but frankly recognizes that she will be an inferior to her cousins. Yet he does not want to see her unnecessarily demeaned and charges Mrs. Norris with the duty to help and thread this difficult needle.

When Fanny settles in at Mansfield Park we are told she "could read, work, and write, but she had been taught nothing more; and as her cousins found her ignorant of many things with which they had been long familiar, they thought her prodigiously stupid" (*MP*, 457). This difference in education is remediable, a fact Sir Thomas recognizes. But Mrs. Norris is no help in remedying the educational deficiency. Moreover, she does nothing to assuage the Bertram sisters' contempt for their cousin, in fact, she encourages it by telling the sisters "you are blessed with wonderful memories, and your poor cousin has probably none at all. There is a vast deal of difference in memories, as well as in everything else, and therefore you must make allowance for your cousin, and pity her deficiency" (*MP*, 458). She also informs the Bertram sisters that they should consider themselves superior to Fanny: "[Y]ou know (owing to me) your papa and mama are so good as to bring her up with you, it is not at all necessary that she should be as accomplished as you are;—on the contrary, it is much more desirable that there should be a difference" (*MP*, 458). This is quite the opposite of Sir Thomas's wishes.

Mrs. Norris's attitude toward Fanny is not benevolent and is not consistent with justice. It is pernicious as it inculcates a bad attitude or disposition in the Bertram sisters, one that deters their moral development. They grow up spoiled, self-centered, and inconsiderate. "Such were the counsels by which Mrs. Norris assisted to form her nieces' minds; and it is not very wonderful that, with all their promising talents and early information, they should be entirely deficient in the less common acquirements of self-knowledge, generosity and humility. In everything but disposition they were admirably taught" (*MP*, 458).[4]

As the novel unfolds Mrs. Norris is unjust and malevolent to Fanny. Edmund Bertram wants Fanny to have a horse so she could exercise for her health; Mrs. Norris objects.[5] When the Bertram siblings and friends plan a visit to the Rushworth estate, Mrs. Norris intentionally excludes Fanny. Austen reports that "Mrs. Norris had no affection for Fanny, and no wish of procuring her pleasure at any time" (*MP*, 493). Smith explains that affection is necessary for benevolence. It is no wonder that Mrs. Norris is incapable of benevolence to Fanny; she has no *affection* for her.

Fanny does end up going on the day trip. On the way home Mrs. Norris takes credit for Fanny's good fortune remarking, "'Well, Fanny, this has been a fine day for you, upon my word,' said Mrs. Norris, as they drove through the park. 'Nothing but pleasure from beginning to end! I am sure you ought to be very much obliged to your aunt Bertram and me for contriving to let you go'" (*MP*, 508). What an irritating old biddy.

Aunt Norris is constantly demeaning Fanny in front of everyone. Fanny does not want to be part of the play the other young people are arranging. Edmund defends her choice telling his aunt it is not fair to pressure her, to which Mrs. Norris replies "'I am not going to urge her,' replied Mrs. Norris sharply; 'but I shall think her a very obstinate, ungrateful girl, if she does not do what her aunt and cousins wish her—very ungrateful, indeed, considering who and what she is'" (*MP*, 532). When the group is busily working on the play, Mrs. Norris complains in front of all that Fanny is not helping enough (*MP*, 543–544).

When Fanny is invited to dinner at the nearby parson's home, Austen tells us that Mrs. Norris "seemed intent only on lessening her niece's pleasure, both present and future, as much as possible" (*MP*, 573). She tells Fanny that the only reason she had been invited was because neither of the Bertram sisters were home. "Nor must you be fancying that the invitation is meant as any particular compliment to you; the compliment is intended to your uncle and aunt and me" (*MP*, 573). She insists on informing Fanny of her inferior status: "Remember, wherever you are, you must be the lowest and last" (*MP*, 573). When Sir Thomas asks Fanny when she would like to be picked up for the dinner engagement, "'My dear Sir Thomas!' cried Mrs. Norris, red with anger, 'Fanny can walk.' 'Walk!' repeated Sir Thomas, in a tone of most unanswerable dignity, and coming farther into the room. 'My niece walk to a dinner engagement at this time of the year! Will twenty minutes after four suit you?'" (*MP*, 574).

When Sir Thomas proposes having a ball in Fanny's honor, Mrs. Norris seethes with resentment and anger; "her surprise and vexation required some minutes silence to be settled into composure. A ball at such a time! His daughters absent and herself not consulted!" (*MP*, 592). Yet as with the outing to Mr. Rushworth's home, she is quick to take credit for any success Fanny may have. When Sir Thomas remarks at how well Fanny looks at the ball, "'Look well! Oh, yes!' cried Mrs. Norris, 'she has good reason to look well with all her advantages: brought up in this family as she has been, with all the benefit of her cousins' manners before her. Only think, my dear Sir Thomas, what extraordinary advantages you and I have been the means of giving her'" (*MP*, 603).

Sir Thomas originally planned to keep Fanny's refusal of Crawford's proposal of marriage a secret but when he realizes that was impossible, he fears the effect of the communication on Mrs. Norris. Austen reveals more of Mrs. Norris's antipathy for Fanny after Mrs. Norris learns of Crawford's proposal.

> Angry she was: bitterly angry; but she was more angry with Fanny for having received such an offer than for refusing it. It was an injury and affront to Julia, who ought to have been Mr. Crawford's choice; and, independently of that, she disliked Fanny, because she had neglected her; and she would have grudged such an elevation to one whom she had been always trying to depress. (*MP*, 637)

When Crawford and Mrs. Rushworth (Maria) have their scandalous affair, Mrs. Norris "was but the more irritated by the sight of the person whom, in the blindness of her anger, she could have charged as the daemon of the piece. Had Fanny accepted Mr. Crawford this could not have happened" (*MP*, 705).

The novel ends with Mrs. Norris leaving Mansfield Park and moving in with Maria in a distant county, an arrangement which Austen describes "on one side no affection, on the other no judgment, it may be reasonably supposed that their tempers became their mutual punishment." Mrs. Norris's move "was regretted by no one at Mansfield" (*MP*, 715).

Always selfish at heart and absent any real prudence, benevolence, or justice, Mrs. Norris is condemned to live with her fallen niece who had been under her constant tutelage. Mrs. Norris had little affection for others and therefore has no real benevolence. Having never been kind she is not loved by anyone. She is the antithesis of Smith's model of Prudence, Benevolence, and Justice.

It is interesting to note that at each of the abovementioned illustrations of Mrs. Norris's character either Sir Thomas or his second son Edmund are in some way at odds with Mrs. Norris. If she is the antithesis of Prudence, Benevolence, and Justice, they embody those virtues.

At the very opening of the novel Austen tells us that Sir Thomas had always been willing to help his wife's family "from principle as well as pride—from a general wish of doing right, and a desire of seeing all that were connected with him in situations of respectability . . . " (*MP*, 449). When it is suggested that Fanny move to the neighborhood, "Sir Thomas could not give so instantaneous and unqualified a consent" but not because he was unwilling to support her but from concerns for the rest of his family such as "cousins in love, etc." (*MP*, 450). In contrast to Mrs. Norris who has no intention to make any sacrifice for Fanny, Sir Thomas is "fully resolved" to be Fanny's "real and consistent patron" (*MP*, 452).

Sir Thomas alludes to the possibility the arrangement may not work out if her "disposition"[6] was "really bad" and noted "we must prepare ourselves for gross ignorance, some meanness of opinions, and very distressing vulgarity of manner" and then notes that "but these are not incurable faults . . . " (*MP*, 453). Unlike Mrs. Norris who is actually quite prejudiced against Fanny from the start, Sir Thomas is willing to give her a chance in the belief that most any deficiency can be remediated by proper influence and education. All in all, Sir Thomas is prudent in his considerations of whether to take Fanny in, fair and just in his assessment of her, and by nature benevolent to those who are in his extended family.

Once Fanny moves in no one shows her any real kindness except Edmund. He finds her crying and inquires "'My dear little cousin,' said he, with all the gentleness of an excellent nature, 'what can be the matter?'" (*MP*, 455). He persistently inquires as to the source of her distress and directs her to the library to write a letter to her favorite brother William.

Throughout the novel Edmund is always fair and kind to Fanny and is promoting her happiness, in contrast to the roughshod ways of Mrs. Norris who is intent on diminishing Fanny's happiness. Whether it is Edmund's insistence that Fanny have some means of exercise or be included in an outing, or insisting that her decision not to act in the play be respected, Edmund is her advocate. Is this a matter of justice, or is it a matter of benevolence? No matter. Edmund practices Smithian virtues toward Fanny.

When Sir Thomas returns from Antigua he is prudent, benevolent, and just with Fanny. Unlike Lady Bertram and Mrs. Norris, he finds nothing unusual about the Grants' dinner invitation to Fanny, and in fact wonders why it had not been extended earlier. As noted above he also insists she be taken by carriage. He proposes a ball for Fanny before her brother William leaves Mansfield Park and takes genuine delight in giving the ball.

The most detailed and poignant encounter Sir Thomas has with Fanny is when he interviews her after Henry Crawford has approached him and asked his permission to propose marriage to Fanny. Sir Thomas enters her chamber expecting her to be delighted at the proposal and ready to encourage her to accept it. He is quite upset when she indicates she will refuse the proposal. He scolds her for her intransigence, which is distressing, confusing, and painful to Fanny.

In this sequence of events Austen weaves in a minor sub-plot that is of interest in assessing Sir Thomas's character, especially as it contrasts with Mrs. Norris's. Entering the room, Fanny's usual sitting room, Sir Thomas notices there is no fire even though it is a cold day. He insists the situation be "rectified" (*MP*, 625). Upon further inquiry he finds that the absence of a fire in the room is the usual state of affairs for Fanny. He also discovers this is the doing of Aunt Norris. He notes, "I know what her sentiments have always been. The principle was good in itself, but it may have been, and I believe has been, carried too far in your case.—I am aware that there has been sometimes, in some points, a misplaced distinction . . . " (*MP*, 625–626). Of course, he is referring to the scruple he mandated years ago that Fanny not be treated as the equivalent of her cousins and is expressing that he thinks Mrs. Norris has taken this "too far" in refusing Fanny firewood for her sitting room.

The point of Sir Thomas's visit was not to investigate Fanny's comforts but to fetch her to meet with Henry Crawford who is then at Mansfield. Henry will propose marriage and Sir Thomas expects Fanny will accept. When she fearfully indicates she will refuse the offer, Sir Thomas's first response is "'This is very strange!' in a voice of calm displeasure" (*MP*, 627). He then follows up by scolding Fanny in a very angry tone, indicating that her refusal is not logical and the result of Henry not being up to her "young heated fancy imagines" (*MP*, 629) of some idealized man which is very short-sighted and immature. He tells her she is not considering the interests of others in her family and is "[s]elf-willed, obstinate, selfish, and ungrateful" (*MP*, 630). Fanny bursts into tears. This ends her uncle's chiding. He leaves her to inform Henry Crawford and in "about a quarter of an hour" returns in a much less tempestuous mood.

In this second exchange he is much more gentle with her, tells her to take some time to compose herself, reflect on the situation and, "I advise you to go out: the air will do you good; go out for an hour on the gravel; you will have the shrubbery to yourself, and will be the better for air and exercise" (*MP*, 631). She takes her uncle's advice and goes for a long walk where she collects her thoughts. When she returns to her sitting room she notes, "A fire! it seemed too much; just at that time to be giving her such an indulgence was exciting even painful gratitude. She wondered that Sir Thomas could have leisure to think of such a trifle again; but she soon found, from the voluntary information of the housemaid, who came in to attend it, that so it was to be every day. Sir Thomas had given orders for it" (*MP*, 631).

It is a small gesture, making sure that Fanny has a fire in her room and ordering it daily. We get the sense that even though Sir Thomas was upset with Fanny, was angry and perplexed over her refusal of Crawford, he would never banish her, wish her removed from his patronage, or otherwise shame or humiliate her. Fanny should have a fire; it is just and proper, and the fact she is behaving oddly or inappropriately does not alter this fact. Sir Thomas is benevolent and just toward Fanny.

Sir Thomas encourages Henry to continue his pursuit of Fanny and believes that with enough effort Henry can win her heart. "Sir Thomas resolved to abstain from all farther importunity with his niece, and to shew no open interference . . . " and assures her that he will not try "to persuade [her] to marry against [her] inclinations" (*MP*, 635–636). As events unfold, Fanny's judgment about Crawford is justified by his scandalous affair with Maria, and Sir Thomas's esteem for Fanny undoubtedly rises.

A benevolent man likely assumes the best about those who are around him. Part of prudence and justice includes an ability to engage in measured judgments, to not rely on simple prejudice or refuse to consider new information when it becomes available. It is interesting to see how Sir Thomas's opinion of Mrs. Norris changes over the novel. It further confirms the quality of his character.

Sir Thomas begins with a generous and favorable opinion of Mrs. Norris. The afternoon when he returns from Antigua and arrives at Mansfield Park he indicates he does not want anything to eat until tea time. The ever-meddling Mrs. Norris insists he eat something, interrupting him as he tells a story. Yet his response to Mrs. Norris is kind and respectful as he states, "Still the same anxiety for everybody's comfort, my dear Mrs. Norris I would rather have nothing but tea" (*MP*, 550).

A few days later he comes to know that the playmaking of his children and their friends had actually been encouraged by Mrs. Norris. When he tries to call her to account for it she prevaricates, changes the subject, and evades the charge. He concludes that, "satisfied with the conviction that where the present pleasure of those she loved was at stake, her kindness did sometimes overpower her judgment" (*MP*, 556). He has come to question Mrs. Norris's prudence, yet he still thinks of her as being kind.

After Fanny refuses Henry Crawford, Sir Thomas makes a point of not wanting to inform Mrs. Norris of the situation. "He deprecated her mistaken but well-meaning zeal. Sir Thomas, indeed, was, by this time, not very far from classing Mrs. Norris as one of those well-meaning people who are always doing mistaken and very disagreeable things" (*MP*, 637). His opinion of her prudence has fallen even lower and he is beginning to question her benevolence and justice.

After the divorce between Mr. Rushworth and Maria, Mrs. Norris's departure from Mansfield became

> the great supplementary comfort of Sir Thomas's life. His opinion of her had been sinking from the day of his return from Antigua. . . . she had been regularly losing ground in his esteem. . . . He had felt her as an hourly evil . . . that must be borne forever. To be relieved from her, therefore, was so great a

felicity that, had she not left bitter remembrances behind her, there might have been danger of his learning almost to approve the evil which produced such a good. (*MP*, 715)

At this point, in Sir Thomas's judgment, Mrs. Norris is a really bad character. How bad is she? It was almost worth approving of actions that risked ruining the family reputation to be rid of her.

Mansfield Park is a rich and nuanced story. We have made the case that three of Austen's characters help us to better understand Smith's notions of prudence, benevolence, and justice as a noble and virtuous lifestyle choice. One character, Mrs. Norris, is its opposite; two of the characters, Sir Thomas and his second son Edmund, are following the virtuous path.

NOTES

1. The possible exceptions are Maria Rushworth (nee Bertram) and Henry Crawford in their adulterous affair in *Mansfield Park* which does lead to a divorce. Austen also has a penchant for writing about fifteen-year-old girls getting seduced. Willoughby seduces Eliza, Colonel Brandon's ward in *Sense and Sensibility*. Wickham tries unsuccessfully to seduce Darcy's sister and succeeds in seducing and eventually marrying Lydia Bennet in *Pride and Prejudice*. It is not clear whether this was a violation of the law in its time as twelve seems to have been the legal age of consent. In *Pride and Prejudice* Wickham alleges that Darcy has not followed the law in the disposition of the elder Darcy's estate—a claim which is shown later to be a spectacular slander. Finally in *Northanger Abbey* there is a suspicion of murder which is also proven to be false.

2. Smith makes clear that every virtue *except* justice cannot be perfectly delineated in the sense it is exacting and precise. We think this must refer to justice-as-law not justice as dutiful obligation.

3. See chapter 9 for a discussion of how her "love of directing" is related to Smith's Man of System.

4. At the time of Austen, the word *disposition* implied something about an individual's moral tendencies. It was understood to be about the "whole frame and texture of the mind." A bad "disposition" is hard to remedy but not impossible to correct if one is instructed in right principles. (See Stokes, 1991, 166–168.) The point is that Mrs. Norris is instructing the Bertram sisters in the wrong principles.

5. Dussinger (1990, 97) points out that horseback riding was a "highly recommended treatment for female hysteria" in the time of Austen. Female hysteria was seen as the source of many of women's health problems.

6. See note 4.

Chapter Six

Vanity in *Persuasion*

Austen begins the novel *Persuasion* by describing Sir Walter Elliot as a man who never "took up any book but the Baronetage" (*P*, 1145). The Baronetage is: "A list of the order of baronets; a book giving such a list with historical and other particulars" (OED). Reading this document he "found occupation for idle hours and consolation in distressed ones" (*P*, 1145). Austen paints the picture of a man preoccupied with his rank in the world, a rank that is a pure accident of birth. Sir Walter sees this inalienable birthright as automatically conferring status and privilege to him. Quite naturally such a person is very prone to vanity, and Austen immediately states "Vanity was the beginning and the end of Sir Walter Elliot's character; vanity of person and of situation" (*P*, 1145). Baronet Walter Elliot is not the major character in *Persuasion*. Even so, he gives us insight into Austen's view of the emptiness and vanity of many aristocrats of her time, a view that fits quite well with Smith's view of rank and "that love of distinction so natural to man" (*TMS*, 182).

Vanity has at least two meanings in the English language. One is "the quality of being worthless or futile" (OED). The writer of the Old Testament book of Ecclesiastes, traditionally King Solomon, cries out: "[V]anity of vanities; all is vanity. What profit hath a man of all his labour which he taketh under the sun?" (Ecclesiastes 1:2–3 KJV). This view of the world can lead one to be *splenetic*, defined as "Having an irritably morose or peevish disposition or temperament" (OED).

Smith uses this term *splenetic* in his discussion of human pursuit of wealth, fortune, and advancement. He describes the view that wealth and rank are useless in the final analysis as a "splenetic philosophy which in time of sickness or low spirits is familiar to every man, thus entirely depreciates those great objects of human desire . . . " (*TMS*, 183). We all sometimes

69

believe, as King Solomon did, that all is futile, all is vain; and we likely become very irritating and depressing to everyone around us and to ourselves. But by Smith's reckoning we tend to snap out of these funks and carry on in our pursuits because we are subject to the "*deception* which rouses and keeps in continual motion the industry of mankind" (*TMS*, 183, emphasis added). And recall from chapter 3, Smith sees this deception as a *good* thing.

This segues quite nicely to the second meaning of vanity: "an excessive pride in or admiration of one's own appearance or achievements" (OED). Smith believes vanity is the true object of improving one's position, of gaining status and wealth in the world. "It is the vanity, not the ease, or the pleasure, which interests us" (*TMS*, 50). When we are not splenetic, we are typically indulging our vanity. An embodiment of this vanity is the *coxcomb*, a word Smith and Austen use a number of times in their work, defined as a "foolish, conceited, showy person, vain of his accomplishments, appearance, or dress; a fop; a superficial pretender to knowledge or accomplishments" (OED).

To both Austen and Smith's view vanity is a vice; both men and women are vain and almost everyone is vain in some way. Our exploration of vanity in Austen shall focus on characters, both male and female, who especially characterize vanity. We will discover that again, Austen's descriptions fit well with Smith's framework, and in fact illustrate and embellish Smith's insight into human nature.

Back to *Persuasion*. Sir Walter Elliot had married a "wife of very superior character to anything deserved by his own" (*P*, 1146) who had managed to constrain the worst of his tendencies, managed his affairs, and borne him three daughters, Elizabeth, Anne, and Mary. At the novel's start, Lady Elliot had died thirteen years earlier leaving the three girls under the direction of a very "conceited, silly father" (*P*, 1146). Lady Elliot did have a friend and neighbor, Lady Russell, who took a maternal interest in the three girls upon their mother's passing and formed an especially close bond with the second daughter Anne.

Over the thirteen years since his wife's death, Sir Walter had overspent and accumulated a considerable amount of debt. His financial position was unsustainable. When he poses the question of where to cut back, his oldest daughter Elizabeth, who is also a very vain creature, can only suggest "to cut off some unnecessary charities, and to refrain from new furnishing the drawing-room" (*P*, 1149). The father and daughter both see their extravagant lifestyle as an entitlement and are appalled at the suggestion they should retrench. "[Elizabeth] felt herself ill-used and unfortunate, as did her father; and they were neither of them able to devise any means of lessening their expenses without compromising their dignity, or relinquishing their comforts in a way not to be borne" (*P*, 1149).

Austen makes a clear distinction between the attitudes of the father and oldest daughter Elizabeth with that of Lady Russell and the second daughter Anne. Lady Russell and Anne had both set up a spending plan that would reduce the debt of the estate over time. Anne's was harder on her father than Lady Russell's: "Every emendation of Anne's had been on the side of honesty against importance. She wanted more vigorous measures, a more complete reformation, a quicker release from debt, a much higher tone of indifference for everything but justice and equity" (*P*, 1150). But Lady Russell suggested they argue for her more modest plan, although she concurred with Anne's sentiments that honesty and justice should trump importance and ostentation. "'If we can persuade your father to all this,' said Lady Russell, looking over her paper, 'much may be done. If he will adopt these regulations, in seven years he will be clear . . . for after all, the person who has contracted debts must pay them; and though a great deal is due to the feelings of the gentleman, and the head of a house, like your father, there is still more due to the character of an honest man'" (*P*, 1150).

Elizabeth and Sir Walter reject Lady Russell's plan, offering no viable alternative and complaining that the retrenchments "could not be put up with—were not to be borne. 'What! every comfort of life knocked off! Journeys, London, servants, horses, table—contractions and restrictions everywhere. To live no longer with the decencies even of a private gentleman!'" (*P*, 1151). The necessary retrenchment is finally accomplished when Sir Walter agrees to rent his country estate to a suitable tenant while he and his family move to other accommodations in Bath, a resort town popular among the wealthy. But even here vanity and appearances are of first order to Sir Walter; his agent is not to "advertise" the availability of the house in a public newspaper (*P*, 1152). As a war had just ended, Sir Walter's agent, Mr. Shepherd, speculates there were many admirals who would be available as tenants.

When Admiral Croft is found, Sir Walter finally assents to this plan noting it will not harm his status. "An admiral speaks his own consequence, and, at the same time, can never make a baronet look small" (*P*, 1157). Austen wryly notes, "In all their dealings and intercourse, Sir Walter Elliot must ever have the precedence" (*P*, 1157). We have little sympathy with the plight of the Elliots, and we suspect that neither Austen nor Smith felt much either; but we can understand the horror that Sir Walter and Elizabeth experienced. The vain person, as Smith teaches, always wants to be the object of attention and have the approval of others. "The rich man glories in his riches, because he feels that they naturally draw upon him the attention of the world, and that mankind are disposed to go along with him in all those agreeable emotions with which the advantages of his situation so readily inspire him" (*TMS*, 50–51). To be popular and to be the object of much attention you must

appear prosperous especially as compared to your peers. How true today and
true then. [1]

When Anne finally arrives at Bath after Sir Walter and Elizabeth have
been there for several months, she notes her sister and father are quite happy
there. They vainly assert:

> Their house was undoubtedly the best in Camden-place; their drawing-rooms
> had many decided advantages over all the others which they had either seen or
> heard of; and the superiority was not less in the style of the fitting-up, or the
> taste of the furniture. Their acquaintance was exceedingly sought after. Every
> body was wanting to visit them. They had drawn back from many introduc-
> tions, and still were perpetually having cards left by people of whom they
> knew nothing. (*P*, 1222)

Upon Anne's arrival quite by coincidence two distant relatives of higher
status, Lady Dalrymple and her daughter Miss Carteret, arrive in Bath. Sir
Walter and Elizabeth obsequiously court their company much to Anne's
dismay. She actually wishes they had more pride and notes:

> Had Lady Dalrymple and her daughter even been very agreeable, she would
> still have been ashamed of the agitation they created, but they were nothing.
> There was no superiority of manner, accomplishment, or understanding. Lady
> Dalrymple had acquired the name of "a charming woman," because she had a
> smile and a civil answer for everybody. Miss Carteret, with still less to say,
> was so plain and so awkward, that she would never have been tolerated in
> Camden-place but for her birth. (*P*, 1229)

Smith tells us why the vain cozy up to prestigious relatives: "The remembrance of such illustrious relations flatters not a little the family pride of them
all; and it is neither from affection, nor from any thing which resembles
affection, but from the most frivolous and childish of all vanities, that this
remembrance is so carefully kept up" (*TMS*, 223).

Smith gives us the insight that those of rank and wealth are usually judged
more leniently than those of meaner conditions. "We frequently see the respectful attentions of the world more strongly directed towards the rich and
the great, than towards the wise and the virtuous. We see frequently the vices
and follies of the powerful much less despised than the poverty and weakness
of the innocent" (*TMS*, 62). A conversation between Anne and her distant
cousin, the heir apparent to the Elliot estate, makes a similar point. Anne
says: "My idea of good company, Mr. Elliot, is the company of clever, well-
informed people, who have a great deal of conversation; that is what I call
good company." "You are mistaken," said he gently, "that is not good company; that is the best. Good company requires only birth, education, and
manners, and with regard to education is not very nice" (*P*, 1229). Mr. Elliot
goes on to note that despite the defects of Lady Dalrymple and Miss Carteret,

"they will move in the first set in Bath this winter, and as rank is rank, your being known to be related to them will have its use in fixing your family (our family let me say) in that degree of consideration which we must all wish for" (*P*, 1229).

It is much to Anne's credit that her actions reflect her disdain for the social climbing rank-based obsession of her father and older sister. Upon arriving at Bath, Anne became re-acquainted with "an old school-fellow" whose kindness to Anne "could never be remembered with indifference" (*P*, 1230). The friend, now Mrs. Smith, "was a widow and poor . . . afflicted with a severe rheumatic fever, which, finally settling in her legs, had made her for the present a cripple . . . " (*P*, 1231). Anne's visits were a great comfort to Mrs. Smith and the two set a regular time for visits. One day Anne's father and sister arrive home "with a sudden invitation from Lady Dalrymple for the same evening, and Anne was already engaged, to spend that evening (with Mrs. Smith)" (*P*, 1233).

Sir Walter was very "severe" in his condemnation of Anne, proclaiming outrage that Anne deemed a visit to an unimportant Mrs. Smith " . . . to be preferred by her to her own family connections among the nobility of England and Ireland!" (*P*, 1234). Anne is calmly unaffected by her father's reproach and spends her evening with her friend. Anne is benevolent and just, in marked contrast to her vain relatives.

Both Smith and Austen observe that rank has an untoward appeal in the larger world and they both are rather appalled by the state of affairs.[2] Smith asks, "By what important accomplishments is the young nobleman instructed to support the dignity of his rank, and to render himself worthy of that superiority over his fellow-citizens, to which the virtue of his ancestors had raised them? Is it by knowledge, by industry, by patience, by self-denial, or by virtue of any kind?" (*TMS*, 53). Absolutely not! All the young nobleman has learned, all he can do is, in Smith's words, to "perform all those small duties with the most exact propriety" (*TMS*, 53).

In Austen's depiction, neither Sir Walter nor Elizabeth has ever done anything of merit. At fifty-four years of age, Sir Walter has lived beyond his means, established nothing and accomplished nothing except to continually strive to advance his social status, to feed his incessant vanity; and Elizabeth is following in his footsteps. Austen gives us nothing to admire, nothing to arouse any sympathy with them. Sir Walter and Elizabeth exhibit "a most contemptible vanity."

VANITY IN *SENSE AND SENSIBILITY*

Few characters in Austen are as despicable as Lucy Steele in *Sense and Sensibility*. Lucy is vain and conniving, a combination that is less than attractive. Recall early on in the novel Lucy reveals to Elinor, that she, Lucy, is secretly engaged to Edward Ferrars, the object of Elinor's affection. We suspect that Lucy is very aware that Elinor is her rival because the affable Sir John has shared the local gossip on the matter with Lucy. We also suspect Lucy has shared her secret with Elinor out of motives other than a desire for Elinor's friendship. We are also pretty sure that Elinor is aware of all this. Lucy is conniving as well as vain, and Elinor is no fool.

In the eyes of Edward's sister, Mrs. John Dashwood, and his mother, Mrs. Ferrars, Elinor is far beneath Edward's dignity. While having manners and education, she has little money. Lucy, with no money and no breeding, would surely be several rungs below Elinor in their estimation. Mrs. John Dashwood had observed Elinor and her brother's friendship at the Norland estate. She clearly indicates to Elinor's mother that any thought of a match between Elinor and Edward is out of the question.

Sometime after the Dashwoods have settled at Barton Cottage, Lucy and Nancy Steele appear on the scene at Barton Park. They are distant cousins of Mrs. Jennings, Sir Middleton's mother-in-law. Sir John Middleton, the owner and master of Barton Park, is an affable character and always enjoys new company. No snob, he sees any relative of his wife and mother-in-law as good enough for him, and he offers the hospitality of Barton Park to the Steele sisters.

Lucy and Nancy make great overtures of friendship to Elinor and Marianne, a telltale sign of vanity. They pay inordinate attention to Lady Middleton's already spoiled children[3] and are constantly trying to please Mrs. Jennings, Lady Middleton, Sir John, and everyone else. After several social interactions and before she knows of Lucy's attachment to Edward, Elinor gives a balanced appraisal of Lucy's character:

> Lucy was naturally clever; her remarks were often just and amusing; and as a companion for half an hour Elinor frequently found her agreeable; but her powers had received no aid from education: she was ignorant and illiterate; and her deficiency of all mental improvement, her want of information in the most common particulars, could not be concealed from Miss Dashwood, in spite of her constant endeavour to appear to advantage. (*SS*, 79)

Lucy is a phony; she puts on airs pretending to be something she is not. This is, in Smith's words, "properly called vanity" and leads to the "most ridiculous and contemptible vices, the vices of affectation and common lying" (*TMS*, 115).

Austen goes on to tell us:

> Elinor saw, and pitied her for, the neglect of abilities which education might have rendered so respectable; but she saw, with less tenderness of feeling, the thorough want of delicacy, of rectitude, and integrity of mind, which her

attentions, her assiduities, her flatteries at the Park betrayed; and she could have no lasting satisfaction in the company of a person who joined insincerity with ignorance. (*SS*, 79)

Elinor is too smart to be fooled by Lucy; she sees through her and immediately suspects she is a rather crass opportunistic social climber. However, most everyone else does not. All hail the flattering Steele sisters as a wonderful new addition to their community. Smith calls the vain (wo)man one who "flatters in order to be flattered. [S]he studies to please, and endeavours to bribe you into a good opinion of [her] by politeness and complaisance . . . " (*TMS*, 256).

Later in the novel when the main characters are in London for the season; both the Dashwood and Steele sisters are invited to a dinner with Edward's mother and his sister. Mrs. Ferrars has suspicions of Edward's interest in Elinor. They clearly have no knowledge as to his actual engagement to Lucy. The Dashwood sisters are not particularly solicitous to the proud Mrs. Ferrars because Marianne is not solicitous to anyone, and Elinor feels no need to be as she surmises she has no hope of ever marrying Edward. The evening does not go well for the Dashwood sisters as Marianne lashes out at Mrs. Ferrars for the older ladies' lack of appreciation of the drawings of Elinor. Lucy, as always, is quite solicitous, a trait consistent with both her vanity and scheming nature.

The next day, Lucy goes on and on to Elinor about how well Mrs. Ferrars treated her the previous evening. Elinor "wondered that Lucy's spirits could be so very much elevated by the civility of Mrs. Ferrars;—that her interest and vanity should so very much blind her, as to make the attention which seemed only paid her because she was *not Elinor*, appear a compliment to herself . . . " (*SS*, 141). Yet Lucy persists in expressing this view to Elinor; she is absolutely adamant in insisting that Mrs. Ferrars and her daughter, Mrs. Dashwood, like her very much. She is absolutely convinced that she can soon reveal her engagement to Edward's family and "it will all end well and there will be no difficulties at all" (*SS*, 142).

Soon after the dinner, Lucy and her sister are invited for a stay with Mrs. John Dashwood at the London residence. It appears to Lucy, at least, that she now has a chance to ingratiate herself to Edward's sister and eventually pave the way for a public engagement and eventual marriage to Edward. Elinor notes: "Her flattery had already subdued the pride of Lady Middleton, and made an entry into the close heart of Mrs. John Dashwood . . . " (*SS*, 150).

But this is not the way it all works out. While staying with the Dashwoods, Lucy's sister Nancy "popt it all out" about Lucy and Edmund's long and secret engagement, thinking that as the Dashwoods and Mrs. Ferrars "are so fond of Lucy, to be sure they will make no difficulty about it" (*SS*, 151). Quite the opposite; Edward's sister flew "into violent hysterics" (*SS*, 151) and wanted to immediately eject both sisters from the house. Her husband restrained her, allowing them to gather their things before they made an exit. The Steele sisters had grossly miscalculated.

Yet this is precisely what vain people do; they are deluded about themselves in an irrational manner. As Smith tells us "vanity arises from so gross an illusion of the imagination" (*TMS*, 115). After all is said and done, however, Lucy's vanity coupled with her mercenary cleverness does lead to her profitable marriage—to Edward's younger brother Robert.

By all accounts Robert Ferrars is also vain. In fact Lucy describes him as a "coxcomb" to Elinor (*SS*, 90). When Elinor finally meets him much later in the novel "he was exactly the coxcomb she had heard him described to be by Lucy" (*SS*, 148). Before Elinor had formally met Robert, she had observed him at a jewelry store. The store was quite crowded, so she went to the counter with the shortest queue.

> [O]ne gentleman only was standing there, and it is probable that Elinor was not without hope of exciting his politeness to a quicker dispatch. But the correctness of his eye, and the delicacy of his taste, proved to be beyond his politeness. He was giving orders for a toothpick-case for himself, and till its size, shape, and ornaments were determined, all of which, after examining and debating for a quarter of an hour over every toothpick-case in the shop. . . . At last the affair was decided. The ivory, the gold, and the pearls, all received their appointment, and the gentleman having named the last day on which his existence could be continued without the possession of the toothpick-case, drew on his gloves with leisurely care, and bestowing another glance on the Miss Dashwoods, but such a one as seemed rather to demand than express admiration, walked off with a happy air of real conceit and affected indifference. (*SS*, 131)

This is the picture of a vain coxcomb. It also reminds us of Smith's discussion that the acquisition of "mere trinkets of frivolous utility" that are goal of the misguided poor man's son (*TMS*, 181). In fact Smith specifically refers to an elaborate "tooth-pick" as an item of conspicuous consumption that is not likely to give its owner as much attention and applauds from others as other more visible symbols of prosperity like "palaces, gardens and equipage" (*TMS,* 182). A coxcomb like Robert is not only vain but a rather inefficient buyer of objects that are effective tools to indulge his vanity.

So how did Robert and Lucy get together? After all, this is the turn in the plot that allows for the eventual happy match between Elinor and Edward. Recall, Edward did not disavow or break up with Lucy when their engagement became public knowledge. He resolutely stood by Lucy and his old promise to her. As a result Edward was disowned by his mother and left with only two thousand pounds, which would generate an income of a hundred pounds a year at most.[4]

However, upon Edward's refusal to cancel his engagement to Lucy, Mrs. Ferrars irrevocably and immediately bequeathed an estate that yielded an income of a thousand pounds a year to Robert. It was this comparative knowledge, one hundred pounds versus one thousand pounds a year, while not precisely accurate,[5] that induced Lucy to switch her allegiance to Robert. She somehow convinced Robert to marry her. Edward offered to Elinor "an explanation by supposing, that, perhaps, at first accidentally meeting, the vanity of the one [Robert] had been so worked on by the flattery of the other [Lucy], as to lead by degrees to all the rest" (*SS*, 213). Vanity preys on vanity; vanity is seduced by a more clever vanity.

There is another vain man in *Sense and Sensibility*: Willoughby, the scoundrel who seduces a fifteen-year-old girl, breaks Marianne's heart, and marries only for money. When Marianne falls gravely ill at the Palmers' estate on the sisters' journey to Barton Cottage from London, Willoughby appears and presents an explanation/confession to Elinor for his dreadful behavior toward her sister.

He recalls that during his time at Barton Cottage his intention was to pass the time pleasantly, but Marianne's personality attracted his attention " . . . I must confess, my vanity only was elevated by it. Careless of her happiness, thinking only of my own amusement, giving way to feelings which I had always been too much in the habit of indulging, I endeavored, by every means in my power, to make myself pleasing to her, without any design of returning her affection" (*SS*, 187). Again, a vain man flatters to be flattered and makes himself pleasing to others. In this case, however, the object was not advancement in any material sense, but rather for the caprice, the fun and wicked pleasure of melting a woman's heart.

Willoughby goes on to reflect that while his fortune was always small he had always had expensive tastes and had always "been in the habit of associating with people of better income than myself" (*SS*, 187). According to Smith the vain man "courts the company of his superiors" and "his way of living . . . announce both a higher rank and a greater fortune than really belong to him" (*TMS*, 256). This habit of vanity made Willoughby believe he must find a wife with a large fortune which Marianne does not have.

Yet as time passed at Barton Cottage he developed true feelings for Marianne; he was falling in love with her, and he recalls "the happiest hours of my life were spent with her" (*SS*, 188). At this point he had every intention "of openly assuring [Marianne] of an affection which I had taken pains to display" (*SS*, 188). However, when his rich elderly cousin, Mrs. Smith discovers his shocking dalliance with the fifteen-year-old Eliza, Colonel Brandon's ward, his cousin cut him off from her inheritance and he was "formally dismissed from her favour and her house" (*SS*, 188).

At this point Willoughby panics. He decides, after a few hours' deliberation, to go back to London and pursue the affections of the rich Miss Grey.

"My affection for Marianne . . . was insufficient to outweigh that dread of poverty, or get the better of those false ideas of the necessity of riches" (*SS*, 189). According to Smith, what is the dread of poverty? It is not a fear of starvation or actual suffering but from a "regard to the sentiments of mankind" that look down at those with fewer of the "superfluities" that additional income provides. Smith rhetorically asks "why should those who have been educated in the higher ranks of life, regard [poverty] as worse than death?" (*TMS*, 150). Yet during those short and panicked hours Willoughby does incline that way.

Willoughby is eventually clever enough to recognize, as Smith does, the "false ideas of the necessity of riches," but by the time of his interview with Elinor it is too late for this realization to do him any good (*SS*, 189). His vanity and avarice has condemned him to a life of misery. He opines: "To avoid a comparative poverty which her (Marianne's) affections and society would have deprived all horrors, I have by raising my affluence, lost everything that could make it a blessing" (*SS*, 187).

After Willoughby had made a "full confession" to Elinor she reflects

> on the irreparable injury which too early an independence and its consequent habits of idleness, dissipation, and luxury, had made in the mind, the character, the happiness, of a man who, to every advantage of person and talents, united a disposition naturally open and honest, and a feeling affectionate temper. The world had made him extravagant and vain.—Extravagance and vanity had made him cold-hearted and selfish. Vanity, while seeking its own guilty triumph at the expense of another, had involved him in a real attachment, which extravagance, or at least its offspring, necessity, had required to be sacrificed. (*SS*, 193–194)

So Willoughby is the victim of his own vanity, and is doomed to a miserable life because it.

VANITY IN *MANSFIELD PARK*

Henry Crawford in *Mansfield Park* is in many ways like John Willoughby in *Sense and Sensibility*. In one important respect, however, he is quite different. He is independently wealthy and does not seek womens' hearts for money. He does seek their hearts for his own vanity. Unlike Jane Austen, Adam Smith, to the best of our knowledge, never considers this manifestation of vanity. Smith sees vanity in individuals' behavior and consumption patterns, but not in interactions with members of the opposite sex.

However, Henry Crawford is not immune from the Smithian manifestation of vanity. Later in the novel, Henry rides by the house that Edmund Bertram is planning to live in when Edmund begins his position as a parish minister in the nearby village of Thornton Lacey. Edmund wants to make some modifications and improvements to the property, but Henry proposes a more ambitious plan and provides the following rationale:

> From being the mere gentleman's residence, it becomes, by judicious improvement, the residence of a man of education, taste, modern manners, good connexions. All this may be stamped on it; and that house receive such an air as to make its owner be set down as the great landholder of the parish by every creature travelling the road; especially as there is no real squire's house to dispute the point. (*MP*, 586–587)

True to Smith's insight the purpose of the improvements to the vain man (Crawford) are to give the place an "air" so that the owner will be thought to be a "great landlord" by those who pass by. This is mere pretense and show. It will not even be Crawford's residence, yet he can be vicariously vain. Unlike Robert Ferrars, however, Crawford is smart enough to know what matters, at least in Adam Smith's opinion: houses are more visible symbols of prosperity than toothpick cases.

Austen primarily shows Crawford's vanity in his desire to win the hearts of young ladies. When he settles in at the parsonage of his half-sister and Dr. Grant, he immediately turns his attention to the Bertram sisters. Austen notes that "Mr. Crawford did not mean to be in any danger; the Miss Bertrams were worth pleasing, and were ready to be pleased; and he began with no object but of making them like him" (*MP*, 473). He wants to flirt, to acquire their affection in a rather innocent way; he is doing it for the sport of it. Yes, he wants to keep it all in proper bounds, but his limits of propriety are negotiable. "He did not want them to die of love; but with sense and temper which ought to have made him judge and feel better, he allowed himself great latitude on such points" (*MP*, 473). He does succeed; both Maria and Julia are captivated with him and jealous of each other over his favor and attention. Maria's infatuation with Henry is quite improper as she is already engaged.

Not sated by gaining the attention of the two Bertram sisters, when Henry returns from a two weeks' absence he informs his sister, Mary, the reason for his return—yet another female conquest: "[M]y plan is to make Fanny Price in love with me" (*MP*, 578). Sister Mary replies "Fanny Price! Nonsense! No, no. You ought to be satisfied with her two cousins." But Henry replies: "But I cannot be satisfied without Fanny Price, without making a small hole in Fanny Price's heart."

On the way to winning Fanny's affection for fun, however, he actually falls in love with her. He makes her a sincere marriage proposal that she turns down despite pressures from her Uncle Bertram and cousin Edmund. Her rejection only makes Henry Crawford more adamant; he is quite persistent as well as vain. Fanny continues to resist his charms. When she leaves Mansfield Park for an extended visit to her much poorer nuclear family in Portsmouth, he follows her there. On this visit he begins to make some inroads to her affection. He appears to be more serious and upright. He leaves Portsmouth for his estate in Norfolk with his hopes high, still wanting Fanny's hand; but on the way he stops off in London where he meets up with some friends.

He plans to leave after a day or so to attend to his business in Norfolk but "he was pressed to stay for Mrs. Fraser's party; his staying was made of flattering consequence." The vain man may flatter, but he can also *be* flattered; both Jane Austen and Adam Smith agree on this point. But more to the point if he stayed in London a while longer "he was to meet Mrs. Rushworth there. Curiosity and *vanity* were both engaged, and the temptation of immediate pleasure was too strong for a mind unused to make any sacrifice to right: he resolved to defer his Norfolk journey . . . " (*MP*, 716, emphasis added).

Henry is much more interested in relighting an old flame than engaging prudent estate management (in this Henry shows an absence of self-command). Once committed to remaining in London, he does meet Mrs. Rushworth and "was received by her with a coldness which ought to have been repulsive, and have established apparent indifference between them forever; but he was *mortified* . . . " (*MP*, 716, emphasis added). Smith tells us this is the response of the vain man. "When you appear to view him, therefore, in different colours, perhaps in his proper colours, he is much more *mortified* than offended" (*TMS*, 255, emphasis added).

Henry's vanity and persistence work together to keep him in London pursuing the favor of Mrs. Rushworth because "he could not bear to be thrown off by the woman whose smiles had been so wholly at his command. . . . and make Mrs. Rushworth, Maria Bertram again in her treatment of himself" (*MP*, 716). He consciously calculates a plan to rewin Maria's heart. "In this spirit he began the attack, and by animated perseverance had soon re-established the sort of familiar intercourse, of gallantry, of flirtation . . . " (*MP*, 716). But he runs into a problem; Maria falls for the bait—hook, line, and sinker:

> he had put himself in the power of feelings on her side more strong than he had supposed. She loved him; there was no withdrawing attentions avowedly dear to her. He was entangled by his own *vanity*, with as little excuse of love as possible, and without the smallest inconstancy of mind towards her cousin. To keep Fanny and the Bertrams from a knowledge of what was passing became his first object. Secrecy could not have been more desirable for Mrs. Rushworth's credit than he felt it for his own. When he returned from Richmond, he would have been glad to see Mrs. Rushworth no more. All that followed was the result of her imprudence; and he went off with her at last, because he could not help it. (*MP*, 716–717, emphasis added)

As discussed in chapter 4, Henry's absence of *principles* contributes to his downfall. Austen's description of Henry's experience is also consistent with the Smithian notion that absence of self-command implies one's vices get the better of one. Vanity is an inevitable part of human nature but if left unchecked and unrestrained it is destructive to both the individual and those around him: a point both Smith and Austen confirm.

NOTES

1. Frank (2014) reports although the luxury good market had not completely recovered from the 2008 financial crisis the demand for super-luxury items such as $65 million eighteen-passenger Gulf Stream G650 jets and yachts 250 feet or longer were quite robust in the fall of 2014.

2. We will explore Smith's and Austen's view of rank in more detail in chapter 12.

3. In an amusing passage in chapter 2, the Middleton's three-year-old daughter Annamaria is scratched slightly by a pin in her mother's hair and proceeds to scream uncontrollably. Austen informs us that "The mother's consternation was excessive; but it could not surpass the alarm of the Miss Steeles . . . " who stuffed her mouth with sugar plums. Austen wryly makes a note dear to the heart of the economist: "With such a reward for her tears, the child was too wise to cease crying" until she also obtained some apricot marmalade (*SS*, 76). Even a three-year-old responds to incentives.

4. In chapter 10 we assert a return on government consols of 4 percent, yet the calculations in *Sense and Sensibility* assume a 5 percent rate of return.

5. Lucy apparently did not know that Colonel Brandon had assured Edward a parish that would yield him an income of 200 pounds per year. Austen tells us that Edward had only 2000 pounds of his own (*SS*, 216). At a 5 percent return this would make Lucy and Edward's income a meager but livable 300 pounds. Upon his betrothal to Elinor, Edward's annual income would be an additional 50 pounds as she brought a capital sum of 1,000 pounds to the marriage. Both Edward and Elinor were aware 350 pounds per year would be meager. In fact Austen tells us that "they were neither of them quite enough in love to think that three hundred and fifty pounds a-year would supply them with the comforts of life" (*SS*, 216). However, in due time Mrs. Ferrars forgives Edward and gives the newlyweds an additional 10,000 pounds in capital making their annual income a comfortable 850 pounds a year (*SS*, 219).

Chapter Seven

Pride in *Pride and Prejudice*

Early in Jane Austen's *Pride and Prejudice*, Mr. Fitzwilliam Darcy is deemed to be a proud man. One of the Bennet girls, middle daughter Mary, who is always reading books and affects the air of an intellectual, comments, "Vanity and pride are different things, though the words are often used synonymously. A person may be proud without being vain. Pride relates more to our opinion of ourselves, vanity to what we would have others think of us" (*PP*, 234). Compare this with Adam Smith's comments on pride in *Theory of Moral Sentiments*. "We call it pride or vanity; two words, of which the latter always, and the former for the most part, involve in their meaning a considerable degree of blame. Those two vices, however, though resembling, in some respects, as being both modifications of excessive self-estimation, are yet, in many respects, very different from one another" (*TMS*, 255).

One cannot help but see the similarity between the two; it is certainly plausible that Austen is rather directly paraphrasing Smith through the voice of Mary Bennet. We are not the first to note this overlap. Mohler (1967) makes this exact point in a short note; Knox-Shaw (2004) uses it as he makes a larger point that Smith as well as other Enlightenment writers had an influence on Austen. A similar argument is made by Valihora (2007). Fricke (2014) goes so far as to argue that *Theory of Moral Sentiments* is "a source of inspiration for creating most of the characters for *Pride and Prejudice*."

This chapter's goal will be to offer for our readers a number of examples of the manifestation of *pride* in Austen, noting how she aligns, illustrates, and embellishes Smith's view on the topic. There is no more logical place to begin, than with Austen's work that uses the vice in its title: *Pride and Prejudice*. In fact the novel will also be our ending point. There is much pride in other works of Austen, but *Pride and Prejudice* gives so many examples of pride in action, it alone will fill our purposes.

A central theme in *Pride and Prejudice* is the stormy relationship between Elizabeth Bennet and Fitzwilliam Darcy. Elizabeth is one of five daughters of a small landholder whose estate is entailed to a distant cousin, leaving her and her four sisters with little prospects for wealth. Mr. Darcy, on the other hand, is the master of an estate that yields an income of over ten thousand pounds a year. The two first come into contact with one another at a local party in the village of Meryton. Darcy is staying with a friend, Mr. Bingley, who had just moved into the area. Bingley was exciting much attention since he was a rich, eligible young bachelor. At first Darcy's position as an even wealthier bachelor incline the locals to think on him favorably until

> he was discovered to be proud, to be above his company, and above being pleased; and not all his large estate in Derbyshire could then save him from having a most forbidding, disagreeable countenance. . . . (he) declined being introduced to any other lady (than those he knew), and spent the rest of the evening in walking about the room, speaking occasionally to one of his own party. (*PP*, 229)

This impression is confirmed by a specific interaction between Darcy and Bingley, apparently within earshot of Elizabeth. When Bingley encourages Darcy to be more sociable and to dance with other ladies at the gathering, Darcy responds, "I certainly shall not. You know how I detest it, unless I am particularly acquainted with my partner. At such an assembly as this, it would be insupportable. Your sisters are engaged, and there is not another woman in the room whom it would not be a punishment to me to stand up with . . . " (*PP*, 229). This is not shyness, it is plain arrogance and pride. Or as Smith tells us "The proud man . . . never flatters, and is frequently scarce civil to any body" (*TMS*, 257).

When Bingley insists that there are many lovely young ladies, not the least of whom is the sister of the young lady he had been dancing with, Darcy asks "'Which do you mean?' and turning round, he looked for a moment at Elizabeth, till catching her eye, he withdrew his own and coldly said, 'She is tolerable; but not handsome enough to tempt me; and I am in no humour at present to give consequence to young ladies who are slighted by other men'" (*PP*, 230). Austen notes that upon hearing this Elizabeth left with "no very cordial feelings toward him" (*PP*, 230). We certainly can see why.

We can link Darcy's actions to Smithian insights about the proud man described in chapter 3: "He disdains to court your esteem. He affects even to despise it, and endeavours to maintain his assumed station, not so much by making you sensible of his superiority, as of your own meanness. He seems to wish, not so much to excite your esteem for himself, as to mortify that for yourself" (*TMS*, 255).

The next day at the Bennet house a group of ladies who had been at the ball gather to talk about the events of the previous evening. Elizabeth's friend Charlotte Lucas offers an insight about Darcy.

"His pride," said Miss Lucas, "does not offend *me* so much as pride often does, because there is an excuse for it. One cannot wonder that so very fine a young man, with family, fortune, everything in his favour, should think highly of himself. If I may so express it, he has a *right* to be proud." "That is very true," replied Elizabeth, "and I could easily forgive *his* pride, if he had not mortified *mine*." (*PP*, 234)

Could it be that Elizabeth also suffers from pride? Austen seems to follow the theme in the next social encounter between Elizabeth and Darcy at Bingley's estate, Netherfield. Miss Bingley is Mr. Bingley's eligible sister who is very interested in Darcy. After dinner when Elizabeth leaves the company for an interval: "Miss Bingley began abusing her as soon as she was out of the room. Her manners were pronounced to be very bad indeed, a mixture of pride and impertinence . . . " (*PP*, 243).

Upon Elizabeth's return she and Darcy enter a discussion on what it means for a young lady to be "accomplished." Darcy indicates he thinks the term grossly overused and proceeds to make a list of characteristics necessary to be so qualified, commenting that he knows scarcely less than a half a dozen who possibly deserve the appellation. Elizabeth responds that given his standard it is surprising he knows any. Upon another exit of the room Miss Bingley accuses her of practicing a trait Smith links to the proud. "'Eliza Bennet,' said Miss Bingley, when the door was closed on her, 'is one of those young ladies who seek to recommend themselves to the other sex by undervaluing their own, and with many men, I dare say, it succeeds'" (*PP*, 246).

This banter between Elizabeth and Darcy continues as the novel unfolds. It is not surprising that it takes many months for the two proud protagonists to come to amiable, and eventually amorous, terms with one another. As Smith wryly notes when we come across a proud or vain person, "their self-estimation mortifies our own. Our own pride and vanity prompt us to accuse them of pride and vanity, and we cease to be the impartial spectators of their conduct" (*TMS*, 246). This Smithian principle, that the proud cannot be impartial about others who are also proud, informs our view of Elizabeth.

A few days later Elizabeth and Darcy have another repartee. She and Miss Bingley begin to walk around the room together and tease Darcy, intimating he lacks a sense of humor and is not willing to be made fun of by others. As Smith notes, "Pride is always a grave, a sullen, and a severe [passion]" (*TMS*, 257). Darcy responds to this noting that jokesters often ridicule the "wisest and best" of men and their actions and notes it "has been the study of my life to avoid those weaknesses which often expose a strong understanding to ridicule." To which Elizabeth responds "Such as vanity and pride." To which Darcy replies, "Yes, vanity is a weakness indeed. But pride—where there is a real superiority of mind, pride will be always under good regulation." To which Elizabeth responds, "I am perfectly convinced by it that Mr. Darcy has no defect. He owns it himself without disguise" (*PP*, 256–257).

Our proud, clever, and biting Elizabeth has made her attack well, as Smith predicts. "The proud man is commonly too well contented with himself to think that his character requires any amendment. The man who feels himself all-perfect, naturally enough despises all further improvement" (*TMS*, 258). Nothing can shake a proud man as much as to accuse him of believing in his own perfection; he is too proud for that. Darcy's response implies Elizabeth has hit a jugular vein, as he begins to list his view of his flaws:

> No . . . I have made no such pretension. I have faults enough, but they are not, I hope, of understanding. My temper I dare not vouch for. It is, I believe, too little yielding—certainly too little for the convenience of the world. I cannot forget the follies and vices of others so soon as I ought, nor their offenses against myself. My feelings are not puffed about with every attempt to move them. My temper would perhaps be called resentful. My good opinion once lost, is lost forever. (*PP*, 257)

It is interesting that Darcy mainly couches his flaws as a kind of virtue. He has no tolerance for "follies or vices" and immunity from being "puffed up" by flattery, but he does admit he has a resentful temper. This is straight from Smith: when the proud man does not receive the respect he instinctively believes he deserves, "he is more offended than mortified, and feels the same indignant resentment as if he had suffered a real injury" (*TMS*, 255).

Elizabeth retorts, "*That* is a failing indeed! . . . Implacable resentment *is* a shade in a character. But you have chosen your fault well. I really cannot *laugh* at it. You are safe from me." To which Darcy replies, "There is, I believe, in every disposition a tendency to some particular evil—a natural defect, which not even the best education can overcome" (*PP*, 257).[1]

Elizabeth comes right back at him. "And *your* defect is to hate everybody." But Darcy is not to be outdone. "And yours," he replied with a smile, "is willfully to misunderstand them" (*PP*, 257). What sparring partners are Mr. Darcy and Miss Elizabeth Bennet!

A few days later the Bennet girls' Aunt Phillips throws a party for a number of young people in the area including a contingent of officers garrisoned in the local village. Elizabeth is introduced to the handsome and amiable officer George Wickham. The subject of Mr. Darcy comes up in their conversation and Wickham remarks that "It is impossible for me to be impartial" (*PP*, 268) about Mr. Darcy. Of course, proud Elizabeth is nowhere near an "impartial spectator" about Darcy so she is inclined to believe the worst about him.

Darcy and Wickham grew up together, Wickham's father being an estate manager for Darcy's father. The older Mr. Darcy is described as just, amiable, and very fond of George Wickham. According to Wickham, the younger Mr. Darcy has failed to provide what his late father intended for Wickham, namely, financial support for a clerical education and access to a lucrative parish. Wickham has been cheated, but can do nothing because of the deference the world gives to the elegant and wealthy Darcy. When Elizabeth inquires, "But what," said she after a pause, "can have been his motive?—what can have induced him to behave so cruelly?" (*PP*, 270). Wickham spins his story:

> A thorough, determined dislike of me—a dislike which I cannot but attribute in some measure to jealousy. Had the late Mr. Darcy liked me less, his son might have borne with me better; but his father's uncommon attachment to me, irritated him I believe very early in life. He had not a temper to bear the sort of competition in which we stood—the sort of preference which was often given me. (*PP*, 270)

The conversation continues and Elizabeth is reeled in. She finds the story credible. For she notes, "I wonder that the very pride of this Mr. Darcy has not made him just to you!—If from no better motive, that he should not have been too proud to be dishonest,—for dishonesty I must call it" (*PP*, 271). Note that Elizabeth believes a proud man is not generally dishonest. Wickham also feigns to marvel concurring in this assessment of pride (note won-der-*ful* in this context means to make one wonder). "It is wonderful," replied Wickham "for almost all his actions may be traced to pride;—and pride has often been his best friend. It has connected him nearer with virtue than any other feeling. But we are none of us consistent; and in his behaviour to me, there were stronger impulses even than pride" (*PP*, 271).

"Can such abominable pride as his, have ever done him good?" asks Elizabeth.

And Wickham replies, "Yes. It has often led him to be liberal and generous,—to give his money freely, to display hospitality, to assist his tenants, and relieve the poor. . . . " Wickham later reinforces the point, stating, "His pride never deserts him; but with the rich, he is liberal-minded, just, sincere, rational, honourable, and perhaps agreeable,—allowing something for fortune and figure" (*PP*, 271–272).

In other words, according to Wickham, Darcy cheated and ruined him, going against the wishes of his own father out of jealous spite. Darcy lies about Wickham, but because he, like most proud men, is generally a man of his word and generous to boot no one will believe he had been cruel to Wickham. And anyway Wickham would not want to shame the memory of his dear departed godfather, the late Mr. Darcy. Young Darcy comes off well to the rest of the world despite his injustice to the ill-used Wickham.

Compare this interaction between Wickham and Elizabeth to an insight of Smith about the proud man. "To do the proud man justice, he very seldom stoops to the baseness of falsehood. When he does, however, his falsehoods are by no means so innocent. They are all mischievous, and meant to lower other people. He is full of indignation at the unjust superiority, as he thinks it, which is given to them" (*TMS*, 257). According to Smith proud men don't generally lie or cheat, but when they do, they are vicious about it, intending to destroy the target of their wrath. So if I were to tell a lie about a proud man, I would admit the proud man is generally truthful. But then claim the proud man had cause to "destroy me" or "keep me down" and so intimate that the proud man lies about me with impunity.

Isn't it interesting that the structure of Austen's narrative follows Smith's insight almost point for point? A liar trying to defame a proud man would weave a story such as Wickham did. What a slippery eel is Mr. Wickham! In addition, as Smith suggests, a proud person is likely to fall for such a story about a person they think is too proud, precisely because they can no longer be impartial. And this is exactly what Austen tells us Elizabeth does. "Elizabeth allowed that [Wickham] had given a very rational account" (*PP*, 272).

Elizabeth and Darcy have another extensive set of interactions during her extended visit with her friend Mrs. Collins, the former Charlotte Lucas who married Elizabeth's cousin Mr. Collins. Darcy spends some time at nearby Rosings, the estate of his aunt the Lady Catherine de Bourgh. They continue in their verbal sparring and Elizabeth is surprised by Darcy's persistent but taciturn visits to her at the Collins' parsonage. As his stay is coming to an end, Darcy professes his love to Elizabeth and asks her to marry him. He informs her that despite her lack of wealth and family connection and despite his exertions to not fall in love with her, he had found his feelings for her "impossible to conquer" (*PP*, 332) and is therefore compelled to ask her for her hand. Austen informs us Elizabeth perceived that "he had no doubt of a favourable answer" (*PP*, 332).

Elizabeth refuses him and indicts him for more than his insufferable pride. She accuses him of blocking further interactions between her sister, Jane, and his friend, Mr. Bingley, for snobbish motives; and also accuses him of ill-using the long suffering Mr. Wickham. Darcy makes little defense to either charge but does tell Elizabeth that she was the one whose "pride [had] been hurt" (*PP*, 334) by his frank admission of the problem of their difference in wealth and status. She tells him that he is the "last man in the world" (*PP*, 334) she would ever think of marrying and he takes his exit.

The next morning Elizabeth encounters Darcy again and he hands her a handwritten note dated eight a.m. of that day. She opens the note, not quite knowing what to expect, and finds a point-by-point rebuttal and explanation of her accusations. He had discouraged his friend Bingley from further pursuits of Jane because he believed at the time she did not return his affections.

He notes "I did not believe her to be indifferent because I wished it; I believed it on impartial conviction." He also discouraged Bingley from pursuing Jane, not so much because of the lack of wealth and status of the Bennet family, but because of "that total want of propriety so frequently, so almost uniformly betrayed by [your mother and] by your three younger sisters" (*PP*, 337).

As to the more serious charge of his misdeeds toward Wickham, he notes that he had long questioned Wickham's principles. Nevertheless, when Darcy's father died he endeavored to fulfill his father's will by preparing to grant Wickham "a legacy of one thousand pounds" (*PP*, 338) to support his entry into the ministry. However, Wickham indicated that he no longer wanted to enter the ministry and expressed an interest in going into law. Darcy then fulfilled his father's wishes in letter and spirit by providing Wickham with three thousand pounds. Wickham then disappeared from view and fell into "a life of idleness and dissipation" (*PP*, 339). Three years later he reappeared and "was now absolutely resolved on being ordained" (*PP*, 339) asking for financial resources to promote that end. Wickham was refused. Wickham began to court the affection of Darcy's sister, Georgiana, who was "persuaded to believe herself in love, and to consent to an elopement. She was then but fifteen . . . " (*PP*, 339). The elopement was prevented, and Darcy reports "Mr. Wickham's chief object was unquestionably my sister's fortune, which is thirty thousand pounds" (*PP*, 339). Darcy also confirms in the letter that all his assertions and claims could be corroborated by his cousin Col. Fitzwilliam.

Elizabeth is bowled over by the letter. The first half of it, which cast aspersions on her family, angers her. The second half of the note, which reveals Darcy's side of the Wickham story, causes her a great deal of consternation. At first she rejects it as false, puts the note away and vows to never read it again. But within a "half-minute" she is reading it again and finds herself in a "mortifying perusal of all that related to Wickham" (*PP*, 341). Over the next two hours Elizabeth re-reads and re-examines Darcy's letter and compares it to her recollection of Wickham's account. She puts aside her prejudice and "weighed every circumstance with what she meant to be impartiality" (*PP*, 341). She is finally and painfully convinced that Darcy is telling the truth, and Wickham is lying. Austen tells us, "She grew absolutely ashamed of herself.—Of neither Darcy nor Wickham could she think without feeling she had been blind, partial, prejudiced, absurd. 'How despicably I have acted!' she cried; 'I, who have prided myself on my discernment!'" (*PP*, 342–343).

We note that Elizabeth's pride has been broken; she has been taken down a peg in her own self-estimation. Even her anger as to the first portion of the letter is softened. To her credit she feels pain but recognizes the truth of how her pride and vanity have deluded her. "How humiliating is this discovery!

Yet, how just a humiliation! . . . Till this moment I never knew myself" (*PP*, 343).

As the rest of the novel unfolds, Elizabeth and Darcy have occasion for many more encounters. When taking a tour of the English countryside with her Aunt and Uncle Gardiner, the three pay a visit to Darcy's estate, Pemberley. Darcy unexpectedly arrives at the estate and is hospitable, amiable, and charming to their party. Toward the end of the visit, they are made aware of a scandal unfolding in the Bennet family. Young and wild sister Lydia has eloped with none other than Wickham. After all is said and done Darcy ensures that the marriage between the two is sufficiently provided for by discreetly paying off Wickham's debts. All this leads Elizabeth to admire Darcy and develop true affection for him. She regrets her former disapprobation. "Oh! how heartily did she grieve over every ungracious sensation she had ever encouraged, every saucy speech she had ever directed toward him. For herself she was humbled; but she was proud of him. Proud that in a cause of compassion and honour, he had been able to get the better of himself" (*PP*, 409).

It is very interesting to note that Elizabeth is humbled alongside her growing regard, respect and love for Darcy. By novel's end, Darcy is also humbled by events. He confesses to Elizabeth that he had been excessively proud and that by her influence he was properly humbled.

> I have been a selfish being all my life, in practice, though not in principle. As a child I was taught what was right, but I was not taught to correct my temper. I was given good principles, but left to follow them in pride and conceit. . . . By you, I was properly humbled. I came to you without a doubt of my reception. You showed me how insufficient were all my pretensions to please a woman worthy of being pleased. (*PP*, 434)

This mutual humbling allows the two of them to fall in love and also paves the way for a felicitous match between sister Jane and friend Bingley. It is also interesting to note that humbling of oneself is not the same thing as humiliation. In Elizabeth's case, though, her self-perceived humiliation is part of her humbling at the beginning. If one is too proud, if one's estimation of one's own abilities, insights, and virtues is excessive it is proper and good for them to be realigned more realistically. By becoming more humble Elizabeth and Darcy not only ensure their match, they both become more virtuous, better adjusted and happier.

As Smith states, "That degree of self-estimation, therefore, which contributes most to the happiness and contentment of the person himself, seems likewise most agreeable to the impartial spectator. The man who esteems himself as he ought, and no more than he ought, seldom fails to obtain from other people all the esteem that he himself thinks due" (*TMS*, 261). To Smith, some degree of pride is proper and necessary,[2] but when it is excessive it becomes a delusion that shields one from knowing the truth about others, or as Elizabeth recognizes, the truth about herself.

It is interesting to compare Elizabeth's view of the situation between Bingley and Jane with the observations of Elizabeth's friend Charlotte. Much can be said about Jane and Charlotte but no one would accuse them of excessive pride. Early on in Bingley and Jane's relationship Charlotte warns Elizabeth that Jane is too demure and ought to show more affection toward Bingley. "Bingley likes your sister undoubtedly; but he may never do more than like her, if she does not help him on" (*PP*, 235). Elizabeth objects to this, arguing that Jane's intentions should be obvious to Bingley.

When it appears that Bingley has abandoned his interest in Jane it is Elizabeth who is offended, sure that Bingley is being unjustly influenced by his sister and Mr. Darcy because they "wish him to marry a girl who has all the importance of money, great connections, and pride." But Jane, who is most affected by the situation, has a more balanced view of the preference by Miss Bingley and Mr. Darcy and refuses to automatically impugn their motives. "'Beyond a doubt, they do wish him to chuse Miss Darcy,' replied Jane; 'but this may be from better feelings than you are supposing. They have known her much longer than they have known me; no wonder if they love her better'" (*PP*, 302).

Although we suspect that Elizabeth is smarter, cleverer, and more capable in many ways than Jane or Charlotte, her pride blinds her; it prejudices her, it keeps her from seeing the reality of situations. The proud person's ability to be other-regarding and to truly assess the situation and feelings of those at the other end of a transaction are limited. This is the costs of excessive self-estimation.

However, it is important to remember that Smith tells us that some pride is good and that "In almost all cases, it is better to be a little too proud, than, in any respect, too humble" (*TMS*, 261–262). Austen seems to concur, as Elizabeth is the heroine of *Pride and Prejudice* and not Charlotte Lucas. This is precisely because Elizabeth is capable of directing her own life and willing to stand up to others who are proud—as we have seen in her interactions Darcy and will observe in her dealing with both Mr. Collins and Lady Catherine. Elizabeth refuses to be ill-used by others; she will not be bullied. Those with deficient pride are in Smith's words "much more liable to every sort of ill-usage from other people" (*TMS*, 261)—a price that neither Smith nor Austen seem prepared to pay. Indeed, Elizabeth exhibits what Smith calls "respectable virtues" common among those who are proud that include "a high sense of honour" and "the most inflexible firmness and resolution" (*TMS*, 258).

OTHER FORMS OF PRIDE: MR. COLLINS AND LADY
CATHERINE DE BOURGH

There are at least two other characters in *Pride and Prejudice* for whom pride is a central characteristic: the proud but ridiculous Mr. Collins, and the proud and malevolent Lady Catherine de Bourgh. First to Mr. Collins. At the end of Adam Smith's commentary on pride and vanity, he notes,

> Those two vices being frequently in the same character, the characteristics of both are necessarily confounded; and we sometimes find the superficial and impertinent ostentation of vanity joined to the most malignant and derisive insolence of pride. We are sometimes, upon that account, at a loss how to rank a particular character, or whether to place it among the proud or among the vain. (*TMS*, 259)

On first impression we are at a loss in an apt description of Mr. Collins. Is he vain or proud? A case can be made for classifying him either way, or as a mixture of both. Mr. Collins has a number of faults. He is long-winded, he flatters everyone around him, he apologizes for any offense however minor or imagined, and he is constantly referring to his connection with the wealthy and rich Lady Catherine de Bourgh. This makes him seem first and foremost a vain man, but Austen's own account is somewhat different and tips the balance toward pride, but the peculiar pride of a fool.

Recall Mr. Collins is the heir of the entailed Bennet estate. As is the case in an entailed estate, Collins becomes the legal owner of the estate upon Mr. Bennet's death. It is hardly surprising that Mrs. Bennet views him with contempt because if Mr. Bennet dies, Mr. Collins has the right to expel her and her five daughters from the estate immediately.

Collins arrives on the scene early in the novel. He sends a letter to the family announcing he plans a visit and sets the date of his arrival. Apparently the Bennets have never met him. When Mr. Bennet reads the letter to the family Elizabeth comments, "He must be an oddity, I think. . . . I cannot make him out.—There is something very pompous in his stile." To which her father comments that he sees in Collins a "mixture of servility and self-importance" (*PP*, 261).

Austen informs us "Mr. Collins was not a sensible man, and the deficiency of nature had been but little assisted by education or society." Collins grew up under the influence of a tyrannical father who taught him to be quite submissive. Although educated at the university he acquired no connections there and his schooling did little to improve his manners, sensibilities, or insights. Ordained in the Church of England he accidentally lands a very lucrative parish where his patron is the very wealthy and arrogant Lady Catherine de Bourgh who is also an aunt of Mr. Darcy's. Austen further describes Collins's character, "his veneration for her as his patroness, mingling with a very good opinion of himself, of his authority as a clergyman, and his right as a rector, made him altogether a mixture of pride and obsequiousness, self-importance and humility" (*PP*, 264).

This is quite a juxtaposition! Collins is proud, but obsequious. How can this be? His pride is founded on his rank as a clergyman and his connection to one of higher rank, Lady Catherine de Bourgh. He is constantly foisting these two facts on everyone as if they alone make him praiseworthy. He is proud because he sincerely and quite foolishly believes they do. We recall Smith's quip about the proud, "The proud man is sincere, and, in the bottom of his heart, is convinced of his own superiority; though it may sometimes be difficult to guess upon what that conviction is founded" (*TMS*, 255).

Yet Collins is also by nature and upbringing obsequious. He acts in such a manner, flattering and apologizing to everyone, despite a posture that is arrogant and presumptuous. Elizabeth is right, it is an oddity. Austen tells us he is not a "sensible" man (*PP*, 261). Recall this means he has never learned to properly take into account the feelings of others. He is oblivious to their disdain for him. He lives in a delusion, a self-delusion, believing his collar and connection with the de Bourgh family impress others as much as it does him. There is hardly a scene or a passage where Mr. Collins does not mention his connection with Lady Catherine. Collins never absorbed Smith's advice that "a certain reserve is necessary when we talk of our own friends, our own studies, our own professions. All these are objects which we cannot expect should interest our companions in the same degree in which they interest us. And it is for want of this reserve, that the one half of mankind make bad company to the other" (*TMS*, 33–34).

After dinner on his first evening at the Bennet's the topic of Lady Catherine's daughter arises. Collins informs them that when he learned the de Bourgh daughter had not been presented at court in London, he assured Lady de Bourgh that the daughter's absence has "deprived the British court of its brightest ornament" (*PP*, 263). This is polite flattery at best and obsequious nonsense at worst, but Collins takes pride in reporting he is always offering up these "little things which please her ladyship" (*PP*, 263). In response the sardonic Mr. Bennet inquires "and it is happy for you that you possess the talent of flattering with delicacy. May I ask whether these pleasing attentions proceed from the impulse of the moment, or are the result of previous study?" (*PP*, 263). We can recast this as Mr. Bennet asking, so do you make these silly, foolish, and insincere comments because you are stupid by nature or do have to work on how to be that idiotic beforehand? Collins's self-delusion ensures that far from taking offense, he responds in all sincerity, "They arise chiefly from what is passing at the time, and though I sometimes amuse myself with suggesting and arranging such little elegant compliments as may be adapted to ordinary occasions, I always wish to give them as unstudied an air as possible" (*PP*, 263). To which Austen tells us, "Mr.

Bennet's expectations were fully answered. His cousin was as absurd as he had hoped, and he listened to him with the keenest enjoyment, maintaining at the same time the most resolute composure of countenance, and, except in an occasional glance at Elizabeth, requiring no partner in his pleasure" (*PP*, 263).

Austen is a master of subtle humor and no so more than with the comedy that Mr. Collins unintentionally gives to *Pride and Prejudice*. His impregnable delusional pride also emerges when he insists on introducing himself to Mr. Darcy at the ball at Mr. Bingham's estate, again to comic end. Collins becomes aware that Darcy is Lady Catherine's nephew and insists on greeting Darcy without a proper introduction. Elizabeth suggests he not do so, knowing Darcy's proud disposition but Collins insists that his status as clergy and his connection with Lady Catherine make it mandatory; in fact he plans to apologize for not having done so earlier.

> And with a low bow he left her to attack Mr. Darcy, whose reception of his advances she eagerly watched, and whose astonishment at being so addressed was very evident. Her cousin prefaced his speech with a solemn bow, and though she could not hear a word of it, she felt as if hearing it all, and saw in the motion of his lips the words "apology," "Hunsford" and "Lady Catherine de Bourgh."—It vexed her to see him expose himself to such a man. Mr. Darcy was eyeing him with unrestrained wonder, and when at last Mr. Collins allowed him time to speak, replied with an air of distant civility. Mr. Collins, however, was not discouraged from speaking again, and Mr. Darcy's contempt seemed abundantly increasing with the length of his second speech, and at the end of it he only made him a slight bow, and moved another way. Mr. Collins then returned to Elizabeth.
>
> "I have no reason, I assure you," said he, "to be dissatisfied with my reception. Mr. Darcy seemed much pleased with the attention. He answered me with the utmost civility, and even paid me the compliment of saying that he was so well convinced of Lady Catherine's discernment as to be certain she could never bestow a favour unworthily. It was really a very handsome thought. Upon the whole, I am much pleased with him." (*PP*, 280–281)

This reminds of us Lucy and Nancy Steele from *Sense and Sensibility*. They misinterpret the civility of Mrs. Ferrars and Mrs. Dashwood for esteem. This error leads Nancy to spill the beans about Lucy's engagement to Edward. Mr. Collins's error is greater, though, as he misinterprets moderate *incivility* by Darcy as affection. Whether this is pride or vanity, it is self-delusion that is impervious to modification.

The comedy continues when Collins proposes to Elizabeth. Collins makes clear that he came to visit in order to find a bride among the Bennet sisters and that she, Elizabeth, was his first choice among the five girls.[3] He then told her he thought it "advisable" to tell her why he wanted to marry:

My reasons for marrying are, first, that I think it a right thing for every clergyman in easy circumstances (like myself) to set the example of matrimony in his parish. Secondly, that I am convinced it will add very greatly to my happiness; and thirdly[4]—which perhaps I ought to have mentioned earlier, that it is the particular advice and recommendation of the very noble lady whom I have the honour of calling patroness. Twice has she condescended to give me her opinion (unasked too!) on this subject; and it was but the very Saturday night before I left Hunsford—between our pools at quadrille, while Mrs. Jenkinson was arranging Miss de Bourgh's foot-stool, that she said, "Mr. Collins, you must marry. A clergyman like you must marry." (*PP*, 285)

How absurd to include in a proposal of marriage mention of Lady Catherine, much less the details of her daughter's foot-stool. When Elizabeth politely but firmly declines his offer Collins insists that he knows full well that ladies decline the first offer when they truly intend to accept. Collins is best characterized by pride because he is oblivious to any notion that Elizabeth could possibly reject him. He will own the Bennet estate, he is ordained and with a good parish, he has the esteem of none other than the Lady Catherine de Bourgh, so it can only be feminine delicacy that is holding Elizabeth back. He is confident of his merit. He offers several appeals to Elizabeth all including some version of the condescending expressions of *I know you really will say yes eventually*. Austen tells us this makes Elizabeth angry. "To such perseverance in wilful self-deception, Elizabeth would make no reply, and immediately and in silence withdrew" (*PP*, 287).

Recall according to Smith, when a vain man is confronted he is mortified, when a proud man is confronted he remains aloof. Austen's description of what occurs when it becomes clear to Collins that Elizabeth means just what she says reveals him to be proud. "As for the gentleman himself, *his* feelings were chiefly expressed, not by embarrassment or dejection, or by trying to avoid her, but by stiffness of manner and resentful silence. . . . The morrow produced no abatement of Mrs. Bennet's ill-humour or ill health. Mr. Collins was also in the same state of angry pride"[5] (*PP*, 290–291).

As the novel progresses Mr. Collins plays an even less-important role, but it is still one that amuses us and informs us of his ridiculous character. Upon Elizabeth's refusal of his proposal he seeks and obtains the hand of Elizabeth's prudent and unromantic friend, the twenty-seven-year-old Charlotte Lucas. Elizabeth and Charlotte's family visit the Collinses' household soon after their marriage, and as expected all centers on Mr. Collins's relationship with Lady Catherine de Bourgh. The whole company is invited for dinner at her nearby estate and Austen tells us, "Mr. Collins's triumph in consequence of this invitation was complete. The power of displaying the grandeur of his patroness to his wondering visitors . . . what the glazing altogether had originally cost Sir Lewis De Bourgh" (*PP*, 315–316).

No doubt there is a measure of vanity in Mr. Collins; he enjoys bragging about how much his patroness spends on things.[6] The Lucas family was overwhelmed and mortified before and during most of the engagement. At dinner "[h]e carved, and ate, and praised with delighted alacrity; and every dish was commended, first by him, and then by Sir William, who was now enough recovered to echo whatever his son in law said, in a manner which Elizabeth wondered Lady Catherine could bear. But Lady Catherine seemed gratified by their excessive admiration" (*PP*, 317).

Later on in the novel when Lydia runs off with Wickham, Mr. Collins feels called upon to offer his insight and advice to the Bennets. In his first communication he states, "The death of your daughter would have been a blessing in comparison of this" (*PP*, 391). What a comfort to the Bennets! In another missive when Collins is aware that the couple is married he implores, "You ought certainly to forgive them as a Christian, but never to admit them in your sight, or allow their names to be mentioned in your hearing." To which Mr. Bennet replies with amusement and amazement, "That is his notion of Christian forgiveness!" (*PP*, 430–431).

Collins's relationship with the Lady Catherine de Bourgh is a study in what we might today call neurotic co-dependence. She seems to thrive on his toadying and sycophancy as illustrated in the dinner conversation at Rosings mentioned above. Lady Catherine is, in modern parlance, a real piece of work and a study in yet another manifestation of pride. Readers of *Pride and Prejudice* do not meet Lady Catherine until midway in the novel, but they have been dutifully warned of her pride and arrogance. When Elizabeth and the dinner party finally do meet the Lady, Elizabeth reflects that "she believed Lady Catherine to be exactly what . . . had [been] represented" (*PP*, 317).

Not all in her company necessarily go along with Lady Catherine's sentiments. We get a trace of Mr. Darcy's character when at an engagement at Rosings Lady Catherine publicly dresses Elizabeth down for not practicing enough on the piano. "Mr. Darcy looked a little ashamed of his aunt's ill breeding, and made no answer" (*PP*, 323).

The most interesting insight on Lady Catherine's pride is to examine her one-on-one with Elizabeth at the Bennet estate. Lady Catherine has heard a rumor that Darcy and Elizabeth are to be wed. She comes all the way to Longbourne to instruct Elizabeth in no uncertain terms that this is not to be. Lady Catherine asks Elizabeth two questions: Is she engaged to Darcy? And does she promise to never be? To the former Elizabeth responds, no, she is not; to the later, "I will make no promise of the kind" (*PP*, 427).

True to Smith's form of the proud "not so much to excite your esteem for (her)self, as to mortify that for yourself" (*TMS*, 255), Lady Catherine spends much of the visit demeaning Elizabeth and her family. She notes, "You have a very small park here" (*PP*, 424). She insults the layout of the house. "This must be a most inconvenient sitting room for the evening, in summer; the windows are full west" (*PP*, 424). When Elizabeth is not obsequious and fully forthcoming on her relationship with Darcy, Lady Catherine proceeds to slur her. "The upstart pretensions of a young woman without family, connections, or fortune. Is this to be endured!" (*PP*, 426). And later in the conversation the entire Bennet family is castigated because her mother's family is not among the gentry and because of her younger sister's recent elopement.

However, we know Elizabeth is also proud. She explains to Lady Catherine that "[Darcy] is a gentleman; I am a gentleman's daughter; so far we are equal" (*PP*, 426). She finally ends the conversation with Lady Catherine by telling her: "You can now have nothing farther to say. . . . You have insulted me in every possible method. I must beg to return to the house" (*PP*, 427).

Elizabeth will not be intimidated by Lady Catherine and she exhibits some of the best attributes of what Smith calls pride in the "good sense." According to Smith, "Where there is this real superiority, pride is frequently attended with many respectable virtues; with truth, with integrity, with a high sense of honour, with cordial and steady friendship, with the most inflexible firmness and resolution" (*TMS*, 258).

Of course *Pride and Prejudice* ends with Darcy and Elizabeth marrying and living happily ever after. Aunt Catherine de Bourgh sends them an insulting note, which angers Darcy who ends all contact with his aunt. Elizabeth eventually suggests Darcy should reconcile with his aunt, which he does. Lady Catherine reluctantly receives them. However, the crowning point of the marriage and the nature of both pride and prejudice is perhaps given by Mr. Bennet, Elizabeth's father, in a letter to his insufferable cousin, Lady Catherine's toady parson Mr. Collins, after Darcy and Elizabeth's marriage is announced:

DEAR SIR,

I must trouble you once more for congratulations. Elizabeth will soon be the wife of Mr. Darcy. Console Lady Catherine as well as you can. But, if I were you, I would stand by the nephew. He has more to give.

Your's sincerely, &c. (*PP*, 442).

NOTES

1. This is exactly the flaw he recognizes he has overcome by the book's end (see Stokes, 1991, 38).

2. Later in the same passage Smith argues that to be a little excessive in one's pride is likely better than to be a little deficient in pride.

3. His claim is untrue. He only asked Elizabeth because he was informed by her mother, Mrs. Bennet, that the oldest sister, Jane, is likely to be engaged. Collins does not love any female; he simply wants a wife.

4. See James Wood's "God Talk" in the *New Yorker* magazine for a description of how Collins's proposal is "a narcissistically exaggerated version of the Prayer Book's liturgy."

5. Recall the source of Mrs. Bennet's ill-humour. If one of the girls had agreed to marry Mr. Collins, Mrs. Bennet would have been assured a home, so she is quite naturally upset at Elizabeth's refusal.

6. When Collins met Aunt Phillips he mentioned that at Rosings a "chimney-piece alone had cost eight hundred pounds" (*PP*, 267).

Chapter Eight

Greed and Promises
in *Northanger Abbey*

Gordon Gecko in the movie *Wall Street* tells us that "Greed is Good!" Not so fast, according to Jane Austen. In her novels, characters' greed causes them to break promises and hurt others; avarice usually also ends up hurting the greedy person in the end. The richest examples of the negative effects of avarice are found in *Northanger Abbey* through the greedy siblings, Isabella and John Thorpe, and the Abbey's owner, General Tilney. Each of these characters meets with misfortune as a result of their greed.

We meet Isabella when she befriends the somewhat younger and much more inexperienced Catherine Morland and shepherds her through Bath society. Isabella is first interested in Catherine's brother James and they eventually become engaged. Immediately after the engagement is revealed, we see that Isabella appears to have an inflated view of James's financial situation. She is not confident that Mr. and Mrs. Morland will approve of the match, fearing that "my fortune will be so small; they never can consent to it. Your brother, who might marry any body!" (*NA*, 1068). Her implication is that James has some fortune coming to him. In fact she goes on to claim that were their situations reversed, and that she had millions, she would still choose James out of love. Bordering on protesting too much, she further insists that "[w]here people are really attached, poverty is wealth: grandeur I detest" (*NA*, 1068). Upon hearing of the Morlands' approval, though, her delusions of grandeur take over. "She saw herself at the end of a few weeks, the gaze and admiration of every new acquaintance at Fullerton, the envy of every valued old friend in Putney, with a carriage at her command, a new name on her tickets, and a brilliant exhibition of hoop rings on her finger" (*NA*, 1070).

Such hopes are dashed once Isabella learns the true nature of James's financial situation. His father has promised him a living of only about four hundred pounds in a few years, so the couple will have a long engagement followed by a life of relatively limited means. Isabella takes the news "with a grave face" (*NA*, 1076), but she manages to convince Catherine that her disappointment is with the delay of the marriage rather than with the size of the living. Isabella soon breaks her engagement promise to James and turns her attention to Captain Tilney, an eldest son who will inherit Northanger Abbey. Captain Tilney, though, is only toying with Isabella's heart for sport. The captain's younger brother Henry sees Isabella's true colors. He predicts that "she will be very constant [in her love for Captain Tilney], unless a baronet should come her way . . . " (*NA*, 1116). Henry also believes that Isabella must be telling the truth about her engagement to his brother because he has "too good an opinion of Miss Thorpe's prudence, to suppose that she would part with one gentleman before another is secured" (*NA*, 1116). Her greed backfires on her, though. The reader only hears details of how the love triangle goes astray through letters to Catherine. James reports to Catherine that Isabella has broken things off with him to become engaged to Captain Tilney. Isabella reports to Catherine that the captain, who she now "abhor[s]" (*NA*, 1122) has finally left Bath. She further writes that she is concerned that she has not heard from James lately, and implores Catherine to intervene. It seems that Isabella forgot that a bird in the hand is worth two in the bush, so she ends up without either James or the captain as a husband.

Like his sister, John Thorpe hides his avarice by pretending not to care for money. "Let me only have the girl I like, say I, with a comfortable house over my head, and what care I for all the rest? Fortune is nothing. I am sure of a good income of my own; and if she had not a penny, why, so much the better" (*NA*, 1071). Of course he says this to Catherine to assess whether or not she would marry someone less wealthy than her. Thorpe's "[a]varice over-rates the difference between poverty and riches," as Adam Smith predicts (*TMS*, 149), and John, like Isabella, assumes the Morland family to be richer than they are. His greed over the imagined fortune causes him to make Catherine break her promise to go for a walk with the Tilney siblings. Furthermore, when John first meets General Tilney, John's "vanity induced him to represent the family as yet more wealthy than his vanity and avarice had made him believe them" (*NA*, 1138). Thorpe's greed, then, leads him to exaggerate the extent of the Morlands' riches as long as he thinks he has a chance with Catherine. Catherine is never taken with John, though, and only tolerates his company for the sake of her brother's and Isabella's romance.

General Tilney's greed is even greater than that of the Thorpes'; he is already rich, but he still goes after more. In addition to owning Northanger Abbey, it is revealed early on that he had married well to a woman with "a very large fortune" (*NA*, 1038). He is so very well off that his children do not need to go into a profession. The general's greed is further evident in his refusal to sanction the marriage between his daughter, Eleanor, and her unnamed longtime love—until the suitor unexpectedly inherits a fortune and becomes a viscount. Eleanor and her brother Henry seem to be fully aware of their father's avarice. When Catherine compliments the general for his liberalness of mind and predicts that he will sanction an engagement between Captain Tilney and Isabella, she exclaims, "He told me the other day that he only valued money as it allowed him to promote the happiness of his children" (*NA*, 1116). At that, the narrator notes, "The brother and sister looked at each other."

After hearing from John Thorpe that Catherine is well situated, General Tilney thinks her a good match for his son Henry. The general further infers that since the wealthy and childless Allens were hosting Catherine in Bath, of course, that meant she would receive a sizeable fortune from Mr. Allen. This overestimation, we later learn, is the impetus for the general's invitation for Catherine to visit with them at the Abbey. With his designs on Catherine as a daughter-in-law, he makes sure to give her a tour of his grand home, being careful to point out all of the luxuries along the way. Throughout the tour, he is careful to ask Catherine to compare his estate to that of the Allens (so that he can better assess the extent the future fortune he imagines for Catherine).

General Tilney later re-meets John Thorpe in London after Thorpe is spurned by Catherine and after the break up of James and Isabella. With no hope of ties to the Morlands, Thorpe no longer overestimates their financial situation. In fact he errs in the reverse direction, making them out to be poor out of spite. Upon hearing this news, the general is furious that his greedy plans are for naught. His disappointed avarice causes him to "disturb the peace of society" and to "violate the rules of either prudence or of justice" just as Adam Smith predicts of a "person under the influence" of greed (*TMS*, 149). The general abruptly turns Catherine out of the Abbey (breaking a promise to host her) and she is left to make her way home as best she can.

Unlike his father, Henry Tilney believes in keeping his word, even when it is not explicitly expressed. After learning of Catherine's expulsion from his home, Henry refuses to accompany his family on the planned trip to Herefordshire and instead heads to Catherine's home to propose. Austen tells us that "He felt himself bound as much in honour as in affection to Miss Morland, and believing that heart to be his own which he had been directed to gain, no unworthy retraction of a tacit consent, no reversing decree of unjustifiable anger, could shake his fidelity, or influence the resolutions it prompted" (*NA*, 1140). In his mind, then, even *tacit* promises are to be kept. Once his engagement to Catherine becomes formal, the couple patiently waits to marry until both families approve. That approval only comes after the General's greed is sated, for the moment, by Eleanor marrying her viscount.

Through General Tilney and the Thorpe siblings, Jane Austen is clearly showing us the dangers of avarice. These characters give us a rich depiction of greed as a vice earlier outlined by Adam Smith. A caricature of Smith's views on greed stems from the most famous Smith quote: "It is not from the benevolence of the butcher, the brewer, or the baker, that we expect our dinner, but from their regard to their own interest" (*WN*, 26–27). Here Smith is offering a defense of commercial society based on efficiency grounds. Markets turn self-interested behavior (which may be greed) into service to others (which is invariably good). Most people, unfamiliar with Smith's moral philosophy like Gordon Gecko, mistakenly shorten this thought into *greed is good*. On the contrary, as we have explained in chapter 2, Smith's moral philosophy is built on human sympathy, not self-interest. Greed, or avarice, is what causes us to put undue value on becoming rich which is one of "[t]he great source[s] of both misery and disorders of human life" (*TMS*, 149). Avarice, along with vanity, is one of those selfish and "extravagant passions" that may cause us to "disturb the peace of society" to get what we want (*TMS*, 149). Motivated by greed, we may also "violate the rules of either prudence or of justice" that ends up causing us shame and regret (*TMS*, 149). Greed, then, is actually bad for us!

According to Smith, history and experience has proven that misfortune comes to those who are greedy; we should be content and thankful for what we already have. Smith makes an important distinction between greed and ambition. In both cases, we want to make ourselves better off, but ambition, as long as it is tempered by prudence and justice, "is always admired in the world" (*TMS*, 173). Austen understands this distinction as evidenced by Elizabeth Bennet in *Pride and Prejudice* who attempts to find the fine line between prudence and greed in her response to her aunt, Mrs. Gardiner. Upon learning that Wickham has deserted Elizabeth to pursue the wealthy Miss King, Mrs. Gardiner expresses dismay that Wickham might be mercenary in his approach to marriage. Elizabeth replies, "Pray, my dear aunt, what is the difference in matrimonial affairs, between the mercenary and the prudent motive? Where does discretion end, and avarice begin? Last Christmas you were afraid of his marrying me, because it would be imprudent; and now, because he is trying to get a girl with only ten thousand pounds, you want to find out that he is mercenary" (*PP*, 312).

When we are greedy, we often break promises to others. According to Smith, the "most sacred rule of justice, [is that] which commands the observance of all serious promises . . . " (*TMS*, 330). Furthermore, people who don't take promises seriously deserve disapprobation. "The man who was quite frank and easy in making promises of this kind, and who violated them with as little ceremony, we should not chuse for our friend and companion" (*TMS*, 331). Such disapprobation, once received, is hard to undo and the shame will follow the promise breaker forever. "He has broke a promise which he had solemnly averred he would maintain; and his character, if not irretrievably stained and polluted, has at least a ridicule affixed to it, which it will be very difficult entirely to efface; and no man, I imagine, who had gone through an adventure of this kind would be fond of telling the story" (*TMS*, 333).

Much of Smith's thought on promise keeping is found in his *Lectures on Jurisprudence*, rightly so for a tome explaining a theory of law. Specifically the keeping of promises is part of contract law. A contract creates an expectation that a promise will be kept. "Thus if one promises to give another five pounds, this naturally creates an expectation that he will receive five pounds from him at the time promised: and here the promiser must be bound to make up to him any loss he has suffered by this expectation" (*LJ*, 12). With a contract, then, if a promise is broken, amends must be made.

Most of the promises made by Austen's characters do not fall within the realm of contract law, however, these promises do create expectations on the part of the promisee. Smith distinguishes between small promises, say to drink tea or go for a walk with someone in the afternoon, and large promises, such as borrowing money. Smith recognizes that we might promise to go for a walk and have every intention of keeping that promise, but sometimes circumstances change that make it inconvenient for us to follow through. Think of Catherine Morland's promise to walk with the Tilneys before being tricked by John Thorpe. Smith admits that this kind of promise breaking may result in a person being "thought to have acted amiss and in an ungentlemanly manner; and might perhaps be thought to have put a slight affront on the person, but not such an injury as would merit a very high resentment, or give sufficient cause for a suit at law" (*LJ*, 92). Indeed, the Tilney siblings forgive Catherine's slight immediately.

Smith maintains that even promises we make that we never intend to keep are still binding because when we make a promise, we create that expectation in the other person. "A promise is a declaration of your desire that the person for whom you promise should depend on you for the performance of it. Of consequence the promise produces an obligation, and the breach of it is an injury" (*LJ*, 472).

Austen's criticism of greed and promise breaking is sprinkled throughout her work. In addition to the prime examples from *Northanger Abbey*, we find interesting examples of this criticism illustrated by characters in *Mansfield Park*, *Persuasion*, and *Sense and Sensibility*. In these novels Austen contrasts the detrimental effects of avarice against the honor earned by promise keeping.

GREED IN *MANSFIELD PARK*

One such greedy character is Mary Crawford of *Mansfield Park* who admits early on that she puts herself before others to an extreme. But, as she explains, "Selfishness must always be forgiven, you know, because there is no hope of a cure" (*MP*, 487). This greedy attitude, however, is part of the reason why she loses out on a relationship with Edmund. She has never been particularly fond of Edmund's chosen profession, the clergy, and urges him to take on something with more distinction, such as the law. She fully admits to him that she plans to be rich and that "[a] large income is the best recipe for happiness . . . " (*MP*, 569). She wrongly assumes that, like for most second sons, Edmund must have a rich uncle or grandfather to leave him a fortune. Most shocking is her reaction to Edmund's brother Tom's serious illness. She openly admits to Fanny that she would have preferred that Tom not recover from his illness so that Edmund could become the Bertram heir. Fanny concludes, "She had only learnt to think nothing of consequence but money" (*MP*, 698). In true Austen form, the greedy Mary Crawford ends up alone at the end of the novel, losing out to the generous Fanny.

GREED AND PROMISES IN *PERSUASION*

Greed is a big motivation for the widow Mrs. Clay in *Persuasion*. As the daughter of Sir Walter Elliot's advisor, Mr. Shepard, Mrs. Clay is very familiar with the extent of the Elliot estate. Becoming a constant companion to Sir Walter's daughter Elizabeth endears her to the father and daughter so much that they prefer to take *her* to Bath instead of their daughter/sister Anne. Mrs. Clay hopes to someday be Lady Elliot, mistress of Kellynch Hall, so she does her best to capture Sir Elliot's attention. She even takes his recommendations regarding which face cream to use to diminish her freckles! Her patience runs out before the novel ends, though, as she accepts an offer from Mr. William Elliot, the heir to Kellynch, to be "established under his protection in London" (*P*, 1289).

William Elliot, a widower himself, is also a picture of avarice. As the heir to the Baronetcy, it was expected that he would marry Elizabeth, but he bristles at being roped into the Elliot family. "Instead of pushing his fortune in the line marked out for the heir of the house of Elliot, he had purchased independence by uniting himself to a rich woman of inferior birth" (*P*, 1148). By marrying a rich woman, he obtained the riches he desired, without taking on the family he did not. By the time we meet Mr. Elliot again, first in Lyme and then in Bath, he seems to have changed his tune. This time, though, he has his eyes set on marrying Anne. Lady Russell makes it clear to Anne that she approves of such a match. Anne sees things differently. "'Mr. Elliot is an exceedingly agreeable man, and in many respects I think highly of him,' said Anne; 'but we should not suit'" (*P*, 1235). Anne later finds out that her instincts were right. According to Anne's schoolmate, Mrs. Smith, the reason Mr. Elliot had earlier spurned Elizabeth was because he "at that period of his life, had one object in view: to make his fortune, and by a rather quicker process than the law. He was determined to make it by marriage" (*P*, 1259). Elliot's greed made him too impatient to wait to inherit the Baronetcy. He took the short cut to wealth by marrying rich. That his wife's family earned their riches in a low way ("Her father was a grazier, her grandfather had been a butcher" [*P*, 1260]) was of no consequence to him.[1] "Money, money, was all that he wanted" (*P*, 1260). His wife was in love with him, but Mr. Elliot did not return the affection and only showed concern for "the real amount of her fortune" (*P*, 1260). Once his wife dies, he decides to pursue his birthright after all. After hearing about Mr. Elliot's checkered past from Mrs. Smith, Anne concludes that Mr. Elliot is "a disingenuous, artificial, worldly man, who has never had any better principle to guide him than selfishness" (*P*, 1264).

Mrs. Smith reveals to Anne that Mr. Elliot is also the reason for her current state of poverty. "Mr. Elliot had led his friend [Mr. Smith] into expenses much beyond his fortune" (*P*, 1264). It seems that Mr. Smith was caught up in the conspicuous consumption that characterizes a vain man (see chapter 6). In trying to keep up with the Joneses, or in this case the Elliots, Mr. Smith is led to financial ruin. The full extent of the difficulties is not discovered until after Mr. Smith's death. Further compounding things is the fact that Mr. Elliot is the executor of Mr. Smith's estate, but he has yet to fulfill his promise to act on this responsibility. Mr. Smith has some property in the West Indies that, if accessed, could provide a comfortable living for Mrs. Smith. It is not until Captain Wentworth gets involved that Mrs. Smith's financial troubles are resolved.

The greedy characters Mr. Elliot and Mrs. Clay end up scheming for the same fortune; Mr. Elliot goes after Anne while Mrs. Clay has designs on Sir Walter. Mr. Elliot buys off Mrs. Clay by setting her up in London in order to keep her away from Sir Walter. The joke may ultimately be on Mr. Elliot, the narrator points out. "She has abilities, however, as well as affections; and it is now a doubtful point whether his cunning, or hers, may finally carry the day; whether, after preventing her from being the wife of Sir Walter, he may not be wheedled and caressed at last into making her the wife of Sir William" (*P*, 1289). So it remains to be seen whose greed wins out in the end with this pair.

Of course it is poor Anne Elliot who bears the full weight of breaking a promise. Early in the novel we learn that she had been persuaded by her mentor, Lady Russell, to break her engagement to Captain Wentworth. Greed was not a motivator here, but rather vanity. Both Lady Russell and Anne's father thought the match "a very degrading alliance" (*P*, 1158) due to their differences in station. Anne feels the negative effects of her promise breaking for most of the novel, and she never moves on to find another mate. "Her attachments and regrets had, for a long time, clouded every enjoyment of youth; and an early loss of bloom and spirits had been their lasting effort" (*P*, 1159).

Anne tried to delude herself into thinking that the decision to break off the engagement was a good thing for Captain Wentworth. Austen writes, "it was not a merely selfish caution, under which she acted, in putting an end to it. Had she not imagined herself consulting his good, even more than her own, she could hardly have given him up. The belief of being prudent, and self-denying, principally for his advantage, was her chief consolation, under the misery of a parting" (*P*, 1159). Here Anne is acting just as Smith predicts. When we fall short of our moral ideal, we deceive ourselves into thinking it is all right. We want so much to be worthy of admiration that we hide from the truth. Roberts (2014, p. 64) maintains that we have a tendency to convince ourselves that "what seems good for me is actually good for you." Such self-delusion is explained by Smith. "This self-deceit, this fatal weakness of mankind, is the source of half the disorders of human life" (*TMS*, 158). We need this self-delusion in order to be able to look ourselves in the mirror. "We could not otherwise endure the sight" (*TMS*, 159). Anne's struggle over the course of the novel gives us keen insight into the predominance and danger of such self-delusion.

GREED AND PROMISES IN *SENSE AND SENSIBILITY*

Sense and Sensibility begins with a prime example of greed and promise breaking. In the very first chapter, we learn of John Dashwood's death bed promise to his father that he "would do every thing in his power to make them [the soon to be widowed Mrs. Dashwood and her three daughters] comfortable" (*SS*, 10). He sets his mind on giving them three thousand of the ten thousand pounds per year he will inherit.[2] His wife Fanny, who is "more narrow-minded and selfish," has other ideas (*SS*, 10). Immediately after the funeral, she swoops in with their small son and takes over Norland, the family home. Austen describes in painful detail how Fanny wheedles John's intended gift of three thousand a year down to five hundred. In going along with his wife, John deludes himself in true Smithian fashion to believe that "it would be better for all parties, if the sum were diminished" (*SS*, 12). In Mr. and Mrs. John Dashwood, then, we see Jane Austen illuminating the importance that Adam Smith gave to promise keeping, especially the honoring of death bed wishes. Smith was adamant that his friends honor his own death bed wish to burn the draft of his book on justice, which is why we only have his *Lectures on Jurisprudence* published from notes taken at his lectures.

Two other characters in *Sense and Sensibility* break promises concerning inheritances: Mrs. Ferrars and Mrs. Smith. Mrs. Ferrars disinherits her son

Edward after hearing of his engagement to the vulgar Lucy Steele. Through Edward's response, Austen shows us the importance of *keeping* promises. Edward sticks by his promise to Lucy, even though one might argue that his engagement was a youthful indiscretion. He even keeps the engagement despite meeting, and falling in love with, Elinor. Finally, in his choice of a profession, Edward will be making a sacred promise when he becomes ordained.

Elinor shows that she is a perfect match for Edward because she, too, keeps her word in three promises throughout the novel. Her first promise is to Lucy Steele. When Lucy confides in Elinor that she and Edward are engaged, she expresses confidence in Elinor's discretion saying, "I have no doubt in the world of your faithfully keeping this secret . . . " (*SS*, 82). To which Elinor replies, "I certainly did not seek your confidence, . . . but you do me no more than justice in imagining that I may be depended on. Your secret is safe with me . . . " (*SS*, 82). Elinor keeps Lucy's secret for the next four months, never even hinting at the truth to her sister, Marianne. Elinor's second promise is to Colonel Brandon who asks Elinor to convey the message to Edward that he will offer him a living at the rectory in Delaford that has just become vacant. Therefore, once Edward takes his orders, he can be supported by at least two hundred pounds per year despite the disinheritance. This small amount, the Colonel points out, would still not be enough to support a wife, but it is better than nothing and may lead to more in the distant future. Despite knowing that this living might make it possible for Edward and Lucy to eventually marry, Elinor keeps her word and delivers the news to Edward in person. Elinor's third promise made and kept is to Willoughby, who asks her to convey to Marianne the tale of his "misery" and "penitence" that he confesses to Elinor (*SS*, 193). Elinor intends to keep her promise, but is unsure as to *when* to relate Willoughby's story to her sister due to Marianne's fragile health. She only does so after Marianne recovers and sets out a plan for improvement. The time is right when Marianne pines, "If I could but know *his* heart, everything would become easy" (*SS*, 203).

In contrast to the trustworthy characters of Edward and Elinor, John Willoughby and Lucy Steele provide examples of greed and promise breaking. In chapter 6 we describe these characters as being exemplars of vanity, but Willoughby's and Lucy's vanity also manifests itself as avarice and causes them to break promises.

Throughout much of the novel, Willoughby is seen as the love of the passionate Marianne. Everyone, even members of her family, presume that they are engaged. Willoughby, though, is not interested in marrying for love. While his fortune never was large, he consistently lived beyond his means until his only hope was "to re-establish [his] circumstances by marrying a woman of fortune" (*SS*, 187). He is disinherited by his rich cousin, Mrs. Smith, after she learns of his scandalous seduction of Colonel Brandon's

young ward, Eliza. In response, Willoughby abruptly cuts things off with
Marianne, setting her off on a downward spiral of depression leading to
illness. He instead pursues the wealthy Miss Grey; with a fortune of fifty-
thousand pounds, Miss Grey is too hard to resist, despite the pain caused to
Marianne. Technically Willoughby and Marianne were never engaged, so an
explicit promise was not broken. Nonetheless, he did give Marianne strong
reason to believe that they were a couple by giving her a horse and asking for
a lock of her hair. Smith would maintain that the key here is that Willoughby's actions created an expectation in Marianne (and in almost everyone else
who had observed the young lovers). He admits to Elinor that his actions
have hurt not only Marianne, but also himself, saying, "I have, by raising
myself to affluence, lost every thing that could make it a blessing" (*SS*, 187).
His greed, then, turns out to hurt not only those he loves, but also himself.
Austen, like Smith, is teaching us that greed is bad for you.

Lucy Steele also greedily marries for money. First she manages to obtain
a youthful engagement to Edward Ferrars, the eldest son and heir. Edward
honors this earlier commitment despite his later meeting Elinor and falling in
love. After Edward's mother finds out about the engagement to Lucy, she
disinherits Edward. Undeterred in her quest for the Ferrars' riches, Lucy
breaks her engagement to Edward and quickly switches her affections to the
new heir, Edward's younger brother, Robert. Now free from his engagement
to Miss Steele, Edward is able to propose to his true love, Elinor. In a way,
then, Lucy's greed paves the way for Elinor and Edward's happiness. That
Lucy's opportunistic pursuit of her self-interest has unintended positive outcomes for others is reminiscent of Adam Smith's invisible hand of the marketplace (Knox-Shaw, 2004, 145). Or to paraphrase Smith, *It is not from the
benevolence of Miss Steele that Edward expects to be free to marry Elinor,
but from Lucy's regard to her own interest.*

As Smith explains, a market participant "intends only his own gain, and
he is in this, as in many other cases, led by an invisible hand to promote an
end which was no part of his intention" (*WN*, 456). When we try to improve
our own standard of living, we end up promoting the interests of others by
serving them. Furthermore in a market, buyers and sellers, again motivated
by self-interest, trade with each other and the result is the determination of a
market equilibrium price. The market order is, thus, an unintended consequence of self-love. As we discuss in chapter 3, the concept of the invisible
hand is first found in *Theory of Moral Sentiments* where Smith illustrates
how the vain consumption by the rich increases the demand for products and
services, leading to employment and prosperity for the masses who produce
those things. A certain amount of vanity has unintended good consequences
for society as a whole. As for avarice, though, Smith and Austen show us that
greed can lead people to hurt others and can even lead to personal misfortune. For both authors, then, greed is certainly not good.

NOTES

1. See chapter 11 for insights into why earning a living through trade was considered to be "low."

2. See chapter 10 for a discussion of annual incomes.

Chapter Nine

Man of System and Impartial Spectator in *Emma*

Emma is a busybody who thinks she knows what is best for her friends. "The real evils, indeed, of Emma's situation were the power of having rather too much her own way, and a disposition to think a little too well of herself" (*E*, 723). The reader begins to see Emma's addiction to managing the lives of others in the beginning of the novel when Emma deludes herself into thinking that she played a major role in arranging a match between her former governess Miss Taylor to the eligible widower Mr. Weston. This early matchmaking success leads Emma to attempt to find a husband for her protégé, Harriet Smith, a likable-enough girl of uncertain parentage. Harriet receives an offer of marriage from Mr. Robert Martin, who farms part of Mr. Knightley's estate, but Emma believes this match to be below Harriet, at least below the level to which Emma aspires for her friend. Harriet had earlier formed an attachment to Mr. Martin during a stay with his family. Ever insisting that she will not offer Harriet any advice on whether to accept or reject the proposal, Emma nonetheless makes it appear that Harriet comes to Emma's choice (rejection) all on her own. Even in the writing of the refusal letter, "though Emma continued to protest against any assistance being wanted, it was in fact given in the formation of every sentence" (*E*, 752).

Emma sets her sights on the new clergyman, Mr. Elton, as a proper match for Harriet. So convinced that her plan for the couple is the right one, Emma is oblivious to the fact that Mr. Elton is actually courting her instead of Harriet. After Elton declares his love for Emma, her confidence in her own ability to manage the lives of others makes it hard for her to believe that she was so wrong. "She looked back as well as she could; but it was all confusion. She had taken up the idea, she supposed, and made every thing bend to it. His manners, however, must have been unmarked, wavering, dubious, or she could not have been so misled" (*E*, 799). On the one hand, then, Emma starts to realize that she was so sure that her plans for Harriet were the right ones that she only saw what she wanted to; but on the other hand, Emma still clings to the idea that Mr. Elton had been partially at fault.

This setback actually makes Emma doubt her ability to control the lives of others and sets her on a slow path toward giving up her meddling ways. In the aftermath of the Elton debacle she even recognizes that while, yes, she is distraught over being wrong about the match, she is much more upset that her actions negatively affected her friend.

> Such a blow for Harriet!—that was the worst of all. Every part of it brought pain and humiliation, of some sort or other; but, compared with the evil to Harriet, all was light; and she would gladly have submitted to feel yet more mistaken—more in error—more disgraced by mis-judgment, than she actually was, could the effects of her blunders have been confined to herself. (*E*, 799)

It takes the rest of the novel, however, for Emma to completely reform. Despite her failure with the Elton match, Emma is insistent that she was correct to steer Harriet away from Mr. Martin. Emma even catches herself immediately considering a different match for Harriet with a young lawyer, William Coxe, but is able to restrain herself from following through—this time. Right after losing interest in Frank Churchill for herself, however, Emma begins to think of him as a proper match for Harriet. Here again, Emma's conceit in her ability to plan for others makes her see and hear only what fits in with her predisposed notions. When Harriet talks of being rescued by her love interest, Emma wrongly believes Harriet is talking about when Frank Churchill saves her from an attack by a band of gypsies during a walk. On the contrary, Harriet was thinking about Mr. Knightley gallantly stepping in to dance with her after she was snubbed by Mr. Elton at a ball. Once Harriet openly admits her feelings for Mr. Knightley, Emma is struck by the realization of her own love for Mr. Knightley and finally sees the folly of her interfering ways. "With insufferable vanity had she believed herself in the secret of every body's feelings; with unpardonable arrogance proposed to arrange every body's destiny. She was proved to have been universally mistaken; and she had not quite done nothing—for she had done mischief" (*E*, 960). In the redemption of Emma, Austen is teaching us that to aspire to control others is not only doomed to failure but is immoral. Enlightenment virtue requires that we respect the liberty of others to choose and plan for themselves.

Adam Smith had a phrase to describe controlling people like Emma—a "man of system" (*TMS*, 233). Smith begins his explanation of the man of system in his section on virtue in *Theory of Moral Sentiments*. First he describes why we tend to show more benevolence toward people we know well and less benevolence toward strangers. Then he uses this familiarity principle to explain why people tend to develop a love of country that results in more concern for fellow citizens than for foreigners. Our love of country also makes us value our particular system of government for the way it serves us. We both respect our laws (the process), and are concerned for the well-being of our fellow citizens (the outcome). In peaceful times, our respect for the process is not in conflict with our concern about the outcome of the process. For example, there may be general agreement that the government should enforce private property rights. In this case when we respect the rules and do not trespass on our neighbors' yard, the outcome is seen as just. What is legal and what is thought to be just are harmonized. However, when public disagreements arise, say, over whether or not our neighbors' property would be better used as a site for a new school, then conflict arises. In this case, some people might consider it proper to override the private property rights of their neighbor in order to build the school for the public good. Others (presumably the neighbor, at least) might see things differently.

Smith maintains that two types of political leaders would have very different responses to the case of public disagreement over process versus outcome. The first type of leader is benevolent and is motivated by concern for the public interest and the second is described as the "man of system" (*TMS*, 233). When the former, the benevolent leader, has views different from his people, he uses "reason and persuasion" to convince them that he is right (*TMS*, 233). He does not resort to force to pursue his agenda. The man of system, however, is so convinced that his desired outcome is the correct one, that he imposes it regardless of the opposition. As Smith puts it in this rather long but important excerpt:

> The man of system, on the contrary, is apt to be very wise in his own conceit; and is often so enamoured with the supposed beauty of his own ideal plan of government, that he cannot suffer the smallest deviation from any part of it. He goes on to establish it completely and in all its parts, without any regard either to the great interests, or to the strong prejudices which may oppose it. He seems to imagine that he can arrange the different members of a great society with as much ease as the hand arranges the different pieces upon a chess-board. He does not consider that the pieces upon the chess-board have no other principle of motion besides that which the hand impresses upon them; but that, in the great chess-board of human society, every single piece has a principle of motion of its own, altogether different from that which the legislature might chuse to impress upon it. If those two principles coincide and act in the same direction, the game of human society will go on easily and harmoniously, and is very likely to be happy and successful. If they are opposite or different, the game will go on miserably, and the society must be at all times in the highest degree of disorder. (*TMS*, 234)

Anyone familiar with the above reference to the man of system arranging people's lives like pieces on a chessboard is struck by the resemblance to Emma's matchmaking machinations.[1] For the man of system, it is his way or the highway. For example, there may be general agreement that a healthy diet does not include a lot of sugary soft drinks, but in a free society, people can still buy large sodas. A publicly spirited leader might begin an education campaign to convince people to give up their Big Gulps; a man of system would outlaw the sale of them directly.

Smith goes on to point out that, yes, some degree of a general plan of government is most likely necessary. "But to insist upon establishing, and upon establishing all at once, and in spite of all opposition, every thing which that idea may seem to require, must often be the highest degree of arrogance" (*TMS*, 234). In this way the man of system thinks "himself the only wise and worthy man in the commonwealth, and that his fellow-citizens should accommodate themselves to him and not he to them" (*TMS*, 234).

Smith concludes that this arrogance on the part of the man of system is one of the dangers of sovereign rule. Of course, as the examples provided above illustrate, it is not just royalty who arrogantly attempt to circumvent the rules to suit their own interests. Political wrangling to obtain certain outcomes regardless of the rules happens frequently in democratically elected governments, too. Smith's condemnation of the man of system is part of the larger Enlightenment theme of questioning authority and valuing individual liberty. The men on the chessboard that the man of system tries to manipulate have their own plans that ought to be respected, as Emma eventually learns.

While in Emma we see the fullest representation of why Smith's man of system is not a model to follow, Austen includes this theme on a smaller level in other novels as well. There are several characters that stand out as suffering from man-of-system syndrome. These characters, however, do not undergo the moral transformation as Emma does, so they end up alone, clinging to their delusions of power.

MRS. NORRIS AS MAN OF SYSTEM IN *MANSFIELD PARK*

One of these such characters is Mrs. Norris of *Mansfield Park* who sees herself as indispensible to the Bertram family and is described as having an "inclination" for managing (*MP*, 671). She is the sister of Lady Bertram, who married well to Sir Thomas; and of Mrs. Price, who married poorly to a lieutenant of the Marines who now lives on a disability pension. Mrs. Norris married somewhere in between, to a local parson. Upon hearing that Mrs. Price had chosen such a lowly mate, Lady Bertram was ready to let the relationship with her sister die a natural death. Mrs. Norris, though, "had a spirit of activity" (*MP*, 451) that makes her write a heated letter to Mrs. Price that led to a long period of estrangement between Mrs. Price and her two sisters. Many years and many children later, Mrs. Price swallows her pride to write to Lady Bertram pleading with her to take in one of the nine Price children, perhaps one of the sons as an apprentice to Sir Thomas. While the letter is addressed to Lady Bertram, the response comes from Mrs. Norris. Mrs. Norris ignores the suggestion that Sir Thomas take on one of the Price sons and instead arranges for the eldest daughter, Fanny, to be chosen. Since it was Mrs. Norris's idea to bring Fanny to Mansfield Park, Sir Thomas assumes that Fanny would live as a companion at the Parsonage to the childless Mr. and Mrs. Norris. Mrs. Norris, however, has other plans. She insists that Fanny be brought into the Bertram family, albeit as a second-class member. Of course, as the narrator notes, "nobody knew better how to dictate liberality to others" as Mrs. Norris (*MP*, 452).

Mrs. Norris usually gets her way, and when others change her plans she takes it personally. For example, when Edmund proposes that he stay home with his mother so that Fanny can go along on an outing to visit the Rushworths, Mrs. Norris was against the plan merely because she did not think of it first. "[H]er opposition to Edmund *now*, arose more from partiality for her own scheme, because it *was* her own, than from anything else. She felt that she had arranged everything extremely well, and that any alteration must be for the worse" (*MP*, 493). When Mrs. Grant offers to stay with Lady Bertram, freeing up both Edmund and Fanny for the outing, Mrs. Norris pretends that was her plan all along.

Even when others make plans that are perfectly reasonable, Mrs. Norris takes credit for doing the planning. After making arrangements for carriage rides home after a ball, she explains the plan to Sir Thomas who "could not dissent, as it had been his own arrangement, previously communicated to his wife and sister; but *that* seemed forgotten by Mrs. Norris, who must fancy that she settled it all herself" (*MP*, 591).

Mrs. Norris takes it upon herself to improve upon the doings of others, no matter how inconsequential. At the outing to the Rushworths', Mrs. Norris quickly takes charge. She accompanies the housekeeper on the shopping errands for dinner, finagling free portions of the wares along the way, and upon meeting the gardener, was happy to have "set him right as to his grandson's illness, convinc[ing] him it was an ague" (*MP*, 507). Later in the novel she is caught "in fresh arranging and injuring the noble fire which the butler had prepared" (*MP*, 604).

While Mrs. Norris enjoyed taking over things at the Rushworths', once the Bertram siblings begin working on their theatrical production, Mrs. Norris is in man-of-system heaven. Her efforts to control the production of the play lead her to neglect her chaperone duties toward the Bertram daughters. She finds herself "too busy in contriving and directing the general little matters of the company, superintending their various dresses with economical expedient, for which nobody thanked her, and saving, with delighted integrity, half a crown here and there to the absent Sir Thomas, to have leisure for watching the behaviour, or guarding the happiness of his daughters" (*MP*, 541).

As an aspiring man of system, Mrs. Norris finds it vexing when her authoritative role is ignored. When Sir Thomas finally returns from Antigua, Mrs. Norris is surprised when he enters the home at Mansfield Park to greet his family without greeting her first and letting her share the good news of his return. Yes, she was happy he was home, but "she was vexed by the *manner* of his return. It had left her nothing to do" (*MP*, 550). She "felt herself defrauded of an office on which she had always depended" (*MP*, 550). Likewise, Mrs. Norris is astounded to learn that Sir Thomas is planning to throw a ball for Fanny and William Price without consulting her. She quickly rebounds from the shock, however, when she realizes that the actual details of the ball would be left to her. "*She* must be the doer of everything" (*MP*, 592).

Later in the novel it becomes apparent to Mrs. Norris that her careful planning for the bright future for the Bertram sisters has gone awry, and she is devastated. She becomes "an altered creature, quieted, stupefied, indifferent to everything that passed" (*MP*, 705). She is especially upset over the news of Maria's affair with Mr. Crawford because Maria's marriage match to Mr. Rushworth was of "her own contriving" (*MP*, 705). During Sir Thomas's long absence Mrs. Norris had "all the house under her care" but in the end that was "an advantage entirely thrown away; she had been unable to direct or dictate, or even fancy herself useful" (*MP*, 705). Of course, Mrs. Norris does not blame herself for the undesired outcome; instead she furiously blames Fanny for deviating from Mrs. Norris's grand plan. Earlier in the novel, when Mr. Crawford asks for Fanny's hand in marriage, Mrs. Norris tells her it is her duty to accept such an attractive offer in light of Fanny's financial situation. According to Mrs. Norris, if only Fanny had accepted Mr. Crawford as she advised, he would not have been around to lead Maria astray. Things end badly for the presumed man of system in *Mansfield Park*. Mrs. Norris ends up exiled to another country to live out her days with the scandalized Maria.

LADY CATHERINE AS MAN OF SYSTEM IN *PRIDE AND PREJUDICE*

The person who imagines to be able to control the lives of others in *Pride and Prejudice* is Lady Catherine de Bourgh, the local patroness to clergyman Mr. Collins and the aunt of Mr. Darcy. Lady Catherine spends most of the novel in the background, using her role as patroness to exert influence over things both big and small in Mr. Collins's life. As he explains, "thanks to Lady Catherine de Bourgh, I am removed far beyond the necessity of regarding little matters" (*PP*, 272). She seems to have some degree of control over his comings and goings; she allows him to leave his position for short visits to his family and once sends for him to fill out a team at an evening game of cards. When Mr. Collins moves into the parsonage and begins renovations, "she had perfectly approved all the alterations he had been making, and had even vouchsafed to suggest some herself" (*PP*, 264). In addition to providing approval for his renovations, Lady Catherine also provides feedback on his sermons. "She had even condescended to advise him to marry as soon as he could, provided he chose with discretion" (*PP*, 264).

After Mr. Collins marries Charlotte Lucas, the couple is visited by Charlotte's father and sister and her dear friend, Elizabeth, who had earlier refused Mr. Collins's offer of marriage. Much to Mr. Collins's delight, Lady Catherine convenes a dinner party for them all, giving him a chance to show off his relationship with his patroness. After dinner, when the ladies are gathered in the drawing-room, Lady Catherine dominates the conversation,

> delivering her opinion on every subject in so decisive a manner, as proved that she was not used to have her judgement controverted. She enquired into Charlotte's domestic concerns familiarly and minutely, and gave her a great deal of advice as to the management of them all; told her how every thing ought to be regulated in so small a family as hers, and instructed her as to the care of her cows and her poultry. Elizabeth found that nothing was beneath this great lady's attention, which could furnish her with an occasion of dictating to others. (*PP*, 317–318)

She questions Elizabeth about her family situation, even mentioning the entail on the estate, no doubt because she has gotten wind of possible feelings between Elizabeth and Mr. Darcy.

Dictating to others seems to be Lady Catherine's primary occupation. As Elizabeth's stay continues she notes how often Lady Catherine micromanages the affairs of the parsonage, much to the delight of Mr. Collins and quiet resignation of Charlotte. Lady Catherine makes several calls on the Collinses where

> nothing escaped her observation that was passing in the room during these visits. She examined into their employments, looked at their work, and advised them to do it differently; found fault with the arrangement of the furniture, or detected the housemaid in negligence; and if she accepted any refreshment, seemed to do it only for the sake of finding out that Mrs. Collins's joints of meat were too large for her family. (*PP*, 320)

Elizabeth also learns that Lady Catherine proffers her unsolicited advice to all the households in the parish at the behest and with the help of Mr. Collins.

> Elizabeth soon perceived that though this great lady was not in the commission of the peace for the county, she was a most active magistrate in her own parish, the minutest concerns of which were carried to her by Mr. Collins; and whenever any of the cottagers were disposed to be quarrelsome, discontented or too poor, she sallied forth into the village to settle their differences, silence their complaints, and scold them into harmony and plenty. (*PP*, 320–321)

It is hardly a wonder that Lady Catherine is so generous to Collins—he is her primary enabler.

At the end of Elizabeth's stay, Lady Catherine even shares her expertise on how best to travel back home and how best to pack their clothes for the journey. Elizabeth, however, refuses to be treated like a piece on Lady Catherine's chessboard, even balking at revealing her age when asked. When Lady Catherine encourages Elizabeth to extend her stay with the Collinses, Elizabeth insists that she "must abide by our original plan" (*PP*, 344). Of course the most important example of Elizabeth bristling at Lady Catherine's attempts to engineer her life is during the scene when Lady Catherine confronts Elizabeth to determine if the rumor of her engagement to Mr. Darcy is true. She informs Elizabeth in no uncertain terms that she intends for Mr. Darcy to marry her daughter and thus he is not available to marry Elizabeth. After much impertinent banter, Elizabeth finally admits that she is not engaged to Mr. Darcy, but refuses to promise that she would turn him down if asked. Lady Catherine is certainly not used to facing such opposition, leading her at one point to exclaim, "do you know who I am?" (*PP*, 425). She further explains, "You are to understand, Miss Bennet, that I came here with the determined resolution of carrying my purpose; nor will I be dissuaded from it. I have not been used to submit to any person's whims. I have not been in the habit of brooking disappointment." This imagined man of system is used to getting her way, but ultimately after a period of estrangement, she must accept that she cannot control the lives of Elizabeth and Mr. Darcy.

LADY RUSSELL AS MAN OF SYSTEM IN *PERSUASION*

At first glance it may appear that Lady Russell of *Persuasion* is another example of Austen critiquing the man of system. After all, the book's title refers to Lady Russell persuading Anne Elliot to break up with her true love! We contend, however, that Lady Russell is closer in nature to Smith's description of a benevolent leader who is motivated by concern for others rather than a man of system consumed with arrogance.

The novel begins with Lady Russell being instrumental in convincing Sir Walter and his daughters to downsize in order to pay off his debts. Unlike the man of system, her motivation is to save the family's good name while also sparing Sir Walter's pride. She steers them toward Bath, a place that she enjoys to be sure, and she handles the arrangements for securing a residence there, but one of her goals in choosing Bath is to help Anne widen her social circle. Lady Russell is described as being "a benevolent, charitable, good woman, and capable of strong attachments, most correct in her conduct, strict in her notions of decorum, and with manners that were held a standard of good-breeding" (*P*, 1150).

While Lady Russell "had scarcely any influence with Elizabeth" (*P*, 1152), she has undue influence over Anne and has served as her mother figure since Lady Elliot's untimely death. We learn that when Anne became attached to Captain Wentworth at nineteen years of age, Anne is influenced by Lady Russell's perception that the captain was not worthy of the attention of someone of Anne Elliot's stature. Such a match,

> would be, indeed, a throwing away, which [Lady Russell] grieved to think of! Anne Elliot, so young; known to so few, to be snatched off by a stranger without alliance or fortune; or rather sunk by him into a state of most wearing, anxious, youth-killing dependence! It must not be, if by any fair interference of friendship, any representations from one who had almost a mother's love, and mother's rights, it would be prevented. (*P*, 1158)

Anne was convinced by Lady Russell's motherly guidance, on which she had always relied, and she broke things off with Captain Wentworth.

As Anne ages, the amount of influence that Lady Russell has over her begins to fade. At age twenty-two Anne turns down a proposal from Charles Musgrove, who later marries Anne's sister Mary. Lady Russell is disappointed in Anne's refusal, but does not push the matter even though Lady Russell would have been pleased to have Anne settled nearby. Lady Russell continues to show that she does not have man-of-system conceit at the end of the novel when Anne and Captain Wentworth are married at last. Reflecting on her earlier perception of the captain, Lady Russell has "to admit that she had been pretty completely wrong, and to take up a new set of opinions and of hopes" (*P*, 1288). Furthermore, Lady Russell "loved Anne better than she loved her own abilities" (*P*, 1289), hardly the sentiments of a man of system.

EMMA'S ENLIGHTENMENT
THROUGH HER IMPARTIAL SPECTATOR

In the character Emma, we discover that the road to virtue involves shedding oneself of man-of-system arrogance. How does she learn that planning for others is wrong? Through the feedback mechanisms of approbation and disapprobation of her friends, especially Mr. Knightley.

Mr. Knightley is known for implementing disinterested justice as evidenced by his position as a magistrate for the local area. In the relationship between Mr. Knightley and Emma we see the development of Emma's moral conscience as she imagines what Mr. Knightley would think of her behavior (see Michie, 2000, and Knox-Shaw, 2004). "Mr. Knightley, in fact, was one of the few people who could see faults in Emma Woodhouse, and the only one who ever told her of them" (*E*, 726). When Mr. Knightley reproaches Emma for encouraging her protégé Harriet Smith to refuse an offer of marriage from the farmer, Mr. Robert Martin, Emma tries to believe that what she has done is right. But she cannot shake the feeling that maybe Mr. Knightley is correct because "she had a sort of habitual respect for his judgment in general, which made her dislike having it so loudly against her" (*E*, 758). Mr. Knightley also admonishes Emma after her embarrassment of Miss Bates at Box Hill, and it is his approbation that Emma is pleased to receive when he hears that she has been to visit the Bateses the next day to make amends. When Emma reaches out and tries to befriend an upset Jane Fairfax, Emma thinks to herself "that could Mr. Knightley have been privy to all her attempts of assisting Jane Fairfax, could he even have seen into her heart, he would not, on this occasion, have found any thing to reprove" (*E*, 947). Finally, Emma and Mr. Knightley both discuss his influence over her near the end of the novel as they reminisce about her childhood after Mrs. Weston gives birth to a daughter. As to the importance of his guidance Emma declares, "I doubt whether my own sense would have corrected me without it" (*E*, 989). Emma's moral development is thus traced throughout the novel under the approbation (imagined or real) of Mr. Knightley.

The feedback mechanisms of approbation and disapprobation are a key component of Adam Smith's description of how we become moral. Smith's moral philosophy centers on the idea that humans have a social nature and want to be positively viewed by others. "The all-wise Author of Nature has, in this manner, taught man to respect the sentiments and judgments of his brethren; to be more or less pleased when they approve of his conduct, and to be more or less hurt when they disapprove of it" (*TMS*, 128–130). In addition to desiring favorable approval of others, we want to favorably view ourselves. Through interactions with others, we develop a moral conscience that Smith refers to as an impartial spectator that guides our behavior. This conscience is ever present in man who "has never dared to forget for one moment the judgment which the impartial spectator would pass upon his sentiments and conduct" (*TMS*, 146–147).

Recall from chapter 2 that Smith's impartial spectator is "a hero of the Enlightenment" (Broadie, 2001, 101). Remember, the Enlightenment involved people thinking for themselves instead of deferring to political and

religious authorities to think for them. Without the direction of these authorities, what would prevent the self-interested nature of man from devolving
into opportunism? How would a free society avoid collapsing into chaos?
The answer Smith provides begins with our "fellow-feeling" (*TMS*, 10) or
sympathy for others. To sympathize, we must observe (spectate) and imagine
how a similar circumstance would make us feel. From this perspective we are
able to discern between the deserved and the undeserved, or the just and the
unjust. As Evensky (2005, 114) explains, "our sympathy is the standard by
which we assess the propriety or impropriety of others' sentiments. And as
we assess others, so, too, they assess us." We express approval (Smith and
Austen call this *approbation*) for behaviors we approve and disapproval
(*disapprobation*) for behaviors we do not, thus we each provide feedback to
each other about the boundaries of acceptable conduct. This feedback of
approbation and disapprobation helps each of us develop our own internal
impartial spectator, just as Emma does with Mr. Knightley. The guidance of
impartial spectator, then, helps us to improve as moral beings and creates
social order out of the chaos of our passions. According to Montes (2004,
108), "Given that the supposed impartial spectator is the judge of self-
command, Smith is granting self-sufficiency to the individual."

Otteson (2002) characterizes this moral feedback mechanism as similar to
the interplay of market supply and demand where self-interested buyers and
sellers end up inadvertently making each other better off. Furthermore, market order in the form of an equilibrium price results from the self-interested
behavior. In this way a market participant "intends only his own gain, and he
is in this, as in many other cases, led by an invisible hand to promote an end
which was no part of his intention" (*WN*, 456). Likewise, the promotion of
human happiness is an unintended consequence of our attempts to live morally. God created mankind with the intent of making us happy, according to
Smith. When we live morally, "we necessarily pursue the most effectual
means for promoting the happiness of mankind" (*TMS*, 166). Otteson (2002,
6) interprets Smith's main thesis as "that an unintended, or spontaneous,
order emerges from people acting on our two basic drives" namely, the drive
to make ourselves better off (the focus of *Wealth of Nations*) and the desire
for mutual sympathy (the focus of *Theory of Moral Sentiments*).

The impartial spectator provides order in our moral world and the invisible hand provides order in our economic world. With our impartial spectator
as our guide, we are able to practice the virtue of justice (Broadie 2001, 101).
Remember that according to Smith, justice is the "main pillar" of society,
and without justice society would "in a moment crumble into atoms" (*TMS*,
86). The impartial application of justice is what allows a society to move
from the authoritarian pre-Enlightenment rule of man to an Enlightened rule
of law. The impartial spectator is not perfect, however, and Smith describes
how difficult it is for us to move beyond our biases and self-deceptions. Even

Mr. Knightley, our favorite Austen impartial spectator, has trouble overcoming his prejudice against Frank Churchill.

IMPARTIAL SPECTATORS IN *SENSE AND SENSIBILITY, NORTHANGER ABBEY* AND *MANSFIELD PARK*

While Smith's impartial spectator and hero of the Enlightenment is best personified in the character of Mr. Knightley in *Emma*, smaller references to impartial spectators are also found in some of Austen's other novels. In *Sense and Sensibility*, despite Elinor's attempt to teach Marianne the importance of self-command, Marianne seems oblivious to the concept of an impartial spectator. "But to appear happy when I am so miserable—Oh! Who can require it?" (*SS*, 113). When Lucy Steele asks for Elinor's advice about ending her engagement to Edward, she insists that "'Tis because you are an indifferent person . . . that your judgment might justly have such weight with me. If you could be supposed to be biased in any respect by your own feelings, your opinion would not be worth having" (*SS*, 91). Lucy, of course, is actually being disingenuous here because she knows that Elinor is anything but impartial when it comes to Edward.

The important role of the impartial spectator is discussed by Henry Tilney in *Northanger Abbey* (Knox-Shaw, 2004, 111). Henry admonishes Catherine for imagining that his father, General Tilney, is a murderer. He tells her that such behavior would not be possible in their society, telling her to "[r]emember the country and the age in which we live. Remember that we are English, that we are Christians" (*NA*, 1111). Furthermore, he insists that even if such deeds had been done, they certainly would not go unnoticed. "Could they be perpetrated without being known, in a country like this, where social and literary intercourse is on such a footing, where every man is surrounded by a neighbourhood of voluntary spies, and where roads and newspapers lay everything open?" (*NA*, 1111). In other words, our passions are tempered by the recognition that others are judging our behavior.

Henry Crawford in *Mansfield Park* entreats Fanny Price to become his impartial spectator when he tries to woo her. He asks her to judge whether or not he should leave town to take care of some business. Of course he is really just trying to find out if she would miss him while he is gone. In response Fanny exclaims: "I advise! You know very well what is right." Henry responds: "Yes. When you give me your opinion, I always know what is right. Your judgment is my rule of right" (*MP*, 684). To which Fanny makes a very Smithian response: "Oh, no! do not say so. We have all a better guide in ourselves, if we would attend to it, than any other person can be" (*MP*, 684). Here Fanny is echoing Smith who states that "Every man is, no doubt, by nature, first and principally recommended to his own care; and as he is fitter to take care of himself than of any other person, it is fit and right that it should be so" (*TMS*, 82). Henry should consult his own conscience, or if you like his own impartial spectator. Of course, Henry Crawford's impartial spectator is in its infancy, yet he appears to be trying to attain a level of rectitude that will attract Fanny, whose own rectitude he seems to genuinely admire and cherish. Part of Henry's downfall has to do with the fact that he has not learned to develop, listen to, or obey his impartial spectator.

Likewise, Edmund Bertram seems to view his cousin Fanny as his impartial spectator according to Knox-Shaw (2004, 187). When Edmund finally gives in to his siblings' demands that they put on a play, he first seeks Fanny's opinion and twice asks for her approbation for his change of heart. "If you are against me, I ought to distrust myself," he tells her (*NA*, 537). As soon as Edmund deludes himself into thinking he sees a small sign that maybe Fanny agrees with him about putting on the play, he goes on his way. But as Valihora (2007) explains, Fanny is not impartial when it comes to her love for Edmund.

The impartial spectator helps us develop our moral character through feedback from others about our behavior. This is not to say that other people direct our behavior; rather we modify our behavior in order to please others. This feedback mechanism helps social order to emerge without explicit direction by some authority. Some of Austen's characters, however, attempt to explicitly create a human order of their liking and these characters are the personification of what Smith refers to as a man of system. The danger of attempting to plan others' lives is exposed by both Adam Smith and Jane Austen. Not only is it impossible to plan for others with any accuracy, it is also unjust to deprive others of their right to choose for themselves.

By including devastatingly critical depictions of characters who attempt to plan the lives of others, Jane Austen provides rich and illuminating examples of Adam Smith's warning about men of system, especially in Emma. In Mrs. Norris and Lady Catherine, we also see the folly of presuming to know better what is right for others and how attempts to rule others leads to defeat. And in Lady Russell we acknowledge the possibility that even the plans of a benevolent leader can turn out to be wrong. That we ought to be humble about the ability to plan for others is a major theme of the Enlightenment and has its roots in Classical thought. As Smith points out, the men of system "hold in contempt the divine maxim of Plato [against the use of violence by leaders], and consider the state as made for themselves, not themselves for the state" (*TMS*, 234).

NOTE

1. Kiesling (2014) makes a similar point.

III

Economic Life in Smith's and Austen's Times

Chapter Ten

Land Rents, Income, and Entails

What do these people do? This is a question readers of Jane Austen might ask. There are no major protagonists or characters that do much of anything to obtain their incomes. Yet there are continual references to both the annual incomes and capital sums. Like Boston Unitarian ladies who don't buy hats but have hats, these people seem to have money but don't do anything to earn it.

The families of Jane Austen's world were members of the class of people in England who lived off the rent from the land they owned. Some are aristocrats with formal titles either acquired or inherited. Others are land owning but untitled members of the "gentry." Yet others have made money through trade and have acquired land. (See chapter 12 for more details of the workings of the British class system.) More often than not they pay agents to manage their lands and financial affairs.

A few characters direct some attention to ensure their assets earn reasonable returns. In *Mansfield Park* Sir Thomas leaves his English estate and spends a year or so making his Antigua properties more profitable. He takes his eldest son and putative heir Tom on the trip to keep him out of trouble in England and presumably to train him in the management of family affairs. In the same novel Henry Crawford begins to show interest in managing his estate in Norfolk although the lures of London trump this newly found interest. In *Pride and Prejudice* Elizabeth must walk to visit her sister Jane at Netherfield because the horses at the Bennet estate are engaged in harvesting work. The commercial business of the estates occasionally interferes with the real business of the characters: their social and romantic interests.

A second source of income was interest from government bonds. Then as now, governments found borrowing to be a useful and an often-preferred source of revenue. Then as now, the state's power to tax ensured both the principal and interest from government bonds were among the most secure financial asset available. To the best of our reading there is no detailed reference to anyone arranging or managing a portfolio of government securities, although Lady Russell's budget for Sir Walter in *Persuasion* undoubtedly included such calculations. Again enterprise and money are in the background. Although the yield on government bonds could vary, a standard estimate is that they generate an annual income of 4 percent per year, and we will use this estimate for illustrative purposes for the rest of the chapter. [1]

While financial details are in the background, money, wealth, and annual income are of obsessive interest to everybody. In *Pride and Prejudice* Fitzwilliam Darcy is known to have income of ten thousand pounds a year. His friend Bingley has inherited a fortune of a hundred thousand pounds from his late father and will live on four thousand pounds a year. Darcy's sister will take thirty thousand pounds into her marriage. The Bennets live on two thousand pounds a year. In *Sense and Sensibility* the Dashwood sisters will each bring two thousand pounds into their marriages, while at Barton Cottage they live with their mother on five hundred pounds a year (figures from *Jane Austen's World*, 2008). But what do these sums really mean?

SOME BASIC TERMS AND FACTS

The English unit of account then as now is the pound sterling. Large sums such as the value of estates or annual income are denominated in pounds. For example, in *Persuasion*, William Elliot, who will inherit the Elliot baronetcy from his uncle Sir Walter, is quoted as saying "if baronetcies were saleable, anybody should have (mine) for fifty pounds, arms and motto, name and livery included . . . " (*P*, 1260).

Since 1967 the British pound has been subdivided into a hundred pence. Not so in Austen's time, when the pound was subdivided into twenty shillings (Pool, 1993, 20). Mr. Tilney tells Mrs. Allen in *Northanger Abbey*, "I gave but five shillings a yard for it, and a true Indian muslin" (*NA*, 1014). He could have also said "a crown," which was five shillings or a quarter of a pound. Another British monetary unit was the guinea that consisted of a pound plus a shilling. Although there was never an actual guinea coin or note it was a commonly used measure of value. Aunt Norris tells young Tom Bertram that when gambling with Dr. Grant, "though *we* play but half-crowns, you know, you may bet half-guineas with *him*" (*MP*, 517). A half crown would be two and a half shillings and a half guinea was ten and a half shillings.

Shillings are further subdivided into pence; there are twelve pence per shilling. Emma is not very fond of spending time with the spinster Miss Bates, but she does credit her with generosity as she indicated that if Miss

Bates "had only a shilling in the world, she would be very likely to give away sixpence of it" (*E*, 771).

Finally the pence or penny is divided into farthings, with four farthings per pence. Mr. Bennet of *Pride and Prejudice* indicates that he thinks little of his daughter Lydia when he exclaims that "Wickham's a fool, if he takes her with a farthing less than ten thousand pounds" (*PP*, 396). Recall it is his brother-in-law Mr. Gardiner who it appears is "buying out" Wickham to marry Lydia (*PP*, 396).

Another simple fact that everyone seems to know in Jane Austen's world is that capital sums yield an annual interest payment of 4 percent. So Elizabeth Bennet's inheritance of a thousand pounds in *Pride and Prejudice* would yield an annual income of forty pounds (*Jane Austen's World*, 2008).

THE INCOMES OF AUSTEN CHARACTERS AND THE NOT SO RICH AND FAMOUS

The annual income figures for the five Austen characters mentioned above in nominal terms pound sterling terms are reported in table 10.1, columns 2 and 3, below. The first simple comparison is to consider the annual incomes of our characters relative to one another. Each of the Bennet girls were to inherit one thousand pounds upon the death of their mother. If Elizabeth Bennet were to live on the interest of her inheritance of one thousand pounds or 40 pounds a year, how would she fare compared to others? Table 10.1, column 1, gives the ratio of the other characters' income to Elizabeth's.

We note that the Bennet household lived on *50 times* the amount an unmarried Elizabeth would live on if on her own. To be in a similar situation a forty-something female living on $40,000 a year today would have grown up in a household with an annual income of around $2 million. It is no wonder Mrs. Bennet is so frantic about her situation should her husband die. Mr. Collins will inherit the Bennet estate upon Mr. Bennet's passing. Mrs. Bennet will have only five thousand pounds of which each of the girls will receive one thousand after her death. Their income would be only two hundred pounds or a mere 10 percent of their former income. It would be like a household of seven with an annual income of $200,000 being reduced by one member and the remaining members' income cut to $20,000. It would not be a pretty sight. We can appreciate why mothers and daughters in Austen's novels often lived together for extended periods of time after the death of a father.

It is also easy to see Mr. Darcy's assumption of Elizabeth's inferior status from column 1 in table 10.1. His annual income is 250 times the additional income Elizabeth might bring to their union; any love for her cannot be for her money. From her perspective his income is 250 times what she could

Table 10.1.   Income Comparison of Jane Austen Characters

(1) Income as Factor of Elizabeth Bennet's	(2) Austen Characters	(3) Nominal Pound Sterling Annual Income in Novel	(4) Inflation Adjusted into 2015 Pound Sterling	(5) Adjusted into 2015 U.S. Dollars at PPP
250	Fitzwilliam Darcy	10,000£	785,000£	$1,138,250
100	Mr. Bingley	4,000£	314,000£	$455,300
50	Bennet Family of Seven	2,000£	157,000£	$227,650
12.5	Dashwood Sisters and Mother at Barton Cottage	500£	39,250£	$56,913
1	Elizabeth Bennet living on her own	40£	3,140£	$4,553

Sources: Character incomes from *Jane Austen World* (2008); adjustment into current pounds from U.K. Office for National Statistics (2015) and O'Donoghue, Goulding, and Allen (2004); adjustment into U.S. dollars from (OECD 2014) and authors' calculations.

expect to live on if she were single and her mother was dead. Elizabeth may be proud, but she is no gold-digger.

Columns 4 and 5 in table 10.1 report our characters' incomes in inflation adjusted U.K. pounds and U.S. dollars for 2015 given appropriate conversions.[2] Our first calculation uses an average U.K. price level between 1795 and 1815. While this gives us some contemporary notion of how our characters lived, there are all kinds of reasons to suspect these calculations are less than perfect. First, and foremost can we even imagine the lifestyles of 200 years ago? How can we compare candles to lightbulbs, horse-drawn carriages to automobiles, or the medicine and hospitals of the 1810s to medical care in the second decade of the twenty-first century? Second, we do not utilize servants as our forebears did two centuries ago. (Or alternatively, few of us are servants as our forebears were!) The capital good of a dishwasher substitutes for a washwoman in the kitchen. We do not engage in self-provision today in a manner common in Austen's time. This is especially important for those with seemingly low incomes of two centuries ago who obtained a good portion of their food from their own land and gardens, an implicit form of income not counted in money income calculations.

Nevertheless the figures provide readers with some notion of the economic means available to Austen's characters. At the very top we see that Mr. Darcy does have an income that would make him proud. A young bachelor with over $1 million a year in income is doing very well. Of course, we must recall that his estate is extensive, and the description of his manse and grounds implies much of this must be allocated to its upkeep. But he is doing well.

Then comes Darcy's friend Mr. Bingley who lives on a comfortable $455,300. The capital value of his fortune is around $10 million, implying there are few country estates outside his reach. We can see why Austen says "a single man in possession of a good fortune, must be in want of a wife" (*PP*, 225). As long as Mr. Bennet stays alive, he, his wife, and five daughters can live comfortably on the $227,650 of income they have at their disposal. By most standards they are quite comfortable but certainly are not super-rich.

Turning to *Sense and Sensibility*, we can see Elinor's plea for economy at Barton Cottage; 500 pounds or around $57,000 can slip away rather quickly if a budget is not made and adhered to. Elinor is very prudent when she insists that Marianne cannot have the horse that Willoughby offers. It would be like a young man gifting your younger sister with an exotic sports car. Not only is the gift too generous for propriety, its maintenance and insurance are likely too expensive for a middle-class household on a tight budget.

Finally, and perhaps most surprisingly, at 40 pounds a year one would be living on the equivalent of just over $4,500 a year in today's dollars. From this we get a picture of absolute poverty, at least to contemporary middle-class folk in the United States. Today such an income might support a very modest room in a very small town likely shared with another, such as a sister or other female relative with similar income. The ladies will eat very simple food, buy no new clothes, have neither hobbies nor entertainments beyond church socials, and no health insurance or means of transportation beyond walking. The donation of a quarter-hind of cured pork would be a welcome addition as would a ride to an outing with friends. Sounds like the Mrs. and Miss Bates in *Emma*, and could reflect the life of a very poor household today, so poor as to be extremely rare in this day and age.

Yet this leads to another point. How were those outside the immediate circle of Jane Austen's world doing? The answer is much more like the Bateses than Mr. Darcy. Using Williamson (1985) data we report in table 10.2 the estimated nominal income for a number of occupations in 1810 and estimates of their 2015 dollar equivalents.[3] As the U.K. index indicated that prices were rather high in 1810, our estimates of 2015 equivalent pounds will be a bit lower than in the previous estimates.

Note that no occupation attains the $50,000 a year status of the relatively impoverished Dashwood sisters and their mother at Barton Cottage in *Sense and Sensibility*. Of course, we should recall that home production, limited mobility, and other factors make direct comparisons to our lifestyle less than perfect; but one is left with the overwhelming impression that our forebears two centuries ago had much lower living standards than we enjoy today. Another clear implication is that those in Austen's world who were enjoying what seem to us today to be rather large incomes were living *very* large in their time. Darcy was an extraordinarily wealthy man for his time.

The structure of income among the occupations is of interest. Farm laborers and common laborers earn just over 40 pounds a year or just over $4,000 in current dollars using an 1810 U.K. price index. One rung up but with only marginally higher incomes are schoolmasters with $4,879 per annum. The Steele sisters have no income (or tact or education) although their uncle runs a school. Given his pay grade it is hardly surprising that the girls remain uneducated. Those with skills in shipbuilding earn a bit more, around $5,275 per annum, while messengers and porters made $7,258. Then, as now, skills conducive to effectively and reliably communicating information earned a premium.

Then, as now, those in the professions earn multiples of common and semi-skilled labor although the structure of professional pay is somewhat different. Ministers did well in Austen's day, earning $27,107 per annum, above clerks at $17,006 and surgeons and doctors at $20,777. The incomes of the men of the cloth are only surpassed by those of the legal professions that earned an average of $42,728.

Table 10.2.   Income in Merry Old England in 1810 by Occupation

(1) Occupation	(2) Nominal Annual Income in Pounds in 1810	(3) Conversion Into U.S. Dollars in 2015
Farm Laborers	42.04	$4,014
Non-farm Common Laborers	43.94	$4,196
Schoolmasters	51.10	$4,879
Shipbuilding trades	55.25	$5,275
Messengers and Porters	76.01	$7,258
Clerks	178.11	$17,006
Surgeons and Doctors	217.60	$20,777
Clergy	283.89	$27,107
Solicitors and Barristers	447.50	$42,728

Sources: Williamson (1985, 12, table 2.4); and authors' calculations. Uses 1810 price level from O'Donoghue, Goulding, and Allen (2004).

Austen scholar Edward Copeland (Copeland, 1997, 135–137) supplements this picture by his pithy observations as to the annual income necessary to be considered "genteel." At *one hundred* pounds we are looking at "poor curates, clerks in government offices (both only marginally genteel). . . . It could supply a family only with a young maid servant, and at a very low wage." At *two hundred* pounds a household can make "claim to gentility but only with the narrowest style of life." At *three hundred pounds* a year a man is, to paraphrase Colonel Brandon in *Sense and Sensibility* "'Comfortable as a bachelor' but 'it cannot allow him to marry.'" Copeland (1997) also explains the income of the dysfunctional Price household in *Mansfield Park*. At *four hundred* pounds a year, one "approaches the comforts of a genteel life." Unfortunately, Mrs. Price was not as good at managing the household's finances as her sister, Mrs. Norris. At *five hundred* pounds a year this "according to domestic economists (of the time) fills the cup of human happiness. Jane Austen is not so confident." This is the income that the Dashwood women would have had, and similar to the one that Austen and her sisters had to live on after her father's death. At *seven hundred to one thousand* pounds per year, "this higher range of upper professional incomes marks the most prosperous pseudo-gentry families." At *two thousand* pounds per year, one "must hold a tight rein" in a large household with a poor home economist, think Mrs. Bennet in *Pride and Prejudice*, but "everything one could wish for" with Colonel Brandon in *Sense and Sensibility*. At *four thousand* pounds one can "leave behind the cheese-paring" and "enter the realm of unlimited genteel comforts."

How many households in England lived in the styles described above? G. E. Mingy made an estimate of the number of landowning families in various income ranges for the year 1790 (John, 1989). He estimates that 85 to 95 percent of the cultivated land in England is owned by these households.

The price level just less than doubled between 1785–1790 and 1810–1815.[4] It should also be noted that the population rose in England from 7.7 million in 1791 to just under 10 million in 1811 and we presume real income levels were rising. We adjust Mingy's income brackets by a factor of two and speculate that the number of households in those brackets increased by 25 percent to yield an estimate of the number of households in various income levels in 1815 shown in table 10.3.

Even with these generous adjustments and even noting these incomes are of the rural aristocracy and gentry, it is apparent that the number of truly wealthy English households makes a very small circle in a nation of 10 million. If there were at maximum 6,500 households with annual incomes above 2,000 pounds a year and ten residents per household, less than 1 percent of English residents lived in such a manner. Even at the lower ranges of rural gentility (under 2,000 pounds a year) and using the very liberal estimate of 25,000 households, it is difficult to imagine that much more than

Table 10.3.   Number of Landholding Households and Income Brackets

Types of Landholding Household	Number of households	Income Ranges	Austen Example
Great Landlords	500	10,000£ and up	Lady Catherine de Bourgh
Gentry-Wealthy Squires	875–1,000	6,000–10,000£	Fitzwilliam Darcy
Gentry- Squires	3,750–5,000	2,000–6,000£	Mr. Bingham
Gentry-Gentlemen	12,500–25,000	600–2,000£	Mr. and Mrs. Edward Ferras
Freeholders-Better Sort	32,500	300–1,400£	Robert Martin
Freeholders-Lesser Sort	100,000	60–600£	?

Sources: John (1989, 1110, table V.IA) and authors' calculations.

1 to 2 percent of the English population falls into this class. We note, however that the non-gentleman yeoman or freehold farmer class was much more numerous and some had incomes comparable to those in the gentry. However, like Robert Martin in *Emma* they were not part of the social circle of Austen's world. Austen was describing the elite of her time; her impoverished ladies were only impoverished in a relative sense.

THE ENTAIL

In three of the six of Austen's major novels, *Sense and Sensibility*, *Pride and Prejudice*, and *Persuasion* and in the popular television series *Downton Abbey*, a significant component of the plot is that the family estate goes to someone other than the wife or the daughters of the estate owner. If the estate owner dies, then the new owner will be able to eject the ladies from the estate. This appalling state of affairs is attributable to three related factors. First, females could not inherit landed estates *per se*, although they could inherit cash assets or income from said estates. Second, land was passed under a law of primogeniture, meaning the whole estate passed to the first-born son. Third, estates could and often were entailed. An entailed estate meant that the firstborn sons only inherited the income from the estate but could not sell or alienate the estate. What was the reason for these peculiar social institutions?

We suspect it has something to do with a quest for immortality via a family line. I cannot live forever but my family name can, and will, if I have anything to do with it. Estates were entailed to ensure they were passed on to the son and grandson *whole* so as to maintain its integrity, we presume for all time.[5] Scholar F. M. L. Thompson reflects the attitude of the owners of hereditary estates; "the owner of an estate for the time being was steward of a trust for unborn generations and temporary recipient of the fruits of his forbears' endeavours" (Thompson, 1963, 6).

Estate entailment along with primogeniture was seen as essential to maintaining a landowning aristocratic class. Because aristocratic landowners also had seats in the House of Lords, allowing heirs to split and divide estates would "leave many peerages without an estate to support their honours" (Thompson, 1963, 66). It was estimated at the time somewhere between one-half and two-thirds of all estate lands were entailed—and the practice was not confined to the large landowners but also the smaller landholding gentry (Thompson, 1963, 66–67).

Tory or Conservative interests in the nineteenth century supported the entail, while Whig and Liberal interests opposed it. Adam Smith is certainly in the liberal camp on this issue as he condemned the entail and primogeniture:

> But in the present state of Europe, when small as well as great estates derive their security from the laws of their country, nothing can be more completely absurd. They are founded upon the most absurd of all suppositions, the supposition that every successive generation of men have not an equal right to the earth, and to all that it possesses; but that the property of the present generation should be restrained and regulated according to the fancy of those who died perhaps five hundred years ago. (*WN*, 323)

In Jane Austen's world the entail is simply a reality that impacts the prospects of her characters. We suspect that she agreed with Smith's sentiments. In *Sense and Sensibility* the circumstances that left the Dashwood sisters and their mother in relative poverty was the by-product of an old man's whim, not out of an explicit wish to maintain the integrity of a family name.

The owner of the estate of Norland was an elderly single man who invited his nephew Mr. Henry Dashwood, the rightful heir to the estate, and his wife and three daughters—the main protagonists of the novel—to live with him. They live for nearly a decade with the old man and Austen tell us that, "In the society of his nephew and niece, and their children, the old Gentleman's days were comfortably spent" (*SS*, 9).

Henry Dashwood, however, has a son from his first marriage that is next in line to inherit the estate, a Mr. John Dashwood. When the old man died he left the estate to Henry but also entailed the estate so that Henry's grandson, the son of his son from his first marriage had future rights to everything. This precluded Henry from providing anything for his three daughters of his second marriage. Austen tells us:

The whole was tied up for the benefit of this child, who, in occasional visits with his father and mother at Norland, had so far gained on the affections of his uncle, by such attractions as are by no means unusual in children of two or three years old; an imperfect articulation, an earnest desire of having his own way, many cunning tricks, and a great deal of noise, as to outweigh all the value of all the attention which, for years, he had received from his niece and her daughters. He meant not to be unkind, however, and, as a mark of his affection for the three girls, he left them a thousand pounds a-piece. (*SS*, 9–10)

Henry, however, had the misfortune of dying within twelve months of his elderly uncle, precipitating the crisis and basis for the story.

In contrast to the income-constrained characters described so far, Emma Woodhouse reflects the view that a single woman never marrying is no disaster as long as she has ample income. She informs her friend Harriet that:

I shall not be a poor old maid; and it is poverty only which makes celibacy contemptible to a generous public! A single woman, with a very narrow income, must be a ridiculous, disagreeable old maid! the proper sport of boys and girls, but a single woman, of good fortune, is always respectable, and may be as sensible and pleasant as anybody else. (*E*, 770–771)

So we suspect that on this issue as most others, Jane Austen is neither a flame-throwing liberal calling for an overturn of the social order, nor an entrenched conservative who uncritically defends the existing state of affairs. Rather she is a woman of common sense and good education, and a tutor for the generations to come.

NOTES

1. We note in chapter 6 that 5 percent seems to be the rate Austen uses in *Sense and Sensibility*. The 4 percent rate, however, is referred to in other contexts.

2. The method used to calculate the figures in table 10.1 are as follows. The nominal values in pounds for the incomes of Jane Austen characters are transformed into 2015 British pounds from the mean average of 1795–1815 U.K. price index. (Sources: U.K. Office of National Statistics (2015) for 2015 U.K. price index level; O'Donoghue, Goulding, and Allen (2004) for 1795–1815 U.K. price index). We use the average of the U.K. price index over the twenty-year period from 1795 to 1815 which coincides with the time between when Jane Austen wrote her novels and when they were published. This calculation yields us a conversion factor of 78.5. In other words, 1 pound sterling in Jane Austen's novel converts to 78.5 pounds sterling in June 2015. In the twenty-year period any single year's conversion factor range from a high of 107.7 using the U.K. price index for 1798 to a low of 58.2 for 1813. One should view the dollar values as accurate plus or minus 40 percent. To convert British pound values to 2015 U.S. dollars, we use a six-year average purchasing-power parity exchange rate between the dollar and the pound for 2009–2014 from OECD Stats (2015). This calculation converts a U.K. pound sterling into $1.45 USA.

3. In this case we use the U.K price index for 1810 only. This yields a conversion factor of 65.85 2015 pounds to one 1810 pound sterling. This generates an approximate 10 percent difference in baseline calculations. Forty pounds is equated to just over $4,000, whereas it is

just over \$4,500 in table 10.1. The methodology used to calculate dollar values is the same as used in note 1.

4. The British price index was at 7.5 in 1790. Its value was 14.2 in 1814. For the years 1787–1792 its mean average was 7.45, and 13.6 for 1813–1818.

5. Unlike the Scottish entailment system that *did* bind estates in perpetuity, the English system was not so straightforward. The English entail only lasted for three generations. In theory a son could refuse to agree with his father to renew the entail for the next generation, but in practice this rarely occurred. On each generation's renewal of the entail, new provisions would be made for income for future children; future aunts and uncles; future dowagers, etc., and some of the estate property could be sold or otherwise alienated (Thompson, 1963, 64–65). Austen's heroines were typically afforded either a small settlement or were from estates with small incomes; they were not entirely or inherently left destitute by the system.

Chapter Eleven

Representations of Business in Smith and Austen

Adopting the Bourgeois Virtues

As illustrated in chapter 10, people in Austen's gentry culture don't really *do* anything to earn their keep. In general, those of the highest social standing are not engaged in a profession. As Mary Crawford of *Mansfield Park* puts it, a profession is something a man would want to "escape" by owning an estate (*MP*, 540). General Tilney in *Northanger Abbey* however, sees things differently from Miss Crawford as evidenced by his explanation of why his sons have professions.

> Perhaps it may seem odd, that with only two younger children, I should think any profession necessary for him; and certainly there are moments when we could all wish him disengaged from every tie of business. But though I may not exactly make converts of you young ladies, I am sure your father, Miss Morland, would agree with me in thinking it expedient to give every young man some employment. The money is nothing, it is not an object, but employment is the thing. Even Frederick, my eldest son, you see, who will perhaps inherit as considerable a landed property as any private man in the county, has his profession. (*NA*, 1099)

In the general's mind, then, it is not enough to live the life of a wealthy gentleman; one must be productive in order to truly flourish. The general appears to value productive work, but we see later that despite his protestations that "the money is nothing," he actually does place a high value on money when he banishes Catherine Morland upon learning of her lower than expected origins. In the contrast between Mary Crawford and General

Tilney, we see Austen's recognition that the cultural attitudes toward business and the professions were changing during her lifetime—changing from disdain toward respect, a trend that would make Adam Smith very happy.

Smith explains that in pre-commercial society "[t]o trade was disgraceful to a gentleman" (*WN*, 907–908), a sentiment shared by most of Austen's characters. In commercial society, however, trade is seen as both needing and fostering virtue. Smith views people as having two basic motivations: self-interest (in *Wealth of Nations*) and fellow feeling (in *Theory of Moral Sentiments*). We interact with others in market exchanges to satisfy the first drive, but our desire for approval from others encourages us to act virtuously in our business dealings. Especially for the middle and lower classes, "the road to virtue and that to fortune, to such fortune, at least, as men in such stations can reasonably expect to acquire, are, happily in most cases, very nearly the same" (*TMS*, 63). Smith explains that moral traits like prudence and justice are the very same as those that lead to success in business. A seller who serves his customers well develops a good reputation that leads to more sales and profit. "That honesty is the best policy, holds, in such situations, almost always perfectly true" (*TMS*, 63). Furthermore, men in these classes are generally not above the law, so their dealings are within the bounds of justice by necessity. In other words, markets need morality to work and markets make us more moral at the same time.

For men of the upper classes, however, Smith maintains that traits that lead to success in royal circles do not lead to virtue. Here, success depends on how well one can cater to the whims of princes, and "[i]n many governments the candidates for the highest stations are above the law" (*TMS*, 64). In *Wealth of Nations*, Smith is very critical of the cozy relationship between politicians and merchants made possible by regulation of business. He catalogs a long list of "Inequalities occasioned by the Policy of Europe" (*WN*, 135–159) such as limits on the number of apprenticeships and the free movement of labor. He concludes that while it is true that "[p]eople of the same trade seldom meet together, even for merriment and diversion, but the conversation ends in a conspiracy against the public, or in some contrivance to raise prices" (*WN*, 145), the law should not assist merchants in their attempts to collude. "It is impossible indeed to prevent such meetings, by any law which either could be executed, or would be consistent with liberty and justice. But though the law cannot hinder people of the same trade from sometimes assembling together, it ought to do nothing to facilitate such assemblies; much less to render them necessary" (*WN*, 145). To Smith, to earn a living through commerce is virtuous as opposed to obtaining wealth through inheritance or political connections.

Smith's support of open and free trade is thus linked to virtue. To be successful in business, we must predict what others will want; in other words, we must sympathize with them. We become more familiar with people when we make market exchanges, therefore these trades encourage the development of more benevolent feelings, and as markets grow larger and larger, so does our network of familiar associations with others. Otteson (2002, 303) concludes that "[m]arkets thus create incentives to establish and maintain ever more extensive networks of producers and consumers that are founded on mutual interest in, as Smith says, 'the fortune of others.'"

This virtuous nature of trade is not shared by most of the characters in Austen's novels. Generally, earning a living through trade is looked down on in Austen's novels, but every once in a while characters involved in trade are esteemed for their contributions and talents. This tension between disdaining and admiring commerce illustrates that the culture described by Austen was just beginning to embrace what McCloskey (2006) refers to as the virtue of the bourgeoisie. Building on Smith, McCloskey explains how successful participation in markets depends on and encourages virtuous behavior on the part of the individuals involved. Zak (2012, 64) refers to this phenomenon as the "virtuous cycle" of markets. The important link between moral values and commerce in Anglo-Saxon culture had been earlier recognized by Hayek (1944) who cautioned us that a movement toward collectivism erodes those virtues.

In his *Lectures on Jurisprudence* Smith describes how little people in pre-commercial society thought of the trading professions. In these societies warriors are honorable, but merchants are suspect. "To perform any thing, or to give any thing, without a reward is always generous and noble, but to barter one thing for another is mean" (*LJ*, 527). "[E]ven in a refined society [this negative perception toward commerce] is not utterly extinguished" (*LJ*, 527). Smith goes on to explain that as commerce began to be introduced into agricultural economies, it was looked down upon so much that it was thus performed only by people of the lowest ranks. No wonder Austen's characters turn up their noses at trade! Finally, Smith concludes that one of the things holding back countries from prospering is that the horrible reputation of merchants prevents talented people from specializing in trade, and this sort of division of labor is necessary to cause the wealth of nations. For the division of labor to take place, "[e]very man thus lives by exchanging, or becomes in some measure a merchant, and the society itself grows to be what is properly a commercial society" (*WN*, 37).

McCloskey (2010) builds on Smith's conclusion to argue that economists' traditional growth theories (which are based solely upon trade and investment) miss the importance of changes in attitudes toward business. Specifically she traces the explosion of growth in the late 1800s and the growth in China and India today to the adoption of Enlightenment values by the middle class. Only once trade and business professions are seen as dignified, can high levels of economic growth occur.

In Austen's work, we see the evolution of these attitudes. Initially, the choice of professions from which a country gentleman may choose is limited to a very short list of acceptable lines of work. The most common professions referred to for gentlemen in Austen's novels are that of clergyman and military officer. Twelve clergymen appear in Austen's novels: Edward Ferrars and Dr. Davies in *Sense and Sensibility*, Mr. Collins in *Pride and Prejudice*, Edmund Bertram, Mr. Norris and Dr. Grant in *Mansfield Park*, Mr. Elton in *Emma*, Henry Tilney and Mr. Morland in *Northanger Abbey*, and Charles Hayter, Dr. Shirley, and Mr. Wentworth in *Persuasion* (Collins, 1998, 46). The clergy is often seen as a good option for sons who are not lucky enough to be the first born male who would, due to the laws of primogeniture, inherit the family estate. These positions provide a fairly good living (see chapter 10) and do not necessarily require much in the way of religiosity.

Military officers are also generally held in high regard as Mary Crawford maintains in *Mansfield Park* that "[s]oldiers and sailors are always acceptable in society" (*MP*, 511). Acceptable, that is, as long as they are of a high enough military rank, such as admiral, colonel, or captain. Even so, it takes some time for Sir Walter of *Persuasion*, to come around to the idea of renting his estate to an admiral. He is at first offended by the idea stating that the sailing profession is "the means of bringing persons of obscure birth into undue distinction, and raising men to honours which their fathers and grandfathers never dreamt of" (*P*, 1154). Lower ranked military men are not held in high esteem as represented by Fanny Price's father who has coarse manners and is "dirty and gross" (*MP*, 670) despite being a "Lieutenant of Marines" (*MP*, 449). Officers must also earn their fortunes at sea in order to be considered desirable for a marriage, as Captain Wentworth of *Persuasion* discovers when he is deemed not good enough for Anne Elliot by Lady Russell. Lady Russell also disapproves of Wentworth for his optimistic confidence and headstrong nature. Knox-Shaw (2004) maintains that these qualities are ones of a self-made man, and that in her persuasion of Anne, Lady Russell is revealing a prejudice against self-made men of the Enlightenment and a bias in favor of inherited wealth. Lady Russell views Wentworth as "a young man, who had nothing but himself to recommend him, and no hopes of attaining affluence, but in the chances of a most uncertain profession, and no connexions to secure even his farther rise in the profession" (*P*, 1158). Clearly, in Lady Russell's mind, who you know is more important than what you know.

Lawyers and doctors are other acceptable professions that are depicted in Austen's novels, albeit for non-major characters. For women, the list of acceptable professions is limited to that of governess, as Jane Fairfax in *Emma* almost becomes. Excluded from the list of respected professions is anything related to trade which is seen as "low."

For example, in *Persuasion*, Sir Walter Elliot cringes at the very thought of the word *advertise* when discussing the possibility of renting his estate in order to move into more affordable quarters. Marianne Dashwood of *Sense and Sensibility* (*SS*, 29) views "commercial exchange" as a zero sum situation, "in which each wished to be benefited at the expense of the other." Success in business does not elevate one's status. For example, while Mrs. Jennings's husband "had traded with success in a less elegant part of the town" (*SS*, 92), he is perceived as "a man who had got all his money in a low way" (*SS*, 135).

The low status of businessmen is also evident in *Pride and Prejudice*. Yes, the Bingleys are described as a respectable family, but that description is qualified by the recognition that they had earlier made their fortune "by trade" (*PP*, 232). Sir William Lucas had also made "a tolerable fortune" in trade, but once he obtains his knighthood he thinks of business with "disgust" (*PP*, 233). He quickly moves his family away from the bustling village to the newly designated Lucas Lodge "where he could think with pleasure of his own importance, and unshackled by business, occupy himself solely in being civil to all the world" (*PP*, 233).

In Austen's work, we start to see the emergence of respect for business with the case of Mr. Gardiner, Mrs. Bennet's brother in *Pride and Prejudice*. When we are first introduced to him, he is still actively involved in business, unlike the Bingleys and Sir William who forsake trade once they are landed. Nonetheless, Mr. Gardiner is described as "a sensible, gentlemanlike man, greatly superior to his sister as well by nature as education" (*PP*, 304). It is noted that the Bingley sisters "would have had difficulty in believing that a man who lived by trade, and within view of his own warehouses, could have been so well-bred and agreeable" (*PP*, 304). Carnell (2009) points out that Mr. Gardiner is gentlemanly enough for Mr. Darcy to accept as gentry and as a friend. When the two meet during a tour of Mr. Darcy's estate, Elizabeth is pleased to notice Mr. Darcy "should know she had some relations for whom there was no need to blush" (*PP*, 367). Lady Catherine, however, remains unimpressed. She deems the Gardiner's "condition" enough to make impossible any engagement of her nephew and Elizabeth Bennet. Even though Elizabeth is "a gentleman's daughter" (*PP*, 426), her mother's familial link to trade is simply unacceptable.

Sir Thomas stands out in *Mansfield Park* as straddling both the old and new attitudes about trade. He is a baron and a member of Parliament and, thus, an exemplar of the old order, but he is also a successful businessman with interests at home and in Antigua. The other characters in *Mansfield Park*, however, generally view businessmen and tradespeople with suspicion. Mrs. Grant describes the typical tradesman as remote and unpunctual, charging exorbitant prices, and committing fraud (*MP*, 569). The mere motives of businessmen are suspect as well. In a discussion of Mr. Rushworth's embarking upon some improvements to his grounds, Miss Bertram expresses the opinion that "it was infinitely better to consult with friends and disinterested advisers, than immediately to throw the business into the hands of a professional man" (*MP*, 483). Clearly, the impression is that businessmen would only be out for profit, while people you know would care about your needs.

The changing attitudes and rhetoric about trade is woven throughout the novel *Emma*. Emma is disdainful of business describing the Eltons as "nobody" (*E*, 800) because Mr. Elton had to "make his way as he could, without any alliances but in trade" (*E*, 800). Emma also looks down on Mrs. Elton's commercial roots. Her father is described as "a Bristol—merchant, of course, he must be called" (*E*, 825). Here, though, the disdain that Austen shows for the business of Mrs. Elton's family is well deserved. Bristol was known as a port active in the slave trade, and the hesitation inserted before the word *merchant* likely indicates that Mrs. Elton comes from slavers (Byrne, 2013, 221).

The Cole family presents an interesting case about the changing attitudes toward legitimate trade. They are described as "very good sort of people, friendly, liberal, and unpretending; but, on the other hand, they were of low origin, in trade, and only moderately genteel" (*E*, 839). Even though the Cole's business success resulted in their being "in fortune and style of living, second only to the [Woodhouse] family at Hartfield" (*E*, 839), it was clear to Emma that "it was not for them to arrange the terms on which the superior families would visit them" (*E*, 839). Because their material success was earned rather than inherited, the Coles could only rise so far in social standing. Emma hopes to highlight this distinction by refusing their invitation to dinner, but she quickly changes her tune when she learns that the Woodhouses are the *only* family in Highbury society *not* invited to the party. The Coles send along a late invitation, making the excuse that they had been waiting to procure a folding screen to shelter the frail Mr. Woodhouse from the cold before inviting them.

The tension between the disdain for and admiration of trade in *Emma* is most evidenced by the differing attitudes toward the character Mr. Robert Martin, a farmer and businessman who is smitten with Emma's friend Harriet. Harriet, at first, is interested in Mr. Martin and impressed with his business acumen and demeanor. She describes how successful he is in marketing his wool and how fond his family and friends are of him. In addition to his business acumen he is also relatively well read. He keeps up with the *Agricultural Reports*, of course, but is also familiar with literary works including the *Elegant Extracts* that Emma and her father reference later in the novel. In Emma's opinion, however, Mr. Martin is beneath the attention of Harriet and is destined to age into "a completely gross, vulgar farmer,—totally inattentive to appearances, and thinking of nothing but profit and loss" (*E,* 739). Emma's anti-business bias is further illustrated by the fact that she prefers Mr. Elton over Mr. Martin as a match for Harriet, turning a blind eye to Elton's true motive to marry well (Michie, 2000).

In contrast to Emma's disdain for Mr. Martin's livelihood, Mr. Knightley's opinion of Mr. Martin is more in line with Adam Smith's concept of the virtuous nature of trade. When Knightley learns that Emma has successfully convinced Harriet to turn down Mr. Martin's offer of marriage, he is livid and cannot believe that Emma thinks Harriet is above being "married to a respectable, intelligent gentleman-farmer" (*E*, 756). That Mr. Knightley values Mr. Martin's contribution to society is in no doubt a reflection of Knightley's own business experience. Mr. Knightley is part of the landed gentry, having inherited the estate Donwell Abbey. While he rents some of that acreage to the Martins for farming, he reserves some of his estate for a home farm that he is actively involved in running. In addition to his activities as a gentleman farmer, he is also a magistrate responsible for public order in the area (*E*, 779, 913). Indeed Mr. Knightley can be seen as a bridge that Austen is making between the old social order that placed a high value on landed wealth and a disdain for the merchant class and the newer view in which wealth creation through trade is admired.

To read Jane Austen is to immerse oneself into the English countryside culture of her day. Enlightenment thought permeates this world as Knox-Shaw (2004) so thoroughly demonstrates. Part of the Enlightenment spirit is manifested in the changing attitudes about mercantile activity from disdain to respect. Recognizing the dignity of creating value through commerce was an essential component of the success of the industrial revolution in lifting millions out of poverty, as McCloskey (2010) illustrates. Characters such as (perhaps) General Tilney of *Northanger Abbey*, Mr. Gardiner of *Pride and Prejudice*, Sir Thomas of *Mansfield Park*, and Mr. George Knightley of *Emma*, start us down the road to a *bourgeois dignity* that Adam Smith admired.

Chapter Twelve

Social Rank in Smith and Austen

The very idea that people ought to be strictly separated by class or rank in society seems old fashioned and even repugnant to modern-day readers. We are much more egalitarian today, or so we believe. But are we really that far off from the adherence to rank described by Adam Smith and Jane Austen? How many of us are truly friends with people of a much lower or much higher socioeconomic status? From our high school cliques to our college fraternities to our churches and our workplace teams, how integrated and diverse are our close associations? Social rank is emphasized in the works of both Smith and Austen, and an exploration of the role it plays can shed light on our relationships of today.

Smith's famous example of the philosopher and the street porter in *Wealth of Nations* illustrates his belief that we are all of the same basic nature, but become differentiated through nurture. "The difference between the most dissimilar characters, between a philosopher and a common street porter, for example, seems to arise not so much from nature, as from habit, custom, and education" (*WN*, 28–29). We all start off life being rather similar, but then branch off into very different paths. But just because we are all similar underneath, don't think that Smith is arguing here that rank should not matter. Rather, Smith devotes much attention in *Theory of Moral Sentiments* to the importance of rank for preserving social order. Recall that one of the challenging questions that Enlightenment thinkers had to answer is "without the leadership and direction of kings or the Church, how would we avoid chaos?" Smith turns to the ordering of society into ranks as part of the answer.

Remember that Smith's moral theory is centered around the sympathy we have for each other. Smith further maintains that "[it] is because mankind are disposed to sympathize more entirely with our joy than with our sorrow, that we make parade of our riches, and conceal our poverty" (*TMS*, 50). We develop ambition, then, because we get more approval from others for our successes than we get concern for our failures. Our vanity pushes us to try to better our condition beyond that which is needed for mere everyday survival. Just as we want others to admire our success, so too we place in high esteem others who have been successful. The emergence of ranks in society is seen by Smith as arising from this admiration of our superiors. We defer to those who we admire, and we strive to be the one that others admire and defer to, so we don't need authorities to provide social order. Knox-Shaw (2004, 204–205) asserts that the ordering of society by these emergent ranks would be more just than any order imposed by above. We agree that social ranks derived from a meritocracy would be more just than those stemming from an autocracy because rankings based on merit are earned and are voluntarily upheld.

Ironically, Smith points out that such a drive to move up the ranks of society doesn't make us any happier in the end. "[T]he mind of every man, in a longer or shorter time, returns to its natural and usual state of tranquillity. In prosperity, after a certain time, it falls back to that state; in adversity, after a certain time, it rises up to it" (*TMS*, 149). We all have a normal level of happiness, and all of our ambition to climb up the social ladder can't change that. But we keep on trying to improve our station nonetheless. We argue that just as reading Austen's novels can give us insights into the changing attitudes about business during her time, her work can also shed light on the shift from strict adherence to social class based on birth to more mobility among classes based on merit.

The social classes of Austen's world are the nobility, the gentry, the commercial class, the working class, and the poor. Of course there are several gradations within each of these classes, too. At the top of the nobility is the royal family, followed by the various other nobles and their wives and children. As McMaster (1997) points out, a title in Austen's works usually signals a character of all style and no substance, and we argue that Austen is using these characters to criticize a social class structure based on birth rights. An example in *Persuasion* is the Dowager Viscount Dalrymple (widow of the viscount) and her daughter, the Honourable Miss Carteret, both of whom Sir Walter Elliot fawns over during their visit to Bath. Anne Elliot is not lured in by their status, however. She notes that "[t]here was no superiority of manner, accomplishment, or understanding. Lady Dalrymple had acquired the name of 'a charming woman,' because she had a smile and a civil answer for everybody. Miss Carteret, with still less to say, was so plain and so awkward, that she would never have been tolerated in Camden-place but for her birth" (*P*, 1229). Similarly, the Honourable John Yates of *Mansfield Park* "had not much to recommend him beyond habits of fashion and expense" (*MP*, 517). The character most concerned about having "the distinction of rank preserved" is *Pride and Prejudice*'s the Right Honourable Lady Catherine de Bourgh (*PP*, 316).

General Tilney in *Northanger Abbey* is overly concerned about rank and titles as well. He throws poor Catherine Morland out of his house once he learns that she is not the rich heiress he thought she was. And he forbids his daughter Eleanor from marrying her unnamed love interest, only changing his mind once the young man unexpectedly becomes a viscount. "[N]ever had the General loved his daughter so well . . . as when he first hailed her, 'Your Ladyship!'" (*NA*, 1142).

There is an important difference between say, a *Lady Catherine* and a *Lady Russell*. Use of the first name, signifies a daughter of a nobleman, and is a permanent designation because it stems from birth. The use of a last name indicates that the lady is the wife of a baronet or knight, a title that disappears if she remarries (McMaster, 1997, 117). Furthermore, baronets (a hereditary title) and knights (an earned title) are not part of the nobility, but as commoners they are the top tier of the gentry class.

One of the social constructs that emerged in Jane Austen's world to enforce these fine distinctions of rank is the creation of a Master of Ceremonies at the social events in Bath, according to Collins (1998). Bath was a resort town where people of many different ranks would gather; all six of Austen's completed novels at least *mention* people spending time in Bath, and significant scenes in *Northanger Abbey* and *Persuasion* are set there. According to Collins (1998), the aristocratic visitors to Bath were offended by the behavior of the lower gentry classes who were having a larger and larger presence in Bath. The Master of Ceremonies' job, then, was to manage the introduction of people at the events so that people of lower classes would not inappropriately approach someone of a higher rank.[1] There are a couple of explicit references to Masters of Ceremonies in Austen's novels. In *Emma* Mr. Elton attends the "Master of Ceremonies' ball" while in Bath (*E*, 809), and the "master of the ceremonies" introduces Henry Tilney to Catherine Morland in *Northanger Abbey* (*NA*, 1012). More importantly, though, there is a prevalent theme that people of lower ranks should not initiate contact with those above them as will be illustrated in the discussions below.

Most of the characters in Austen's works are from the gentry class, the class in which Austen lived and had the most interaction with personally. At the top of this tier are the Baronets and the Knights who are often portrayed by Austen as being overly proud of their status. For example, *Persuasion* opens with the sight of Sir Walter Elliot immersing himself in the book of the Baronetage, poring over his lineage entry. Likewise Sir William Lucas of *Pride and Prejudice* takes on airs upon receiving his knighthood, relocating his family to the pretentious sounding Lucas Lodge.

The titled gentry are followed in status by the landed gentry, those whose land holdings provide an income, usually by renting the land out to tenant farmers. These families seem to live lives of leisure, but some of the gentlemen are actively engaged in the management of their properties, as Mr. Knightley is in *Emma*. At the lower end of the gentry are people in the professional class. Younger sons in gentry families generally had to take on some sort of profession, usually the clergy, the military, the law, or medicine. Earning a living for these sons was necessary because under the primogeniture laws of the day, only the eldest son (or other designated male heir if there was no son) would inherit the land. These laws insured that family estates would stay intact from generation to generation instead of being repeatedly divvied up among an increasing number of heirs (see chapter 10).

While the gentleman sons either had inheritances or professions, gentry daughters were expected to learn how to perform some home production, such as sewing. Collins (1998, 35) explains that these women, like Jane Austen herself, were mostly taught how to manage a household of servants. Collins (1998) refers to a scene in *Pride and Prejudice* when Mrs. Bennet is trying to impress Mr. Bingley with how well she raised her daughters, particularly Jane. To contrast her daughters with the Lucas girls, possible rivals for Bingley's affection, Mrs. Bennet cattily refers to Charlotte as having to miss dinner with them. "No, she would go home. I fancy she was wanted about the mince pies" (*PP*, 249). Her implication is clear: *her* daughters do not *make* mince pies, they *supervise* servants who do.

For daughters who did not marry or inherit a living, the only means of support would be to become a schoolteacher, like Mrs. Goddard who runs the girls' school in *Emma*, or a governess, like Miss Taylor. Poor Jane Fairfax almost has to take such a position before her engagement saves her from that plight. Despite their limited options, it can be argued that women enjoyed a greater degree of class mobility than men because they are more likely to marry up. As Edmund points out in *Mansfield Park*, "Miss Crawford may chuse her degree of wealth. She has only to fix on her number of thousands a year, and there can be no doubt of their coming" (*MP*, 569). Edmund, on the other hand, does not have that luxury since he "cannot intend any thing which it must be so completely beyond my power to command" (*MP*, 569). Willoughby of *Sense and Sensibility*, however, shows us that men, too, can aim for a certain income through marriage.

Widows could easily lose economic security as is evidenced by Mrs. Bates in *Emma*. The Bateses' place in the gentry society had been secured by Mr. Bates's position as local vicar. Since his death, Mrs. Bates and her daughter live in one floor of a house in the village owned by "people in business" (*E*, 809) and receive generous gifts of food from their richer neighbors. Their economic fall does not mean they also lose their place in society. Rather the Bateses' inclusion in Highbury society is reminiscent of Smith's commendation for those who "accommodate themselves with the greatest ease to their new situation, . . . [those who] rest their rank in the society, not upon their fortune, but upon their character and conduct, are always the most approved of, and never fail to command our highest and most affectionate admiration" (*TMS*, 144). Thus the Bateses are included in the regular guest lists for social gatherings such as those at the Woodhouse home. As McMaster (1997) points out, the relatively poor Bateses actually enjoy a higher standing in term of circulation in society than do the much richer Coles, who owe their economic success to trade.

Within the gentry class, then, there could be vast differences in the standard of living and the level of economic security, as we illustrate in chapter 10. People like Mr. Darcy of *Pride and Prejudice* live in grand estates and are related to nobility, but the Woodhouses in *Emma* with less prestigious properties are also held in highest regard. At the lower level of the gentry class (in which Jane Austen, herself, spent most of her life [Collins, 1998]) stood families like the Dashwoods of *Sense and Sensibility* and the Bennets of *Pride and Prejudice*. Some characters, like Sir Walter in *Persuasion*, take these gradations very seriously. Upon hearing Mrs. Croft's brother, a curate, described as a gentleman, he exclaims "You misled me by the term gentleman. I thought you were speaking of some man of property" (*P*, 1157). Likewise Mrs. Musgrove is dismayed at the thought of her daughter, Henrietta, becoming attached to Charles Hayter who is "[n]othing but a country curate" (*P*, 1187); however, Mr. Musgrove looks on the match favorably because Mr. Hayter is an eldest son who will one day inherit a nice piece of property. In Charles Hayter we see Jane Austen's recognition of the possibility of improving on one's rank in society by deliberate choice of self-improvement, a very Enlightenment sentiment. Even though the rest of his family was not well respected, Charles is described as one "who had chosen to be a scholar and a gentleman, and who was very superior in cultivation and manners to all the rest" (*P*, 1186).

Sir Thomas Bertram in *Mansfield Park* is initially eager to maintain the distinction of rank between his own daughters and that of his poor niece, Fanny, who will be brought up in the same household. He explains to Mrs. Norris that they will have to carefully consider

> how to preserve in the minds of my *daughters* the consciousness of what they are, without making them think too lowly of their cousin; and how, without depressing her spirits too far, to make her remember that she is not a *Miss Bertram*. I should wish to see them very good friends, and would, on no account, authorise in my girls the smallest degree of arrogance towards their relation; but still they cannot be equals. Their rank, fortune, rights, and expectations will always be different. (*MP*, 453, emphasis original)

This distinction is deeply engrained in Fanny. When she learns that she is the one who will open the ball that Sir Thomas is giving for her and her brother, "[s]he could hardly believe it. To be placed above so many elegant young women! The distinction was too great. It was treating her like her cousins!" (*MP*, 605). By the novel's end, though, Sir Thomas recognizes that it is Fanny who has the greater character compared to his daughters.

In contrast, characters like Elizabeth Bennet ignore these subtle distinctions from the start and reflect a more modern attitude toward the leveling of the classes. When Lady Catherine tries to explain to Elizabeth why Mr. Darcy is above her, Elizabeth dismisses the thought, insisting that "He is a gentleman; I am a gentleman's daughter; so far we are equal" (*PP*, 426). Nonetheless, even Elizabeth recognizes Darcy's pride when she cautions Mr. Collins against introducing himself to Mr. Darcy at a ball. Mr. Collins thinks approaching Mr. Darcy without introduction is perfectly fine since they are already connected because Darcy's aunt, Lady Catherine, is Collins's patron. "Elizabeth . . . assur[ed] him that Mr. Darcy would consider his addressing him without introduction as an impertinent freedom, rather than a compliment to his aunt; that it was not in the least necessary there should be any notice on either side, and that if it were, it must belong to Mr. Darcy, the superior in consequence, to begin the acquaintance" (*PP*, 280).

Obtaining land is a way for people in the merchant class to obtain equality with the gentry class as evidenced by Charles Bingley in *Pride and Prejudice*. Bingley had inherited a sum from his father to be used to purchase an estate so that future generations of Bingleys could be included in the gentry class. The fact that Bingley was on his way up, no doubt factored into his sister's fear of an attachment to a lower class gentry woman like Jane Bennet.

In the *Wealth of Nations* chapter entitled "How the Commerce of the Towns contributed to the Improvement of the Country," Smith is highly complementary of the fact that "[m]erchants are commonly ambitious of becoming country gentlemen, [because] when they do, they are generally the best of all improvers" (*WN*, 411). To Smith, merchants were used to seeking profit, so they would make the most efficient use of the capital and land, which helped the countryside to develop and prosper.

Mr. Weston, of *Emma*, is a prime example of a character who rises up through the ranks of society via the commercial class. He is "born of a respectable family, which for the last two or three generations had been rising into gentility and property" (*E*, 728). He joins the local militia where he falls in love with Miss Churchill of Enscombe. His rank of captain, however, does not impress Miss Churchill's closest relatives, her landed brother and sister-in-law, so the marriage leads to estrangement. After Mrs. Weston passes away, their son is adopted by his rich uncle and aunt, and Mr. Weston takes up a living in trade. His business earns him enough to finally purchase a small estate and he joins the Highbury gentry circle. He even has enough wealth "to marry a woman as portionless even as Miss Taylor" (*E*, 729).

Mr. Weston's stint in the militia did not propel him up the social ladder, and other military men in Austen's novels find themselves in the same boat.

Yes, Sir Walter Elliot comes around to the idea of renting his family estate to Admiral and Mrs. Croft, but the Crofts are never accepted as equals. Elizabeth Elliot cautions Sir Walter against introducing the Crofts to their cousin Lady Dalrymple saying, "We had better leave the Crofts to find their own level. There are several odd-looking men walking about here, who, I am told, are sailors. The Crofts will associate with them" (*P*, 1239).

Nonetheless, the military was a way for some men to improve their stations. In Austen's day, military commissions were obtained by purchasing them and by having the right connections, as happens with William Price in *Mansfield Park*. Naval officers were rewarded with prize money from captured ships, as Captain Wentworth describes in *Persuasion*. It is only after Captain Wentworth obtains rank and fortune in this way that Anne Elliot's family deems him "no longer nobody" (*P*, 1288). McMaster (1997) argues that in *Persuasion* Jane Austen is using the example of the navy to promote the idea of a new meritocracy that ought to replace an outdated and unjust system of social rank based on inheritance. Austen "demotes the landed gentry and replaces them with the navy" (McMaster 1997, 121) when she has Admiral Croft take over as the head of the Elliot family home, Kellynch Hall, and when she has Anne Elliot choose Captain Wentworth over the heir to the Elliot estate.

Beneath the gentry class, which again, ranges from the landed and titled to the professional class, is the commercial class, the nouveau riche who threaten to upset the traditional social order. A prime example is the Cole family in *Emma* whose business success elevates their standard of living almost up to that of the Woodhouses. Even so, the Coles are still viewed by Emma as beneath her in station and even beneath the just barely gentry Bates family. Likewise the Gardiners in *Pride and Prejudice* are accepted by some in the gentry class, most notably Mr. Darcy, but still scorned by the likes of Lady Catherine. We argue in chapter 11 that Austen's inclusion of families like the Coles and the Gardiners are her way of reflecting the changing attitudes about business from disdain to respect during her time.

An important social distinction is evident between those large successful merchants and wholesalers of the emerging commercial class and those small retailers and tradespeople who provide goods and services to the gentry and commercial classes (McMaster 1997, 127). Austen's novels are rife with descriptions of various establishments where the gentry can socialize, such as the Pump-room in Bath (*Northanger Abbey* and *Persuasion*), or throw a ball, such as the Crown Inn in Highbury (*Emma*). Innkeepers also provide a place for people to stay during travel. The gentry and merchant classes shop at places like Ford's in Highbury (*Emma*) and Molland's in Bath (*Persuasion*), and they use the services of bakers like Mrs. Wallis (*Emma*). Property managers like Mr. Knightley's steward, Mr. William Larkin, and tenant farmers like Mr. Robert Martin (both in *Emma*) also make up this working class.

Other than business transactions though, there are no social interactions between members of the working class and the gentry and commercial classes. Emma makes this delineation painfully clear to her friend and protégé Harriet by pointing out matter-of-factly that were Harriet to marry Mr. Martin, "it would have been the loss of a friend to me. I could not have visited Mrs. Robert Martin, of Abbey-Mill Farm" (*E*, 751).

In addition to needing the goods and services provided by the working class, the upper classes also depend on a vast array of servants working in the background to keep their households going. For example, Catherine Morland observes during her tour of Northanger Abbey that, "[t]he number of servants continually appearing did not strike her less than the number of their offices. Wherever they went, some pattened girl stopped to curtsy, or some footman in dishabille sneaked off" (*NA*, 1104). In such a prestigious household as the Tilneys', servants are even employed to open the window shutters in the bedrooms of the sleeping gentry each morning to rouse them (*NA*, 1096). Even the relatively poor Bates family in *Emma* has one servant and the rather low family of Fanny Price in *Mansfield Park* employs several servants. Servants included female housekeepers, cooks, and housemaids, and male butlers, gardeners, footmen, and coachmen. Interestingly, most of the servants are unnamed in Austen's novels, but even when they are named, they do not necessarily get much notice or respect. Terry (1988) points out that when William Price visits his sister Fanny at Mansfield Park after seven years' absence, "the first minutes of exquisite feeling had no interruption and no witnesses, unless the servants chiefly intent upon opening the proper doors could be called such" (*MP*, 580). Here the servants do not even count as people! Later in the novel, Mrs. Price is complaining about the quality of her help and she barely acknowledges the humanity of her servant Rebecca saying, "If I was to part with Rebecca I should only get some*thing* worse" (*MP*, 668, emphasis added). One way to explain the invisible nature of the servants in Jane Austen's novels is the same reason that is given for the lack of any scenes involving only men. Austen was careful to write about what she knew. Since she could not have observed men talking among themselves, she did not include any scenes with only men. Likewise, as a gentlewoman, she would not have been able to observe private conversations among the help.

Not being able to employ any servants is a sure sign of poverty in Austen's novels (Terry, 1988). Anne Elliot's former school friend, now the crippled widow Mrs. Smith, is described as "living in a very humble way, unable to afford herself the comfort of a servant" (*P*, 1231). Very little other mention of the poor exists in Austen with the notable exception of the unnamed poor and sick family that Emma and Harriet visit to bring assistance. As is expected of a lady of Emma Woodhouse's standing in the community, Emma pays a charitable visit to a poor family. After the visit, she remarks to Harriet, "These are sights, Harriet, to do one good. How trifling they make every thing else appear! I feel now as if I could think of nothing but these poor creatures all the rest of the day; and yet who can say how soon it may all vanish from my mind?" She goes on to insist, "And really, I do not think that the impression will soon be over" (*E*, 772). However, upon further reflection she explains the futility of dwelling upon the poor family's circumstances. "If we feel for the wretched, enough to do all we can for them, the rest is empty sympathy, only distressing to ourselves" (*E*, 772). Emma's sentiments are reminiscent of Smith's example of a European man's reaction to news of an earthquake in China. Smith explains that "when all these humane sentiments had been once fairly expressed, he would pursue his business or his pleasure, take his repose or his diversion, with the same ease and tranquillity, as if no such accident had happened" (*TMS*, 136). The poor people of High-bury are as far removed (figuratively) from Emma as Smith's earthquake victims are from his man in Europe.

A brief reference to the poor is made in *Pride and Prejudice* as Lady Catherine scolds poor villagers "into harmony and plenty" (McMaster, 1997, 128). Similarly, the laboring class such as farm workers and the like are barely acknowledged except for Mary Crawford in *Mansfield Park* to note with frustration that her maid is unable to hire a horse and cart to deliver her harp because the farmers were too busy with the harvest (McMaster, 1997, 128).

Austen's novels, then, give us a glimpse into the importance of social rank in early nineteenth-century Britain. As a member of the lower gentry class herself, she must have been painfully aware of the fine distinctions of class that governed relationships. In *Emma*, she pokes fun at the idea that people seem more concerned about ranking above others, but less about how others out rank us. When Mr. Elton shocks Emma with his marriage proposal and is offended by her suggestion that he consider Harriet for a match, she wonders how he "should suppose himself her equal in connexion or mind!—look down upon her friend, so well understanding the gradations of rank below him, and be so blind to what rose above, as to fancy himself shewing no presumption in addressing her!—It was most provoking" (*E*, 800). That is, she wonders how Elton could be so concerned about marrying down to Harriet, but oblivious to the impossibility of marrying up to Emma. The joke, of course, is on Emma for being so blind in thinking herself so far above Mr. Elton.

Austen's characters that seem to place the highest value on rank are not shown in a very favorable light, such as Sir Walter Elliot and the Right Honourable Lady Catherine de Bourgh. We conclude that through these characters Austen is poking fun at the overemphasis of rank, a skepticism also found in Smith. Smith teaches us that the "disposition to admire, and almost to worship, the rich and the powerful, and to despise, or, at least, to neglect persons of poor and mean condition, though necessary both to establish and to maintain the distinction of ranks and the order of society, is, at the same time, the great and most universal cause of the corruption of our moral sentiments" (*TMS*, 61). Smith explains that instead of admiring people for being rich and powerful, a truly enlightened person would admire people for being wise and virtuous. Unfortunately most human beings, "the great mob of mankind" according to Smith (*TMS*, 226), have difficulty perceiving wisdom and virtue in others. On the other hand, riches are easy to see. "Nature has wisely judged that the distinction of ranks, the peace and order of society, would rest more securely upon the plain and palpable difference of birth and fortune, than upon the invisible and often uncertain difference of wisdom and virtue" (*TMS*, 226). In other words, we need some sort of ordering of society to replace the authority of kings and the Church. The best ordering would be based on wisdom and virtue, but these are hard for us to perceive, so the best we can do is to rely on riches and power to serve as proxies for wisdom and virtue. Both Austen and Smith are teaching us that since the social ordering of society might not reflect truly deserved rank, we ought not to take these fine delineations too seriously. Perhaps we should pay less respect to the Right Honourable Lady Catherine de Bourgh and more to Miss Bates.

NOTES

1. Collins (1998) explains that eventually the aristocracy gave up on Bath and took up residence in other more posh spa towns, leaving Bath to the gentry folks.

Chapter Thirteen

Reflections on the Intersection between Jane Austen and Adam Smith and Its Relevance for Today

We began this exploration of the intersection between Jane Austen and Adam Smith by first asking "Why these two authors?" and then asking "Why should we care about them today?" Our analysis reveals that the themes found in their classic works have much in common and still resonate with readers today. Smith's nonfiction treatises formed the basis of moral philosophy of the Enlightenment, and he is considered to be the founding father of the economics discipline. Austen's fiction contains a sophisticated use of comic irony and realistic descriptions of gentry society of the Regency era, and is considered to be some of the most widely read works of English literature. Yes, their lives only overlapped by fifteen years, but Enlightenment thought permeated the air of that time and radiates through their work. Enlightenment themes that both Smith and Austen explore include (1) individual thinking/questioning authority; (2) tolerance; and (3) self-improvement/actualization.

These themes from centuries ago remain an important part of current modernization theory which holds that economic development leads to significant cultural change in a predictable way.[1] Economies industrialize due to advancements in science and technology. Such advancements decrease the reliance on supernatural explanations of nature and lead to secularization and the questioning of traditional royal and church authorities. In post-industrial service-based economies another cultural shift takes place due to the value of creativity and knowledge in the workplace. As we become richer, we become less concerned about day to day survival and more concerned about individual freedom and the ability to express ourselves. We develop greater tolerance for diversity and a higher demand for participation in the political process. Economic prosperity, then, gives people the opportunity to develop more meaningful lives. The Enlightenment themes explored in Smith and Austen can still be seen in modern-day events such as the Arab Spring, protests in Hong Kong, and modernization in China and India today.

Both Smith and Austen use general Enlightenment themes in their works, but we specifically investigate how Austen reflects, and more importantly, *illuminates* Smith's moral philosophy. We provide a reading of each of Jane Austen's six completed published novels through a Smithian lens. Smith's moral philosophy begins with the assumption that we humans are social creatures who want to be loved and want to be *deserving* of love. Smith gives us a system of virtues that if we follow, can lead us to a happy, flourishing life. We learn this system of virtues through our interactions with others and our attempts to arrive at mutual sympathy. When we do things that get approval (approbation) from others, we are happy, and when we do things that get disapproval (disapprobation) from others, we are pained. Over time, we develop our own internal judge of our behavior, the impartial spectator. We couple this with reference to general principles of conduct that also guide our behavior. Whether this impartial spectator is purely internal or has an external component is not important to Smith's theory; that it exerts real moral discipline on the individual is all that matters.

Virtues are practices that we follow in order to become virtuous. What are these virtues? Prudence, Benevolence, and Justice, rooted in Self-Command. Self-command, as explained in chapter 3, is the ability to control our passions, our emotions. We naturally exhibit more self-command the less we know the other person. We illustrate, in chapter 4, how Austen gives us a richer view of self-command through her novel *Sense and Sensibility*. Elinor Dashwood is the epitome of self-command, while her sister Marianne's passions are ungovernable throughout most of the novel. Part of Marianne's moral development involves her learning self-command and valuing it in others, such as her sister and Colonel Brandon. We also learn that self-command is much more than simple self-restraint or self-control. It also includes specific strategies for assuaging the underlying cause of the emotional disturbance. These include directing one's attention to other matters, realistically and rationally examining the causes and the consequences of the action that excites the emotional outburst. With effort and exertion one can tame or guide the emotion without repressing it in an unhealthy fashion.

Self-command also means sticking to one's principles, a Smithian theme that is found in *Mansfield Park*. Indeed, the absence of good principles is likely accompanied with poor habits of self-command. Finally, one cannot have self-command if one is self-deluded, a key theme in *Emma*. Indeed, self-command is perhaps best understood as self-government. A useful image is that of a captain piloting a ship; with skills and experience she can sail the ship in most any wind or storm.[2]

The virtue trinity of PB&J—Prudence, Benevolence, and Justice—is explained in chapter 3 and explored in detail through Austen's *Mansfield Park* in chapter 5. In the unpleasant character of Mrs. Norris, Austen shows us the consequences of lacking these important virtues. Instead of being prudent, Mrs. Norris gets caught up in being overly frugal. Throughout the novel she is neither benevolent nor just to Fanny Price. Ultimately, her lack of virtue leads to a life of exile. In contrast, through Sir Thomas Bertram and his son Edmund's treatment of Fanny, we see how we can develop the virtues of prudence, benevolence, and justice.

Keeping us back from a virtuous and flourishing life is our proclivity to the vices of Vanity, Pride, and Greed. In chapter 6 we use Austen's vain characters of Sir Walter and Elizabeth Elliot in *Persuasion* to flesh out Smith's critique of vanity and his theory about the unintended consequences of vanity. Our vanity causes us to want to keep up with (or out do) the Joneses, and that drive leads us to be productive. Of course, money does not buy happiness, but this self-delusion does give us the ambition to strive for improvement. It is important to note, though (as Collins, 1998, also does) that in the end the happiness of *all* of the heroines in Austen's work is *not* dependent on money, but rather on relationships with others. In the case of vain characters like Willoughby in *Sense and Sensibility* and Henry Crawford in *Mansfield Park*, excessive vanity leads to personal misfortune, a point that both Austen and Smith emphasize. The vice of pride is best illustrated with the novel that includes the vice in its title, *Pride and Prejudice*. Smith teaches us that excessive pride blinds us to self-knowledge and an understanding of others, and Austen's novel traces the moral development of Elizabeth Bennet and Mr. Darcy as they overcome their pride and find their way to one another. Greed is a vice closely related to vanity and pride and in chapter 8 we use Austen's greedy characters in *Northanger Abbey*, the Thorpes and General Tilney, to show that neither Austen nor Smith think that greed is good.

We can become more virtuous by practicing the virtues of self-command, prudence, benevolence, and justice and also by observing these virtues in others. In psychology this process of absorbing virtue from others is called *moral elevation*. The idea is that when we see or hear about virtuous behavior, we are more likely to act virtuously ourselves. Evidence for this positive feedback mechanism has been found in modern-day surveys and psychological experiments.[3]

Smith's feedback mechanism is found in the concept of the impartial spectator which is best personified in the relationship between Mr. Knightley and Emma in Austen's novel *Emma*. We explain in chapter 9 that throughout the novel Mr. Knightley provides Emma with the approbation (and disapprobation) that she needs, and that she even imagines what Mr. Knightley would think of her behavior in his absence. Remember, the idea that we can develop our own social order from bottom up interactions with others, instead of requiring top down ordering from some central authority is an important Enlightenment theme. Some folks take this responsibility for order too literally, as Emma does when she tries to act as a Smithian man of system. Part of her moral development involves learning that treating others as pieces on a chessboard is not only presumptuous on her part but shows disrespect for the dignity of others. Aspiring men of system, such as Mrs. Norris from *Mansfield Park* and Lady Catherine from *Pride and Prejudice*, never learn this lesson and remain morally stunted.

Respecting the dignity of others is also an important part of the development of what McCloskey (2006) calls the *Bourgeois Virtues* which we see happening in Austen's novels. In pre-commercial society, wealth was associated with owning land and the family properties were carefully handed down from generation to generation. Some background regarding how income is earned in Smith and Austen's time and the importance of landed property and inheritance is explained in chapter 10. This knowledge is needed in order to understand the changing attitudes about business and the upheaval of social ranks described in chapters 11 and 12, respectively.

Smith explains that business and trade was generally looked down on in these pre-commercial societies. That attitude discouraged virtuous people from engaging in trade and prevented economic development which depends keenly on trade. We show in chapter 11 that in several of Austen's characters, we begin to see commercial activity viewed with respect rather than disdain. This important social and economic development is illustrated especially in the attitudes toward Mr. Gardiner of *Pride and Prejudice*, Sir Thomas of *Mansfield Park*, and Mr. George Knightley of *Emma*, all virtuous men who are actively engaged in trade. Respect for business is sometimes in short supply in our modern times. Who is most likely to be the villain in movies today? Businessmen, of course. We even see this bias against the private sector in proposals to forgive student loan debt; only those employed in public service careers receive this forgiveness in half the time. The clear impression is that it is somehow less honorable to create wealth in business. Smith and Austen caution us against this anti-business attitude.

Closely related to the changing attitudes about commerce is the rise of the merchant class and the upheaval of the social order of Smith and Austen's time which we explore in chapter 12. While both Austen and Smith accept the social ordering of their day, they recognize that these rankings might not be really deserved so we ought not to take them too seriously. Austen makes fun of these rankings through unfavorable characters such as Sir Walter Elliot (*Persuasion*) who pores over the book of Baronetage and the Right Honourable Lady Catherine de Bourgh (*Pride and Prejudice*) who "likes to have the distinction of rank preserved" (*PP*, 316) so much that she prefers her dinner guests to be slightly underdressed. According to Smith and Austen, true respect should be earned, rather than be an accident of birth. These sentiments ring true in the respect given to self-made men and women of today.

What lessons can we draw from Adam Smith and Jane Austen to help us live lives of happiness and significance? Simple. Develop self-command over our passions so we can live a life that balances both sense and sensibility. Be prudent in our affairs but not to the extent of miserliness. Show benevolence toward those we care about, and justice to all. Have pride in our true accomplishments, but do not become too vain or greedy. Show respect to those who earn it. Finally, take those Enlightenment themes to heart by thinking for ourselves, tolerating others, and always striving for improvement.

NOTES

1. For an overview of modernization theory, see Inglehart and Welzel (2005).
2. We thank Patrick Callahan for sharing this imagery with us.
3. See Zak (2012), and Aquino, McFerran, and Laven (2011).

Appendix

A Brief Synopsis of Austen's Six Published Novels

For readers needing a refresher (or introduction) to Jane Austen's novels, we provide a synopsis of each of the six novels in the order of publication: *Sense and Sensibility* (1811), *Pride and Prejudice* (1813), *Mansfield Park* (1814), *Emma* (1816), *Northanger Abbey*, and *Persuasion* (both published posthumously in 1818).

SENSE AND SENSIBILITY

Henry Dashwood owns an estate, Norland, in Sussex. He resides with his second wife and three daughters: Elinor, age nineteen; Marianne, age sixteen; and Margaret, age thirteen. When Henry Dashwood dies, the entail on his estate requires he leave Norland and most of his wealth to his son John Dashwood from his first marriage, although he makes a deathbed plea to his son to take care of his half sisters and stepmother. After his death, Mr. John Dashwood and his greedy wife Fanny Dashwood (nee Ferrars) take immediate possession of Norland but allow the Dashwood sisters and their mother to stay on until suitable arrangements can be made. They do not make any additional provision for the widow Mrs. Dashwood or her daughters.

Fanny's brother, Edward Ferrars, visits Norland. Edward is shy and unambitious; he plans to be a clergyman although his mother and sister are encouraging him to seek more fashionable and important callings. During the visit Edward and Elinor Dashwood appear to be falling in love. Fanny insists that Elinor's lack of wealth and status make a marriage between the two impossible; Edward is far too good for her. Edward leaves Norland without making his intentions clear to Elinor.

A distant relative of the Dashwood mother, Sir John Middleton, offers the Dashwood ladies a home on favorable terms at Barton Cottage near his larger home, Barton Park, in Devonshire. The family moves to Barton Cottage and are greeted amiably by Sir John. His wife, Lady Middleton, is fully devoted to spoiling her children so she pays little attention to the new arrivals, but Lady Middleton's mother, Mrs. Jennings, takes a great interest in the Dashwood sisters. They are introduced to a thirty-five-year-old bachelor, Colonel Brandon, an intelligent but formal man. He takes an immediate interest in Marianne, but she does not reciprocate his affections.

One day Marianne and Margaret take a walk. It rains and Marianne slips, falls, and twists her ankle. Out of the mist a dashing young man on horseback comes and rescues her. He is Mr. John Willoughby, a handsome, elegant, and clever young man who has a wealthy elderly cousin, a Mrs. Smith, who owns an estate in the neighborhood. It is commonly expected that he will inherit that estate upon her death. Willoughby and Marianne appear to fall in love, spending most of their time with one another at Barton Cottage and Barton Park. Marianne and John take unchaperoned rides together and even visit his elderly cousin's estate when she is away. All assume they are soon to be engaged and married.

Colonel Brandon hosts a day outing to which all are invited. In the morning when the group is assembled Brandon receives a message and indicates he must leave immediately. The party is canceled. A few days later Willoughby announces he must leave immediately and gives no timeline for his return. His abrupt departure leads to much emotional distress for Marianne that is very apparent to all. A bit later Edward Ferrars arrives for a short visit. He is distant and seems unhappy during most of his time at Barton and leaves in no better spirits than when he arrived.

The Steele sisters, Lucy and Nancy, distant relatives of Mrs. Jennings, arrive at Barton Park for an extended visit. The sisters are nice enough but not well educated and a bit brash. Lucy approaches Elinor and reveals a great deal of knowledge about the Dashwood sisters. She also inquires of Elinor's knowledge of Mrs. Ferrars, mother of Fanny Dashwood and Edward Ferrars. She requests Elinor to be her confidant and reveals that she, Lucy, has been secretly engaged to Edward Ferrars for more than four years. Elinor is shocked but keeps her composure. She is at first angry at Edmund for not having told her, but then feels sorry for him as she thinks Lucy beneath his education and sensibilities. True to her word Elinor keeps Lucy's secret from everyone, including her own sister Marianne.

Mrs. Jennings has a house in London and plans to go there for the winter season. She invites Elinor and Marianne to stay with her in London. Marianne is delighted as she is sure she can rekindle the flame with her heartthrob

Willoughby as he will certainly be in London. When they arrive in London, Marianne sends Willoughby a number of notes letting him know she is in town. He makes no response, neither a note nor a visit. This continues for a week or so. He does finally make a visit to their abode when they are away and leaves his card. Eventually the sisters and Mrs. Jennings are invited to a party where they run into Willoughby. He greets Elinor modestly and seems uncomfortable. He does not talk to Marianne until she makes a scene crying out "Willoughby. . . . Will you not shake hands with me?" (*SS*, 106). Willoughby hems and haws and finally gets enough composure to make a hasty retreat to a group of friends. Marianne and Elinor leave the ball and Marianne is overcome with grief and despair.

The next day she receives a cold note from Willoughby informing her that he never had anything but friendship for her and was sorry if she had misunderstood but as of now "his affections have been long engaged elsewhere" (*SS*, 106). Marianne is overwhelmed, heartbroken, and stays in bed for days on end. It comes out that Willoughby is engaged to the rich Miss Grey who has a fortune of fifty thousand pounds. Marianne wants to go home but Elinor insists it would be improper and impolite to Mrs. Jennings. Marianne remains incapacitated by her grief.

Colonel Brandon, long in love with Marianne and on good terms with Elinor, visits Mrs. Jennings's house and engages Elinor in a confidential conversation. He tells her of a love he had long ago, Eliza. They had almost eloped to Scotland but the plan was dashed. He went into the navy. She was induced to marry his older brother and the marriage was a disaster. Upon their divorce Eliza fell into ruin. A few years later Colonel Brandon returned to England. He eventually tracked down Eliza and found her when she was in the last stages of consumption. She left behind a child, little Eliza, that Colonel Brandon agreed to care for. He placed her in a respectable home and provided for her education. She recently had visited Bath and had fallen into the company of a man who eventually made her pregnant. And that man was none other than Willoughby, who then abandoned her. Colonel Brandon only learned of all of this "on the very morning of our intended party" (*SS*, 124), which explains his sudden exit. It also explains the soon followed exit of Willoughby as news of it had reached his elderly cousin who proceeded to disown him. In response, Willoughby came to London to renew and cement a liaison with the wealthy Miss Grey. Elinor relays this information to Marianne, who falls into even deeper despondency.

Soon Lucy and Nancy Steele come to London. As it happens the Steele sisters and the Dashwood sisters are all invited to a dinner at John Dashwood's London residence where not only will his wife Fanny be present, but also her and Edward's mother, Mrs. Ferrars. Edward is not at the dinner. It does not go well for the Dashwood girls; they do not make a good impression on the proud Mrs. Ferrars as they contradict her. Lucy and Nancy Steele, however, are treated with cordiality by the stiff-necked Mrs. Ferrars.

A few days later Fanny invites the Miss Steeles to stay at the Dashwood London residence. They are convinced they are in the good graces and highest esteem of both Mrs. Dashwood and Mrs. Ferrars. Nancy Steele imprudently announces that her sister Lucy and Edward Ferrars have been engaged for some time. Fanny is enraged and kicks the sisters out of the house. When the news is leaked out, Edward is confronted by his mother and remains resolute in his intention to marry Lucy. She cuts him off without a penny. He has only two thousand pounds to his name although he is soon to be ordained as an Anglican minister.

Upon receiving the news that Edward and Lucy's engagement and upcoming marriage is public knowledge, Elinor reveals all the details of her prior knowledge of the engagement to Marianne, who is shocked but impressed that her sister had held up so well. She also feels a bit guilty for her own self-centered behavior after being jilted by Willoughby. In the meantime Colonel Brandon hears the news and through Elinor offers a parish near his estate at Delaford with a stable income for Edward and Lucy. Elinor graciously conveys the information to Edward who is delighted at Colonel Brandon's magnanimity and generosity. Elinor and Marianne resolve to leave London accompanied by Colonel Brandon and the Palmers (Mrs. Jennings's other daughter and son-in-law).

The girls arrive at Cleveland, the home of the Palmers, where Marianne falls dangerously ill and nearly dies. Colonel Brandon is gracious and fetches the girls' mother from Barton Cottage. By the time she arrives, Marianne is out of danger.

After Marianne is out of danger but before mother arrives, Willoughby appears at Cleveland and gives a long explanation/confession to Elinor. He regrets his actions and hates his new wife. His object at first with Marianne was his own amusement and vanity, but he later discovered that he did love her after all. He has taken a very bitter pill. Elinor actually feels sorry for him.

Elinor does not reveal Willoughby's visit to Marianne until they return to Barton Cottage. In the meantime, Marianne determines to turn over a new leaf and adopt a more disciplined lifestyle. The family receives the news that Lucy Steele is married from their servant Thomas who ran into her in the village near the Delaford parish. Out of the blue Edward Ferrars visits the Dashwoods at Barton Cottage. The Dashwoods ask about Mrs. Ferrars and Edward indicates his mother is fine. When they ask about the Mrs. Edward Dashwood, he indicates that no such person exists, although there is a Mrs. Robert Dashwood who is well. It becomes apparent that Lucy is married to Edward's brother, Robert. Elinor is so overcome with joy she uncharacteristically runs out of the room. Edward and Elinor marry; Mrs. Ferrars forgives

Edward and accepts Elinor. Marianne falls in love with the steadfast Colonel Brandon and they marry. The novel ends happily for the Dashwood sisters.

PRIDE AND PREJUDICE

The story centers on the Bennet family. Mr. Bennet is a reasonably educated man with a wry sense of humor who owns a small estate, Longbourn. His wife is a garish and often foolish woman who has given him five daughters. His estate is entailed so none of the girls can inherit it, thus Mrs. Bennet is keen on seeing all her daughters married. The oldest daughter, Jane, has a sweet disposition and is quite the beauty. The second daughter, Elizabeth, is the favorite of her father as she is witty, intelligent, and has a biting sense of humor. But she is also rather proud. Mary, the third daughter, is unaccomplished but affects an intellectual air that is offputting to everyone. Kitty and Lydia, the two youngest daughters, are foolish and obsessed with flirting with young men.

The plot opens with the purchase of the nearby estate of Netherfield by a single young man of some fortune. Indeed, Austen's opening line "It is a truth universally acknowledged, that a single man in possession of a good fortune must be in want of a wife" (*PP*, 225) is often considered her most memorable. The new resident, Mr. Bingley, is charming, friendly, and handsome and interested in meeting and socializing with the Bennet family. He is accompanied by his sisters, a brother-in-law, and his friend a Mr. Darcy. Like Bingley, Darcy is young and rich; unlike Bingley, Darcy is aloof and prideful. Not surprisingly everyone takes an immediate liking to Bingley and a dislike to Darcy. Bingley takes a special interest in Jane Bennet, much to Mrs. Bennet's delight.

The heir to Longbourn is a distant cousin, a Mr. Collins, who has recently been ordained as a minister in the Church of England. He announces his intention to visit Longbourn with a not so subtle intention of courting and marrying one of the Bennet girls. Mr. Collins's visit reveals him to be a pompous, foolish, and deluded man obsessed with his connection with the rich and high born Lady Catherine de Bourgh in whose parish he is minister. He first has his eye to marry the oldest Bennet daughter Jane, but when Mrs. Bennet informs him she is likely to become engaged to another (she presumes Bingley) Collins immediately turns his attention to the second-oldest Elizabeth.

Collins makes a rather awkward proposal of marriage to Elizabeth which she refuses. He insists she will change her mind, which infuriates her. She remains adamant in her refusal which he eventually accepts. Undaunted by his failure, just three days later Collins asks Elizabeth's friend, twenty-seven-year-old Charlotte Lucas, to marry him. She, being of a pragmatic mind when it comes to marriage, agrees to the match. Elizabeth is somewhat surprised but in no way offended by Charlotte's choice and agrees to visit Charlotte after the couple is married. The Lucas family, headed by Sir William and Lady Lucas, are neighbors of the Bennets; and Mrs. Bennet and Lady Lucas enjoy a sort of competitive friendship, especially when it comes to marrying off their daughters. Remember that Mr. Collins stands to inherit the Bennet home, and Mrs. Bennet is particularly upset at the thought of losing her home to a Lucas girl.

At the same time, the two eldest Bennet girls are socializing with Bingley and Darcy. Jane is invited for a day visit to Netherfield, but catches cold and stays at Netherfield with the Bingleys until she recovers. Elizabeth comes to Netherfield to nurse Jane and has a number of encounters with Darcy. The two spar over a number of issues and Elizabeth leaves with a heightened dislike of the proud Darcy.

At a social engagement with a number of officers at the home of the girls' Aunt Phillips, Elizabeth meets the handsome and amiable Mr. Wickham. It ends up Wickham knows Darcy, having grown up on the Darcy family estate. Wickham's father was the estate manager for Darcy's father, but both of the fathers are now deceased. Wickham is estranged from Darcy because, according to Wickham, Darcy has cheated Wickham out of his rightful inheritance and prevented him from entering the clergy. This explains why he is in the military. Elizabeth's opinion of Darcy sinks even lower after hearing of his alleged abuse of poor Wickham. Wickham also informs Elizabeth that Darcy is the nephew of none other than Lady Catherine de Bourgh, Mr. Collins's patron, who is as proud and arrogant as Darcy.

Mr. Collins and Charlotte are married and Elizabeth, along with a number of Charlotte's family, visit the Collinses' parsonage which is adjacent to the magnificent estate of Rosings, home of Lady Catherine de Bourgh. They are invited to Rosings a number of times and Elizabeth comes into contact with both Darcy and his cousin, Colonel Fitzwilliam.

During this visit, to Elizabeth's shock and dismay, Darcy reveals that he is madly in love with her despite his superior social status and he asks for her hand in marriage. She refuses and subsequently accuses him of misconduct on two counts. First, he has persuaded his friend Bingley to stop courting her sister Jane, which is unfair to both Bingley and Jane because they are in love. Second he has ill-used Mr. Wickham. Darcy leaves in a huff, but the next morning delivers a long letter to Elizabeth that responds in detail to both charges. Elizabeth is angered, perplexed, but ultimately convinced by the letter. She begins to change her opinion of Darcy concluding that "she had been blind, partial, prejudiced, absurd" (*PP*, 342).

Some months later Elizabeth, along with her Aunt and Uncle Gardiner, take a vacation touring the English countryside. Her aunt is interested in visiting Pemberley, the home of Darcy. Elizabeth is relieved to learn that

Darcy is not to be at the estate at the time of their visit. Upon the visit she is impressed by the house and grounds. She is also impressed by the high esteem in which the servants at the estate hold Darcy. As they are ending their visit to Pemberley, Darcy suddenly and unexpectedly returns. To Elizabeth's relief he is charming, attentive, and hospitable to her and her aunt and uncle. He invites them to see more of the grounds and encourages her uncle to fish at his leisure in its ponds and streams.

When Darcy accompanies the party back to their inn in nearby Lambton, they receive some very disturbing news. Lydia, the youngest and most unbridled of the Bennet daughters, has run away with none other than Wickham. Elizabeth and the Gardiners return to the Bennet estate and Mr. Gardiner and Mr. Bennet go to London to try to sort out the affair. Wickham is eventually persuaded to marry Lydia, in no small part because Darcy secretly assumes Wickham's debts. Lydia and Wickham, now married, move to his military unit in Newcastle.

Darcy and Bingley return for a visit to Bingley's estate Netherfield and they visit the Bennet family at Longbourn. Bingley proposes to Jane and she accepts to the delight of everyone. Lady Catherine de Bourgh visits the Bennet home to see Elizabeth. It seems Lady Catherine has heard a rumor that Elizabeth and her nephew Darcy are engaged and she wants Elizabeth to know that a marriage between the two of them is impossible. Elizabeth finds Lady Catherine's manners and demeanor high-handed and arrogant, so she is cheeky and coy in her responses to the Lady's inquiries. Elizabeth finally confesses that she is not engaged to Darcy but will not promise she will never become engaged to him. Lady Catherine leaves as indignant as when she arrived.

Darcy visits a few days later and he and Elizabeth declare their love for one another and agree to marry. They recognize the problems of their own pride and prejudice and how they have both changed since their first meeting. Elizabeth and Darcy eventually reconcile with Lady Catherine and live a happy life.

MANSFIELD PARK

Three sisters married into very different circumstances. One became Lady Bertram, the wife of a prosperous and high-ranking Sir Thomas Bertram, and takes her place at Mansfield Park giving birth to four children. A second became Mrs. Norris, wife of a middling clergyman Reverend Norris at a parish church near Mansfield Park. The couple remains childless. The third became Mrs. Price, the wife of a low-ranking and rather dissolute navy officer, and has a large and unmanageable brood of children and a rather small income.

At the behest of Mrs. Norris, the Bertrams are persuaded to help the Price family by offering a home at Mansfield Park for one of the Price daughters, ten-year-old Fanny. When she arrives she is overwhelmed by her new surroundings and it takes some time to adjust to her new circumstances. Her cousins are Thomas, age seventeen, Edmund, age sixteen, Maria, age fourteen, and Julia, age thirteen. She is not treated badly by any of them, or by Sir Thomas and Lady Bertram, but she forms a close attachment only to Edmund. As Fanny grows up, she becomes deeply in love with Edmund, a love which is not requited by him. Fanny is also under the constant rule of Aunt Norris who treats her as an inferior to her two female cousins.

Several years after Fanny's arrival in Mansfield Park, Reverend Norris dies and Mrs. Norris moves into a cottage even closer to the Park. The new vicar, Dr. Grant, is accompanied by his wife and eventually two of her half-siblings, Henry and Mary Crawford. The two have moved out of the home of their uncle, Admiral Crawford, upon the death of their aunt as the admiral has invited his mistress to live in his home in London. Henry and Mary are well situated, independently wealthy, urbane, and sophisticated, and considered to be quite eligible. Sir Thomas and eldest son Tom embark on a voyage to the family estate in Antigua.

Before the Crawford siblings arrive, Maria Bertram has become engaged to the dull-witted but quite wealthy Mr. Rushworth. The Bertrams and Crawfords make a plan for a day trip to the Rushworth estate of Sotherton to advise Rushworth on possible improvements to his property. Mrs. Norris is obsessed with arranging the plans for the day. She originally wishes to exclude Fanny, but Edmund figures out a way for Fanny to be included. When the group arrives, it appears that Maria, despite being engaged to Rushworth, is competing with her sister Julia for the attention of Henry Crawford. Crawford, enjoying the attention, encourages them both. Mary Crawford speaks rather disrespectfully about the role of church and clergy in society, much to the chagrin of Edmund who plans to become a clergyman. These actions make Fanny very suspicious of both of the Crawfords. Nevertheless Fanny's love, cousin Edmund, seems to be in love with Mary Crawford.

The older son Tom Bertram comes home from Antigua early, leaving his father behind. Tom devises a plan for his siblings and friends, including the Crawfords, to plan and produce a play using the billiard room and library of the absent Sir Thomas as the set. Edmund thinks putting on a play is inappropriate, as does Fanny. Nevertheless the set construction and rehearsals proceed with the approval of Mrs. Norris, and the reluctant participation of Edmund. Fanny, though, will not agree to take a role. Fanny continues to observe Henry Crawford's flirting with both Julia and the engaged Maria and sees it as less than innocent. When they are a day or so from the first showing of the play, Sir Thomas arrives home and puts a stop to the whole project.

A while later Maria and Mr. Rushworth are married and sister Julia accompanies them on their honeymoon. Mary Crawford strikes up a friendship with Fanny, and Henry Crawford begins to take an interest in Fanny, first as a lark, but his interest in her grows over time. Fanny's older brother, navy officer William, arrives at Mansfield for a visit. Sir Thomas decides to give a ball in Fanny's honor which is a social success. Henry and William leave after the ball to visit Henry's uncle, Admiral Crawford, in London. This encounter leads to William's promotion in the navy. Henry informs Fanny of her brother's promotion and declares his love for her, asking for her hand in marriage. Fanny rejects his offer in no uncertain terms. She is soon visited by her uncle who condemns and scolds her for not accepting Henry's proposal and encourages her to reconsider. This upsets Fanny greatly. Sir Thomas encourages Henry Crawford to continue to court Fanny, but he is otherwise resolved to no longer pressure Fanny on the matter. Over the next week both Edmund and Mary Crawford encourage Fanny to reconsider Henry Crawford's proposal.

Fanny is sent to visit her family in Portsmouth, whom she has not seen for nearly a decade. Part of Sir Thomas's design is for the return to her humble roots to make Fanny appreciate her lifestyle at Mansfield Park, which he hopes will give her reason to acquiesce to marriage to Henry Crawford. During her visit at Portsmouth, she becomes reacquainted with her family and becomes a mentor to her sister, Susan. Henry Crawford calls on her at home and restates his affections for her. Fanny notes that he seems more serious and is slowly beginning to consider him in a different light. Meanwhile, Tom Bertram becomes dangerously sick, due to his excessive partying in London, and his extended illness is partly responsible for the Bertrams extending Fanny's stay in Portsmouth. Fanny soon learns that after Henry left Portsmouth, he visited friends in London and was persuaded to stay a few days. He meets up with Maria Rushworth (nee Bertram) at her home and the two begin a scandalous and shocking affair. Maria and Henry run away together and Mr. Rushworth sues for divorce. Edmund meets with Mary Crawford and is shocked to find she is much more interested in rehabilitating the errant Maria and Henry to polite society than in holding them accountable for their perfidy. Edmund confesses to Fanny his rejection of Mary. Fanny is vindicated in her judgment of the Crawford siblings as Edmund realizes he has feelings for Fanny and the two are married. The Crawfords leave the scene. Mrs. Norris and the errant Maria are banished to the distant countryside doomed to live with one another.

EMMA

In *Emma*, Jane Austen tells the story of a wealthy and self-deluded young woman who, while having no romantic inclinations of her own, fancies herself as a successful matchmaker. The novel takes place in the village of Highbury, England, about sixteen miles from London (*E*, 724). Austen introduces the title character to the reader in the very first line of the novel. "Emma Woodhouse, handsome, clever, and rich, with a comfortable home and happy disposition, seemed to unite some of the best blessings of existence; and had lived nearly twenty-one years in the world with very little to distress or vex her" (*E*, 723). Emma lives with her indulgent father, the ever careful of his and everyone else's health Mr. Woodhouse, on the Hartfield estate and they enjoy the highest social standing in the area. Emma's mother had died when Emma was a little girl, and the development of Emma and her older sister, Isabella, was supervised by their governess, Miss Taylor. Perhaps *supervised* is too strong of a word, as Emma has been mistress of Hartfield since Isabella married. "The real evils, indeed, of Emma's situation were the power of having rather too much her own way, and a disposition to think a little too well of herself (*E*, 723).

Emma begins to think of herself as a matchmaker when Miss Taylor marries Mr. Weston who lives in a neighboring estate. In Emma's mind, the two would not have found each other if it were not for Emma's constant encouragement, especially since many thought the widower would never remarry. With one successful match under her belt, Emma sets her sights upon finding a match for Mr. Elton, the vicar of Highbury. The intended match for Mr. Elton is Harriet Smith, a girl of uncertain parentage who Emma takes under her wing.

Observing Emma's efforts and offering cautionary counsel against such meddling is Mr. George Knightley, a close friend of the Woodhouses both in terms of proximity and degree of intimacy. Mr. Knightley's estate is walking distance to Hartfield; he visits almost daily. The connection between the families is further strengthened by Knightley's brother, John, being married to Isabella Woodhouse. Mr. George Knightley is a kind and benevolent gentleman very well regarded throughout Highbury.

Despite Mr. Knightley's advice that Mr. Elton is quite capable of finding a wife on his own, Emma presses on with her scheme. She manages to convince Harriet to turn down an offer of marriage from the yeoman farmer, Mr. Robert Martin, without Harriet ever suspecting that she had been influenced by Emma at all. Mr. Knightley and Emma quarrel over her interference with what, in Knightley's mind, is a very beneficial match for Harriet. Mr. Knightley knows and respects his tenant farmer Mr. Martin for his character and business acumen.

The match between Mr. Elton and Harriet goes awry when Mr. Elton misperceives Emma's attentions on behalf of Harriet as feelings of romance from Emma to Mr. Elton directly. Managing to ride home with Emma alone from a dinner party one evening, Mr. Elton proposes to her instead of Harriet. Not only must Emma suffer the embarrassment of turning away a suitor in whom she has no interest and who is beneath her in social standing, she must also break the news to her protégée who has developed feelings for Mr. Elton under Emma's tutelage. Emma urges Harriet to practice "self-command" in the face of the considerable embarrassment and disappointment over the failed match (*E*, 874). Mr. Elton leaves town after Emma's rejection and quickly becomes engaged to Miss Augusta Hawkins from a mercantile family in Bristol.

Despite Emma's protestation that she would never marry, she for a time begins to think she is in love with the dashing Mr. Frank Churchill, Mr. Weston's son from his first marriage. Emma is initially drawn in by his charming nature and his affinity for teasing Miss Jane Fairfax. Jane is Emma's age but the two are acquaintances instead of friends. "Why she did not like Jane Fairfax might be a difficult question to answer; Mr. Knightley had once told her it was because she saw in her the really accomplished young woman, which she wanted to be thought herself" (*E*, 815). Indeed Jane shows herself to be a more accomplished pianist and singer at a dinner party given by another Highbury family, the Coles. Jane normally lives with her adopted family, the Campbells, who took her in after her parents died, but she is in Highbury for an extended stay with her aunt, Miss Bates, and the widowed Mrs. Bates. Mr. Bates was a former vicar of Highbury, and the economic status of the Bates family has sunk considerably since his passing. Despite their relatively low income, Mrs. and Miss Bates remain part of the gentried society of Hartfield and receive discreet support from the Woodhouse family and Mr. Knightley in the form of occasional gifts of food and the like. During the Coles' party, Frank and Emma speculate about the anonymous and lavish gift of a pianoforte to Jane.

That Emma should attend a party given by the Coles is surprising since they are "of low origin, in trade, and only moderately genteel" (*E*, 839). In fact, Emma expected that the Coles would not invite families superior to them and planned to decline the invitation if they so dared to extend one. However, upon hearing that the Westons and Mr. Knightley had been invited, and only the Woodhouses left out, Emma is disappointed until at last the invitation arrives. During the party, Mrs. Weston confides in Emma that she is following in Emma's footsteps at matchmaking by making a pair out of Jane Fairfax and Mr. Knightley. This news sparks protestations on Emma's part that Mr. Knightley should never marry.

Emma's feelings for Mr. Churchill fizzle once he leaves town. Absence, in this case, does not make the heart grow fonder. With the passing of her fancy for Mr. Churchill, Emma instead sets her sights on him as a prospective husband for Harriet. Frank, unaware of Emma's designs, continues his very public flirtation with Emma during the group outing to Box Hill, one of the more famous scenes in the novel. Participating in the picnic are Emma and Harriet, Mr. Churchill, Mr. Knightley, Mr. and (the newly) Mrs. Elton, and Mr. Weston, as well as Miss Bates and Miss Fairfax.

During the Box Hill outing Mr. Churchill devises word games to keep Emma amused and flattered. At one point in the games Emma cannot resist blurting out a stinging barb toward the unsuspecting Miss Bates who becomes visibly taken aback and embarrassed. Mr. Knightley later lambasts Emma for being so uncharacteristically cruel to someone beneath her in stature. Very quickly Emma is distraught at having hurt her old friend Miss Bates and, more importantly, at having disappointed Mr. Knightley.

Mr. Churchill, it is later revealed, has been secretly engaged to Miss Jane Fairfax all along (he had given her the pianoforte), and his actions toward Emma had been merely a smokescreen. Once again, Emma cannot believe how much she had been mistaken. She is left with the unpleasant task of informing Harriet that the intended match will not occur. Harriet's affections, however, had not been for Mr. Churchill as Emma had presumed, but rather for Mr. Knightley. Upon learning of Harriet's feelings, Emma realizes that she, herself, is in love with Mr. Knightley!

The novel ends, then, with the unraveling of all the misdirected pairings. Mr. Knightley, who has been in love with Emma well before she realized her own feelings, proposes to her once he is convinced that she is not in love with Churchill. And Harriet ends up happily accepting a second offer of marriage from Mr. Martin, her first love.

NORTHANGER ABBEY

The heroine of *Northanger Abbey* is Catherine Morland, the eldest daughter in a family of ten children, who "had reached the age of seventeen, without having seen one amiable youth who could call forth her sensibility, without having inspired one real passion, and without having excited even any admiration but what was very moderate and very transient" (*NA*, 1007). All of that changes when the Morlands' childless neighbors, Mr. and Mrs. Allen, invite her to accompany them to Bath for a six-week stay.

Catherine's introduction to bustling Bath includes shopping for the latest styles and attending various social events. Initially the Allens find that there are none of their acquaintances in town, so there are no dance partners for Catherine at the balls. When they visit the Lower Rooms, however, the master of ceremonies introduces Catherine to Mr. Henry Tilney who humorously flirts with Catherine. Mr. Allen approves of Tilney as a friend to

Catherine upon learning that Mr. Tilney is both a clergyman and from a good family. Catherine, of course, is smitten with Mr. Tilney and looks for him in vain the next day at the Pump-room where the crowds assemble.

In the Pump-room, Mrs. Allen finally comes across someone she knows, an old school friend, Mrs. Thorpe, who is in Bath with her three daughters. The eldest, Isabella, takes an immediate liking to Catherine whom she recognizes as taking after Catherine's older brother James, a schoolmate of Isabella's brother, John Thorpe. Isabella, at four years Catherine's senior, is happy to shepherd Catherine through Bath society. They share a love of novels with romantic and mysterious plots, especially those by Mrs. Radcliffe, a Gothic author of Jane Austen's time.

James Morland and John Thorpe soon arrive in Bath. Since James and Isabella are constant companions, John and Catherine are somewhat thrown together, much to Catherine's chagrin. Catherine holds out hope that she will see Mr. Tilney again, and when she finally spies him at a ball, she learns that he had left Bath briefly to fetch his sister Eleanor and his father, the rather gruff General Tilney. Catherine is very pleased when Mr. and Miss Tilney invite her to go for a country walk the next day, weather permitting.

Before the Tilneys arrive to pick up Catherine for their walk, however, Isabella, John, and James swoop in with the expectation that Catherine will join them on an excursion to Blaize Castle. John convinces Catherine that he just saw Mr. Tilney and his sister heading out of town in a carriage. Thinking that the Tilneys had decided the weather was not right for a walk, and being excited about a visit to a Gothic-style castle like those she has read about in Mrs. Radcliffe's novels, Catherine joins the group for the drive. On their way out of town, who should they pass but the Tilneys heading toward the Allens' to pick up Catherine for their walk? Catherine, realizing she has been duped, begs John to stop so that she can join them, but her pleas only make him go faster.

Catherine calls on Miss Tilney the next day to apologize, but is told by the servant that Miss Tilney is not at home. After then seeing Miss Tilney leave the house with her father, Catherine concludes that her offense was unforgivable. She is finally able to apologize in person that evening at the theater when she comes across Mr. Tilney. He is charmed by the sincerity of her apology, and further explains that his sister did not mean to snub her at all; General Tilney had merely been in a hurry to leave, so he had instructed the servant to offer the white lie. They then make plans to reschedule the walk. Catherine's evening is made even more perfect when she later hears from John Thorpe that "the General thinks you the finest girl in Bath" (*NA*, 1054).

The country walk with the Tilneys is finally made, despite another attempt by John, Isabella, and James to engage Catherine in yet another outing. During the walk, Mr. Tilney continues his playful teasing of Catherine, the three discover a mutual interest in novels, and Catherine is invited to join the Tilney family at dinner the next day. That day, Isabella shares the good news that she is engaged to Catherine's brother and that James has gone home to seek his parents' approval for the match. In discussing the engagement with Catherine, hints made by John Thorpe about a match with Catherine go completely over her head.

Meanwhile, the Tilneys' brother, Captain Tilney, has come to Bath and seems most interested in Isabella at a ball. Henry asks Catherine for an introduction for his brother, unaware of Isabella's engagement. Catherine turns him down and then is shocked to see Isabella from across the ballroom dancing with the very captain! They soon hear from James that while his parents approve of the engagement, the 400-pound-a-year living Mr. Morland has arranged for James will not begin for a couple of years, so the engagement will have to be a long one. Isabella seems disappointed at the size of the living, but assures Catherine that her disappointment is instead with the delay. Catherine begins to have her doubts about Isabella's fidelity as she observes further interactions between her friend and Captain Tilney.

With the Allens's six-week stay in Bath nearing its end, Catherine fears that she will lose touch with Mr. Tilney. How delighted she is, then, when General Tilney invites her to join his family for a visit at their home, Northanger Abbey. Before leaving Bath, however, Catherine learns from Isabella that John Thorpe is, in fact, in love with her and mistook her conversation about Isabella's engagement as encouragement of his affection. Catherine makes it clear to Isabella that she is in no way interested in her brother.

On the drive to Northanger Abbey, Henry cannot resist sparking Catherine's imagination about the horrors she may encounter in such a grand old Abbey, echoing the novels Catherine loves to read. While the Abbey is of Gothic style, it is not nearly as scary as Mr. Tilney made it out to be. Nonetheless, Catherine does find a mysterious chest in her room, and General Tilney's gruff manner instills in her a heightened anxiety. The general seems most interested in hearing about the Allens' home in comparison to Northanger Abbey. A stormy night ensues, leaving Catherine spooked with visions from her novels. How embarrassed she is to discover in the calm of the morning that the mysterious chest only held old washing bills and the like. "Heaven forbid that Henry Tilney should ever know her folly!" (*NA*, 1097).

During a walk, Eleanor speaks of her long dead mother and Catherine learns that her portrait is hanging in Eleanor's bedchamber instead of the general's. This information leads Catherine to imagine that something sinister was behind Mrs. Tilney's death. Catherine's morbid curiosity is further piqued by the general's insistence that the tour of the Abbey not take place without his supervision, and his avoidance of showing her the quarters where Mrs. Tilney had died. Catherine even supposes that Mrs. Tilney might still be alive and shuttered away in those very quarters. When Catherine sneaks in to see for herself, she is caught by Henry who reproaches her for her suspicions. She worries that there is no further hope for a romance with Henry, even though he never again mentions the incident.

Catherine's world is again jolted by the news from her brother that he and Isabella are no longer engaged and that Isabella is now engaged to Captain Tilney. A letter from Isabella tells a different story, though, about how she is very happy that the evil Captain Tilney has left Bath, how she has always loved James, and how concerned she is that she has not lately heard from him. Catherine resists Isabella's request to write to James on her behalf.

The general is called away to London, leaving Henry, Eleanor, and Catherine to enjoy a few days of peace. While Henry is away tending to his parsonage nearby, the general returns home unexpectedly and announces that Catherine must leave the premises first thing in the morning. With such short notice, there is no time to inform her family of her imminent return; so she is to go by public carriage with no servant to attend to her. Catherine cannot help but wonder if the general has learned of her earlier suspicions about him.

She learns the reason for the general's cruelty when Henry visits her home to profess his love for her and ask for her hand in marriage. The general had been misled by Mr. Thorpe to believe that she was a young lady of fortune due from her father and Mr. Allen. "Under a mistaken persuasion of her possessions and claims, he had courted her acquaintance in Bath, solicited her company at Northanger, and designed for her his daughter in law" (*NA*, 1138). After Mr. Thorpe is spurned by Catherine, he makes her out to be poor when he sees the general in London. Catherine's parents would approve of her marriage to Mr. Tilney only upon consent from the general, which was not seen to be forthcoming. The general only softens once Eleanor marries into titled family and once he learns that while not rich, Catherine is most decidedly not poor. Thus Henry and Catherine are married at last.

PERSUASION

Anne Elliot, of *Persuasion*, is calm and dependable; there is "no one so proper, so capable as Anne" (*P*, 1210). The same cannot be said of her father, Sir Walter Elliot, and her older sister, Elizabeth. Elizabeth had inherited her father's vanity and penchant for overspending, while Anne took after her departed mother who had been able to keep her husband's extravagance in check. Without the prudence of Lady Elliot, however, Sir Walter finds himself in unsustainable debt. Two trusted friends are called upon to provide advice: Mr. Shepherd, the family lawyer, and Lady Russell, Anne's godmother. They manage to persuade Sir Walter, without him realizing that he is being persuaded, to rent out the family home at Kellynch and take up a smaller residence in Bath in order to economize.

Once Sir Walter is convinced that his pride would not be compromised by renting to Admiral and Mrs. Croft, he approves of their tenancy. Anne is especially interested in this development since Mrs. Croft's brother is Captain Frederick Wentworth, her first and only love. Eight years earlier Captain Wentworth had proposed to Anne, but her family, and especially Lady Russell, did not approve of the match due to Captain Wentworth's low social standing and lack of fortune. Lady Russell also viewed him as "brilliant" but "headstrong," a combination that she feared would result in imprudence (*P*, 1159). Ultimately, Lady Russell uses her strong motherly influence over Anne to convince her to end things. Anne even manages to convince herself that the parting would be best for him in the end. Part of the attraction of going to Bath, for Lady Russell, is the hope that Anne might finally widen her social circle enough to meet eligible gentlemen.

Her plans are postponed, however, by a request from Anne's married younger sister, the hypocondriatic Mary, for Anne to keep her company during her latest illness. An injury to one of Mary's sons further postpones Anne's departure for Bath. Much to Anne's and Lady Russell's dismay, Anne's replacement for the party to Bath is Elizabeth's friend and Mr. Shepherd's daughter, Mrs. Clay. Lady Russell has never approved of Elizabeth's closeness with Mrs. Clay and had hoped that the move to Bath would diminish the friendship. Anne's dislike of Mrs. Clay stems from her suspicion that she has designs on Sir Walter.

The delayed move to Bath means that Anne is still in town when Captain Wentworth comes to stay with the Crofts and becomes friends with Mary's husband, Charles Musgrove. Their first meeting is awkward, and while they soon are "repeatedly in the same circle" (*P*,1179) due to the friends they have in common, their interactions remain strained. Anne believes that Captain Wentworth can never forgive her and is no longer in love with her, especially as she sees him enjoying the company of Henrietta and Louisa Musgrove, Charles's younger sisters.

During a long walk with the Musgroves and Captain Wentworth, Anne overhears the captain and Louisa talking about the importance of remaining true to one's wishes and not allowing oneself to be persuaded into doing otherwise. "My first wish for all whom I am interested in, is that they should be firm," says Captain Wentworth (*P*, 1194). Louisa then reveals that she would have preferred Anne as a sister-in-law and explains that her brother had asked Anne to marry him before turning to Mary. Anne hears Louisa surmise that it was Lady Russell who had persuaded Anne to refuse Charles because he was not "learned and bookish enough" for Anne (*P*, 1194).

Anne looks forward to going to Bath so that she can be spared of further interaction with the man she cannot have, but is thrown once again into close contact when she, Charles, Mary, Henrietta, Louisa, and Captain Wentworth all venture to Lyme for an overnight stay. Louisa, liking to get her own way and knowing that Captain Wentworth values constancy of feeling, relentlessly presses for the visit after hearing Captain Wentworth sing its praises. Captain Wentworth's friends, Captain and Mrs. Harville, are staying in Lyme for the winter with Captain Benwick who had served under Captain Wentworth and who had been engaged to Captain Harville's sister before her untimely death. Anne and Captain Benwick bond over their shared love of reading.

During one of their walks, everyone notices that Anne catches the eye of a gentleman on the steps and they later find out that the mysterious man is none other than the Elliot sisters' cousin, Mr. William Elliot. William is Sir Walter's heir with whom he is estranged. Sir Walter had envisioned William as a good match for Elizabeth years ago, but William "purchased his independence by uniting himself to a rich woman of inferior birth" (*P*, 1148), who has since died.

Before heading back home, the group takes one last walk along the sea. Louisa, who has a habit of jumping from steps into Captain Wentworth's waiting arms, does so until she slips and falls, lifeless, to the ground. Mary and Henrietta lose all composure and the men are stunned into inaction. Only Anne emerges as capable. She provides salts to try to rouse Louisa and suggests getting a doctor. She has the presence of mind to send Captain Benwick in search of one, since he is the only one in the group that knows Lyme. Anne then suggests moving Louisa back to the inn, but the Harvilles meet up with them and offer their home instead for the recovery period.

After much deliberation it is decided that Charles and Mary will stay with Louisa, while Captain Wentworth would take Henrietta and Anne home to inform the elder Musgroves about Louisa's condition. Anne is pleased that the captain seeks and heeds her advice on how to best break the news, but she is relieved to hear that his returning to Lyme will lessen the probability of them spending much time together. Word from Lyme comes that Louisa is slowly recovering and that Captain Benwick still seems interested in Anne. Lady Russell seems more pleased about this revelation than Anne. Furthermore, Lady Russell interprets Captain Wentworth's interest in Louisa as proof that he was not worthy of "an Anne Elliot" (*P*, 1214), so her earlier persuasion of Anne had been for the best.

Finally Lady Russell takes Anne to Bath to be reunited with her family. Lady Russell and Anne are disappointed to find that Anne's arrival does not mean the removal of Mrs. Clay. They also learn that Sir Walter and Elizabeth have since reconciled with William Elliot who has become a frequent companion. He and Anne reminisce about their chance encounter in Lyme, and he becomes "their pleasantest acquaintance in Bath" (*P*, 1228). Lady Russell hopes for a match between Mr. Elliot and Anne so that a Lady Elliot can once again be mistress of Kellynch. Anne is less enthused about the prospect given her steadfast love for Captain Wentworth and her suspicion that Mr. Elliot is not to be trusted. Sir Walter and Elizabeth are excited to hear that their aristocratic cousins arrive in Bath, the Viscountess Dalrymple and her daughter. In contrast Anne pursues a connection with less social standing, the poor, widowed, and invalid Mrs. Smith who was Anne's schoolmate.

After a month in Bath, Anne receives word from Mary that not only has Louisa recovered and returned home, but that she and Captain Benwick have become engaged. While Anne thinks them an odd couple, she is thrilled to hear that there is no future between Louisa and Captain Wentworth. Her spirits are further lifted by the news that the Crofts (and perhaps Captain Wentworth?) are soon to be in Bath.

Yes, Captain Wentworth arrives and in their brief encounters, Anne begins to believe that he might still have feelings for her. Mr. Elliot, however, is still in pursuit of Anne, and his attentions make Captain Wentworth obvious in his jealousy. Word of Mr. Elliot's attachment to Anne even reaches her friend Mrs. Smith who supposes the two to be engaged. Anne quickly sets her straight as to her lack of feeling for Mr. Elliot. Mrs. Smith is relieved at the revelation because she had been holding back information about Mr. Elliot's true character, thinking that her friend loved him. According to Mrs. Smith's sources, Mr. Elliot had aspirations of taking on Sir Walter's baronetcy, and saw a match with Anne as a way to secure his seat, especially given Mrs. Clay's designs on Sir Walter. No room for more than one Lady Elliot at Kellynch Hall! Not only were Mr. Elliot's intentions toward Anne suspect, Mrs. Smith further reports that his inaction at properly executing the estate of her deceased husband is one of the reasons for her current poverty.

Because Mr. Elliot and Mrs. Clay are both scheming and competing for a place at Kellynch Hall, Anne finds it odd to see the two of them in close conversation across the street. She perceives Mrs. Clay as acting somewhat guilty after being asked about the encounter. Meanwhile Anne persists in avoiding Mr. Elliot and relishes any moment spent in the presence of Captain Wentworth.

During one such happenstance of being in the same room as Wentworth while he was composing a letter, Captain Harville and Anne discuss the upcoming marriage of Louisa and Captain Benwick. Harville expresses dismay that Benwick could have forgotten his sister so quickly, and he posits to Anne that men are more constant in their affection than women. He and Anne argue on the subject but ultimately agree to disagree, as Captain Wentworth interestedly eavesdrops. After the captains leave, Anne is surprised to find that the letter Captain Wentworth was writing is addressed to her! In it, he professes his steadfast love and offers his hand to her again after all these years. The news startles her so much that her companions think her to be ill and send her home accompanied by Charles. As luck would have it, they run into Captain Wentworth who walks her the rest of the way, giving the long lost lovers a chance to reconcile.

This time around, Sir Walter has no objection to the match, since Captain Wentworth had since gained rank and a fortune; he "was no longer nobody" (*P*, 1288). Even Lady Russell finds pleasure in Anne's happiness. Of course, Mr. Elliot does not take the news very well. He leaves for London, only to be shortly followed by Mrs. Clay whom he takes "under his protection" (*P*, 1288). By taking Mrs. Clay out of the picture, Mr. Elliot hopes to maintain claim to the Elliot estate. Captain Wentworth and his bride settle into happy married life. He is even able to settle the financial affairs for Mrs. Smith, bringing even more happiness to Anne at last.

Bibliography

Aquino, Karl, Brent McFerran, and Marjorie Laven, "Moral Identity and the Experience of Moral Elevation in Response to Acts of Uncommon Goodness," *Journal of Personality and Social Psychology* 100 (4) (2011): 703–718.

Austen, Jane, *The Complete Novels of Jane Austen*. New York: Penguin Books (1983).

Brissenden, R. F., *Virtue in Distress: Studies in the Novel of Sentiment from Richardson to Sade*. New York: Barnes and Noble (1974).

Broadie, Alexander, *The Scottish Enlightenment*. Edinburgh: Birlinn (2001).

Buer, M. C., *Health, Wealth and Population in the Early Days of the Industrial Revolution*. Oxon, UK: Routledge (1926).

Byrne, Paula, *The Real Jane Austen: A Life in Small Things*. New York: Harper Collins Publishers (2013).

Carnell, Geoffrey, "Early Nineteenth Century: Birmingham—'Something Direful in the Sound,'" in *The Representation of Business in English Literature*, ed. Arthur Pollard. Indianapolis: Liberty Fund (2009): 35–65.

Coase, Ronald H., "Adam Smith's View of Man," *Journal of Law and Economics* 19 (3) (1976): 529–546.

Collins, Irene, *Jane Austen: The Parson's Daughter*. London: Humbleton Continuum (1998).

Copeland, Edward, "Money," in *Cambridge Companion to Jane Austen*, ed. Edward Copeland and Julie McMaster. Cambridge U.K.: Cambridge University Press (1997): 9.

Cox, Stephen, "Sensibility as an Argument" in *Sensibility in Transformation*, ed. Syndy McMillen Conger. Rutherford, N.J.: Fairleigh Dickinson Press (1990): 63–82.

Dostoevsky, Fyodor, *The Brothers Karamazov*, translated by Constance Garnett. Chicago, I.L.: Encyclopedia Britannica, Great Books of the Western World, volume 52 (1987).

Dussinger, John, "Madness and Lust in the Age of Sensibility" in *Sensibility in Transformation*, ed. Syndy McMillen Conger. Rutherford, N.J.: Fairleigh Dickinson Press (1990).

Eliot, T. S., *The Cocktail Party*. New York: Harcourt, Brace and World (1950).

Evensky, Jerry, "Adam Smith's *Theory of Moral Sentiments*: On Morals and Why They Matter to a Liberal Society of Free People and Free Markets," *Journal of Economic Perspectives* 19 (2005): 109–130.

Frank, Robert, "Another Widening Gap: The Haves vs. the Have-Mores," *New York Times*, November 15, 2014, http://www.nytimes.com/2014/11/16/business/another-widening-gap-the-haves-vs-the-have-mores.html?_r=0

Fricke, Christel, "The Challenges of *Pride and Prejudice*: Adam Smith and Jane Austen on Moral Education," *Revue Internationale de Philosophie* 269 (3) (2014): 343–372.

Hayek, F. A., *The Road to Serfdom*. Chicago: University of Chicago Press (1944).

Holy Bible, King James Version (KJV).

Inglehart, R., and C. Welzel, *Modernization, Cultural Change, and Democracy: The Human Development Sequence*. Cambridge: Cambridge University Press (2005).

Jane Austen's World, "Pride and Prejudice Economics: Or Why a Single Man with a Fortune of £4,000 Per Year is a Desirable Husband," https://janeaustensworld.wordpress.com/2008/02/10/the-economics-of-pride-and-prejudice-or-why-a-single-man-with-a-fortune-of-4000-per-year-is-a-desirable-husband/ 2008.

John, A. H., "Statistical Appendix," in *The Agrarian History of England*, gen. ed. Joan Thirsk. *Volume VI, 1750–1850*, ed. G. E. Mingay. Cambridge, U.K.: Cambridge University Press (1989).

Kiesling, Lynn, "Made Every Thing Bend to It: Themes of Design in Jane Austen and Adam Smith" (paper presented at the annual meetings of the Association of Private Enterprise Education, Las Vegas, Nevada, April 13–15, 2014).

Knox-Shaw, Peter, *Jane Austen and the Enlightenment*. Cambridge, U.K.: Cambridge University Press (2004).

McCloskey, Deirdre, *The Bourgeois Virtues*. Chicago: University of Chicago Press (2006).

McCloskey, Deirdre, *Bourgeois Dignity*. Chicago: University of Chicago Press (2010).

McMaster, Juliet, "Class," in *The Cambridge Companion to Jane Austen*, eds. Edward Copeland and Juliet McMaster. Cambridge, U.K.: Cambridge University Press (1997): 115–130.

Michie, Elsie B., "Austen's Powers: Engaging with Adam Smith in Debates about Wealth and Virtue," *Novel: A Forum on Fiction* 34, Autumn (2000): 5–27.

Miller, Matthew, "Adam Smith and Limits of Compassion," Tribune Media Service, downloaded at http://articles.sun-sentinel.com/2005–01–07/news/0501060822_1_moral-sentiments-tsunamis-smith-s-day, dated January 7, 2005.

Mohler, Kenneth L., "The Bennet Girls on Pride and Vanity," *Philological Quarterly* 46 (4) (1967): 567.

Mokyr, Joel, *The Enlightened Economy: An Economic History of Britain 1700–1850*. New Haven: Yale University Press (2009).

Montes, Leonides, *Adam Smith in Context: A Critical Reassessment of Some Central Components of His Thought*. Hampshire, U.K.: Palgrave Macmillan (2004).

O'Donoghue, Jim, Louise Goulding, and Grahame Allen, "Consumer Price Inflation since 1750," *Economic Trends* 604, March (2004): 38–46.

OECD. Stats "Purchasing Power Parities for GDP and related indicators," http://stats.oecd.org/Index.aspx?DataSetCode=PPPGDP (2015).

Otteson, James, *Adam Smith's Marketplace of Life*. Cambridge: Cambridge University Press (2002).

(OED), Oxford English Dictionary On-Line, http://www.oed.com/.

Pool, Daniel, *What Jane Austen Ate and Charles Dickens Knew*. New York: Simon and Schuster (1993).

Porter, Roy, "The Enlightenment in England," in *The Enlightenment in National Context*, eds. Roy Porter and Mikulas Teich. Cambridge: University of Cambridge Press (1981): 1–18.

Raphael, D. D. and A. L. Macfie, "Introduction," in Adam Smith, *The Theory of Moral Sentiments*. Indianapolis: Liberty Fund (1982).

Read, Leonard E., "I, Pencil: My Family Tree as told to Leonard E. Read." Library of Economics and Liberty (1999). Retrieved November 24, 2014, from the World Wide Web: http://www.econlib.org/library/Essays/rdPncl1.html.

Roberts, Russ, *How Adam Smith Can Change Your Life: An Unexpected Guide to Human Nature and Happiness*. New York, Portfolio Penguin (2014).

Robinson, Austin, "John Maynard Keynes 1883–1946," *The Economic Journal* 57 (225) (1947): 1–68.

Schneewind, J. B., *The Invention of Autonomy: A History of Modern Moral Philosophy*. Cambridge: Cambridge University Press (1998).

Skinner, Andrew S., "Adam Smith. Science and the Role of the Imagination," in *Hume and the Enlightenment*, ed. William B. Todd. Edinburgh: Universities of Edinburgh and Texas (1974): 164–188.

Smith, Adam, *An Inquiry into the Nature and Causes of the Wealth of Nations*. Indianapolis: Liberty Fund, 1976 (1776).

Smith, Adam, *Lectures on Jurisprudence*. Indianapolis: Liberty Fund, 1982 (1762–63, 1766).

Smith, Adam, *The Theory of Moral Sentiments*. Indianapolis: Liberty Fund, 1982 (1759).

Solzhenitsyn, Alexander, *The Gulag Archipelego*. New York: Harper and Row Paperback Edition (1974).

Stokes, M., *The Language of Jane Austen*, New York: St. Martins Press (1991).

Terry, Judith, "Seen But Not Heard: Servants in Jane Austen's England," *Persuasions* 10 (1988): 104–116.

Thompson, F. M. L., *English Landed Society in the Nineteenth Century*. London: Routledge and Kegan Paul (1963).

Thompson, James, "Finance and Romance" in *Sensibility in Transformation*, ed. Syndy McMillen Conger. Rutherford, N.J.: Fairleigh Dickinson Press (1990): 147–171.

U.K. Office of National Statistics, "Consumer Price Indices—CPI indices: 1988 to 2015" http://www.ons.gov.uk/ons/datasets-and-tables/dataselector.html?cdid=D7BT&dataset=mm23&table-id=1.1 (2015)

Valihora, Karen, "Impartial Spectator Meets Picturesque Tourist: The Framing of Mansfield Park" *Eighteenth-Century Fiction*, 20 (1) (2007): Article 4. Available at: http://digital commons.mcmaster.ca/ecf/vol20/iss1/4.

Warren, Leland, "Conscious Speakers: Sensibility and the Art of Conversation Considered" in *Sensibility in Transformation*, ed. Syndy McMillen Conger. Rutherford, N.J.: Fairleigh Dickinson Press (1990).

Watt, Ian, "On *Sense and Sensibility*" in *Jane Austen: A Collection of Critical Essays*, ed. I. Watt. Englewood Cliffs, N.J.: Prentice-Hall (1963): 41–51.

Williamson, Jeffrey G., *Did British Capitalism Breed Inequality?* Boston: Allen and Unwin (1985).

Wood, James, "God Talk," *New Yorker*, November 22, 2012. http://www.newyorker.com/magazine/2012/10/22/god-talk?currentPage=al.

Zak, Paul, *The Moral Molecule*. New York: Dutton (2012).

Index

Adam Smith problem, 27, 31
Age of Sensibility, 34
Alexander the Great, 20
ambition, 20, 21, 31, 148, 159; as distinct from avarice, 102
amiable virtues, 23, 24, 29; and vanity, 33–34
approbation, 15, 28, 30, 31; and pride, 33; and vanity, 32, 33; as feedback mechanism, 35, 120, 121, 158, 159; desire for, 12, 18, 31; in *Emma*, 120; in *Mansfield Park*, 49, 123; in *Sense and Sensibility*, 49
Anacin, 40, 54n1
Austen, Jane, 1, 136, 157; Age of Sensibility, 34; Enlightenment, 3, 4, 83, 145, 158; as gentlewoman, 149, 150, 151, 154, 155
avarice. *See* greed
awful virtues, 23, 24, 29. *See also* respectable virtues

Bath, England, 156n1; in *Emma*, 149, 153; in *Northanger Abbey*, 99, 100, 101, 149, 153, 174–177; in *Persuasion*, 71, 72, 73, 104, 119, 148, 149, 153, 178–180; in *Sense and Sensibility*, 165
Bates, Miss: and Emma's moral development, 53, 120, 174; benevolence of, 128–129; income and social rank, 131, 150–151, 153, 154,

156, 173
Bates, Mr.: clergy, 150, 173
Bates, Mrs.: income and social rank, 131, 150, 151, 153, 154, 173
beneficence. *See* benevolence
benevolence, 5, 16, 25, 26, 28, 58, 59, 67, 158, 161; amiable virtue, 24; Anne Elliot, 73; butcher, brewer, or baker, 11, 25, 102, 108; Colonel Brandon, 59, 81n5, 107; compared with justice, 27; Edmund Bertram, 65, 159; feeble spark of, 17–18, 26, 50; in leaders, 113, 118, 123; Lady Russell, 118, 119, 123; Mrs. Norris's lack of, 60, 61, 62, 64, 67, 159; Mr. Darcy, 59; Mr. Knightley, 172; other directed virtue, 23, 24, 27, 60; perfection of human nature, 14, 25, 41, 58; relation to level of familiarity, 25–27, 58, 113, 141
Bennet, Elizabeth: income, 129–130; pride, 85–91, 97, 159; social rank, 96–97, 143, 152, 168
Bennet, Jane: social rank, 3, 89, 91, 152
Bennet, Lydia: imprudence, 90, 96, 169
Bennet, Mary: on pride and vanity, 83
Bennet, Mr.: recognition of Mr. Collins's vices, 92, 93, 96, 97; social rank, 97, 143, 167
Bennet, Mrs.: entail, 98n5, 129, 168; income, 129, 133; servants, 150; social rank, 143

About the Authors

Cecil E. Bohanon is professor of economics at Ball State University. He earned a BA in economics from Wilmington College in Wilmington, Ohio, and an MA and PhD in economics from Virginia Polytechnic Institute and State University. He has published numerous refereed and popular articles, won a number of local and national teaching awards and has directed students in the production of several award-winning films on economic topics. Dr. Bohanon's current academic interests are in applied microeconomic and macroeconomic issues especially as they relate to history and culture. He lives in Muncie, Indiana, with his wife and two sons.

Michelle Albert Vachris is professor of economics at Christopher Newport University. She earned a BA in economics from the College of William and Mary, and an MA and PhD in economics from George Mason University. Previously she was an economist with the U.S. Bureau of Labor Statistics in the International Price Program. She has since served as a consultant to the International Monetary Fund. Dr. Vachris has published many academic articles, is a past-president and Distinguished Fellow of the Virginia Association of Economists, and a member of the Mont Pelerin Society. Her current research program involves economics and literature and public choice economics. She lives in Virginia Beach, Virginia, with her husband and two sons.